CUPCAKES
& COOKIES
GALORE

Jacqueline Bellefontaine & Gail Wagman

spruce

An Hachette UK Company
www.hachette.co.uk

First published in Great Britain in 2013 by
Spruce, a division of Octopus Publishing
Group Ltd
Endeavour House
189 Shaftesbury Avenue
London
WC2H 8JY
www.octopusbooksusa.com

This material in this book was previously
published under the titles *Cupcakes Galore*
and *Cookies Galore*.

Copyright © Octopus Publishing Group Ltd
2013
Text copyright © Cupcakes Galore, Gail
Wagman 2006

Design concept and layout: Clare Barber
Recipe and photography credits: see
page 376

Distributed in the US by
Hachette Book Group USA
237 Park Avenue
New York NY 10017 USA

Distributed in Canada by
Canadian Manda Group
165 Dufferin Street
Toronto, Ontario, Canada M6K 3H6

ISBN 978-1-84601-408-6

A CIP catalogue record for this book is
available from the British Library

Printed and bound in China

10 9 8 7 6 5 4 3 2 1

Publisher's note
Ovens should be preheated to the specific
temperature. If using a fan-assisted oven,
follow the manufacturer's instructions for
adjusting the time and temperature.

This book includes dishes made with nuts
and nut derivatives. It is advisable for those
with known allergic reactions to nuts and
nut derivatives or those who may be
potentially vulnerable to these allergies,
such as pregnant and nursing mothers,
invalids, the elderly, babies and children to
avoid dishes made with these. It is prudent
to check the labels of all pre-prepared
ingredients for the possible inclusion of
nut derivatives.

CONTENTS

INTRODUCTION

When the idea of writing a book on cupcakes was first broached to me, I immediately had visions of those cupcakes of my youth—the ones my mother used to make for the birthday parties of my childhood.

★ ORIGINS ★

You remember—they were usually made with either chocolate or yellow batter, lavished with gobs of pastel frosting and decorated with chocolate sprinkles, coconut, candied fruits, or nuts. They were always served on a big platter with a candle in each one in honor of the birthday girl or boy or brought to school on that special day to be shared with friends during recess. Cupcakes have of course come a long way since then, thanks to the amazing amount of cupcake paraphernalia available on the market, from decorations to cupcake tins, as well as the many recipes expressly designed for them or that can be adapted to them. But we will come back to that later. For the time being, let's set the record straight. Just what is a cupcake? And what isn't? Webster's Dictionary defines a cupcake as follows:

noun*:*

a small cake baked in a cuplike mold

This minimal definition just about sums it up—no more, no less—leaving a great deal of room for interpretation, creativity, and perhaps a little confusion.

★ A CUPCAKE WITH ANY OTHER NAME ... ★

A cupcake is undeniably a "little cake," but all "little cakes" aren't necessarily cupcakes. Unless they are made in a cup-sized mold. And fit the criteria of a "cake," let's say, as opposed to a muffin, which can be made in a cup-sized mold but is basically a quick bread and not a cake. And then again, some cupcake recipes are "quick" but the result is not to be mistaken for a muffin. And does a cupcake require icing to conform to the appellation? Iconographically speaking, I would say yes since the festive character of the beast certainly lends itself to a little "dressing up for the occasion," but it would really be too bad to add anything other than powdered sugar or a little glaze to some of the cupcakes in this book. A number of sources refer to the origin of the humble cupcake as a "cup cake," in other words, a 1 (cup butter)–2 (cups sugar)–3 (cups flour)–4 (eggs) cake, which can certainly be made into cupcakes (provided that you add a little flavoring, a substantial dose of imagination, some yummy frosting, and a decoration or two) but as anyone who has ever made a cake will know, this refers to what is commonly known as a pound cake and no one is mistaking that for a cupcake.

So, if you stick to my definition, you can't go wrong. Just remember the three cardinal rules:

1. cupcakes should be pretty
2. cupcakes should taste good
3. cupcakes should be fun

★ THE PARTY BEAST ★

Defining a cupcake is sort of like defining a pair of shorts (short pants). Or a can of soda (compared to a bottle). Or a bikini (as opposed to a one-piece bathing suit). It is just a smaller version of the original that has taken on a meaning of its own (thus the confusion). When referring to cupcakes, most of the respectable cookbooks that I have consulted agree that nearly all cake batters lend themselves to being baked in individual portions. My experience has certainly proved that to be true. It is a rare cake batter that cannot be metamorphosed into a cupcake with the addition of some sort of topping or decoration. So I have decided to stick with my original idea of the cupcake as a "party beast"—no "savory" cupcakes here—I'll leave that for the muffin department. My two basic criteria were (1) the cupcakes all had to be made with some sort of cake batter (to be defined); and (2) they could be made in a cupcake tin—either with or without a paper, mini, regular, or jumbo. I have added an extra section entitled "Cupcakes Plus" for those "cupcakes"

that may or may not specifically fit those criteria but that can be made in a cupcake tin and/or served in a cupcake paper and that could pass for a cupcake with a little imagination.

I hope you enjoy these recipes. I had great fun writing them and am very excited about sharing them with you. Special thanks to my "testers"—Mark, my son, and his friends at school who received a batch every Monday morning to start off the week, Brigitte and Christian who stopped by on Saturday mornings after the market to try my latest creations and whose detailed tasting notes were invaluable, and to all my other friends who have been on a "cupcake diet" since I started this project. I am forever grateful to Alain, my partner in all culinary endeavors, for having not only tested all of my recipes but for having so patiently listened to the "Cupcake Monologue" during the gestation of this book. And then there is of course my daughter Emily who could leave no cupcake paper unturned and who constantly supplied me with ideas and cupcake paraphernalia while I was writing the book.

SOME RULES
of Thumb

Here are a few helpful hints for the aspiring cupcake baker. So put on that apron and get to work!

★ RECIPES ★

Almost all of the cupcake recipes in this book (with the exception of some of the ones in the "Cupcakes Plus" section) are really cake recipes tailored to a cupcake. As I already mentioned in the introduction, just about any cake recipe can be used to make a cupcake. Only the cooking time will change which is true within the range of cupcake sizes as well—mini cupcakes will take less time than regular cupcakes that will take less time than jumbo cupcakes that will take less time than a cake. Logical, isn't it? Take your favorite cake recipe, bake it in a cupcake tin, add a little frosting, a glaze, some powdered sugar, and a decoration, and you will have your own original cupcake recipe. Let your imagination be your guide.

★ INGREDIENTS ★

As a rule of thumb, all ingredients should be at room temperature unless otherwise indicated (frozen berries, hot milk, etc.). I used all-purpose flour for all of the recipes in this book. If you want to use cake flour, add 2 tablespoons per cup of all-purpose flour. I never use self-rising flour since it already has salt and a leavening agent in it and I prefer to add my own. As for leavening agents, I generally use 1 teaspoon baking powder per cup of flour and fraction thereof. I only use baking soda when there is an acid factor such a buttermilk, sour cream, yogurt, or citrus juice. Otherwise, it apparently serves no purpose. Whenever possible, I mix all of the dry ingredients together before mixing them into the batter. Which brings us to the question—to sift or not to sift? From all that I have read and from my own experience, I don't think sifting adds anything to a recipe except when you are adding small quantities of flour to beaten egg whites with a whisk, allowing you to add the flour slowly and not to deflate the whites. In my old recipe books from the 50s, ingredients are sometimes sifted three times before being measured. I'm not sure what the logic was but I wouldn't waste my time. I only use unsalted butter. I live in France and almost all of the butter available is unsalted. If you are using salted butter, leave the salt out of the recipe. Both salt and cream of tartar are used to stabilize beaten egg whites. Use about $\frac{1}{8}$ teaspoon cream of tartar or a pinch of salt for every 2 egg whites.

★ BAKING TIPS ★

Most of the recipes call for the cupcake papers or molds to be filled $\frac{2}{3}$ full. There are exceptions of course. If you are adding a topping, you will probably want to leave more room (Strawberry-Filled Oatmeal Cupcake, for instance). Unless otherwise stated, I generally suggested preheating the oven to 350°F. Some recipes require a hotter or a cooler oven and, occasionally, the temperature has to be turned down while the cupcakes are baking. In that case, just follow the recipe. I tend to bake just about everything in a moderate, preheated oven. Remember that temperatures vary from one oven to the next, so know your oven and use your common sense. There are just so many variables—weather, altitude, position in the oven, whether it is a first or second batch, etc. I generally insert a tester in my cupcakes to see if they are done. When it comes out clean, remove the cupcakes from the oven. Some cupcakes stay moist in the center (Chocolate Mousse, cupcakes cooked with fruit like the Blueberry and Raspberry Cream Cupcake for the Fourth of July), defying the "tester" test. In any case, when they start to burn, regardless of the recipe, you will know that you have left them in the oven too long!

It is generally advisable to let the cupcakes cool before removing them from the tins. Place them on a rack when you take them out of the oven. Some can be unmolded after about 10 minutes whereas the denser ones should be completely cooled first.

Just remember, any rule that applies to cake baking techniques or ingredients generally applies to cupcakes.

EQUIPMENT

Cupcake paraphernalia can be found in just about any supermarket and in all good kitchen supply stores.

★ CUPCAKE TINS ★

Cupcake tins (also known as muffin tins) come in a variety of sizes but the three major sizes are "mini" (1¼ to 2 inches in diameter, holding ⅛ cup or 2 tablespoons batter), "regular" (2½ inches in diameter, holding ¼ to ⅓ cup batter), and "jumbo" (3½ inches in diameter, holding about ⅝ cup batter). The number of cups in the tin is variable. I have mini-cupcake tins with 20 cups and others with 30. There are usually 12 cups in a regular-size cupcake tin whereas the silicon ones are often smaller. My jumbo tins make six jumbo cupcakes each. Tins come in metal, in which case you have to grease and flour them if you are not using cupcake papers. Although I see no reason not to use cupcake papers and avoid the mess. The new silicon molds are very handy and can be used at high temperatures in an oven without any additional

preparation. They are nonstick and the cupcakes will just pop out as soon as they are cool. They come in rigid and nonrigid varieties and are extremely easy to clean. Just remember to use a baking sheet with the nonrigid ones. I prefer metal tins when using cupcake papers and nonstick silicon molds when I am not.

★ CUPCAKE PAPERS ★

Cupcake papers come in a variety of colors and designs. I have found ones for just about every occasion—Christmas, Valentine's Day, the Fourth of July, St. Patrick's Day, etc. and for every season—fall leaves and spring flowers, just to name a few. There are papers with Barbie dolls, baseball bats, footballs, and some rather unidentifiable objects. Supermarkets seem to carry the pastel ones of my youth whereas many of the specialty stores carry plain white ones which are good

for any occasion. They also come in a full rainbow of colors and in gold and silver. The variety is slightly more limited for the mini and jumbo versions. And plain papers will do just fine. Remember, it is what is inside and on top that counts.

As for any other equipment you will need to make a cupcake, it is basically the same as what you would need to make a cake—spatula, whisk, wooden spoon, measuring cups and spoons, electric or hand beater, electric mixer, and a wide range of bowl sizes. You will also need some equipment to make frosting and decorations, but I will cover that in the section devoted to those topics.

DRESSING UP FOR
the Occasion

Icings, Frosting, Toppings, and Glazes
and, last but not least, Decorations.

★ THE CROWNING TOUCH ★

Is a cupcake a cupcake with nothing on top? Since I'm not quite sure but tend to believe that a cupcake is the sum of its individual parts, I have given at least one alternative for every cupcake in this book—whether it be an icing or frosting as in the majority of the recipes, a topping as in the case of the Apple Crumble or Bourdaloue, a glaze for the Kir or Honey Hazelnut Cupcake, or just a dusting of powdered sugar for the Poppyseed Cupcake—plus some sort of decoration. I have used the terms "frosting" and "icing" interchangeably. Webster's Dictionary gives "icing" as a synonym for "frosting" and vice versa. I just love the definition of "icing" in my Webster's Dictionary and you will see why: "a sweet, flavored and usually creamy mixture used to coat baked goods (as cupcakes) [sic]—called also frosting." Can you believe that? So I guess that cupcakes are just predestined to have some sort of icing/frosting/topping/glaze. After all, they could have said "cakes." But no. They explicitly mention cupcakes. In Alan Davidson's Oxford Companion to Food, he goes into great detail about "icings" but doesn't mention "frosting." The Joy of Cooking has a whole section on "Icings" whereas the Fanny Farmer Cookbook has it all under "Frostings."

Cake/cupcake icing/frosting is an art in itself. As is cake/cupcake decorating. Many books exist on the subject and all good cookbooks will have a section devoted to the topic as well. I have tried to present a full panoply of alternatives, from the simple to the more complicated—easy-to-make-icings with just powdered sugar and a little liquid, to cooked icings that require a bit more skill and time. Ready-made icings can be found in supermarkets and specialty stores if you are in a hurry although some of the recipes in this book can be made in the time it will take you to open the can or read the directions on the ready-made stuff. Fondant is a challenge to even the most skilled baker and I always use one of the brands available on the market, with the addition of a little sugar syrup, flavoring, and coloring, if need may be. Feel free to mix and match as well. And create your own personalized versions by changing the flavors. For example, replace the mint in the Mint Butter Cream Frosting with lavender or lemon extract, or a few drops of orange flower water or rose water, and invent your own recipes. A little imagination will go a long way.

And speaking of imagination—a word on cupcake decorations! I guess you could just say "awesome." On a recent trip to the States, I was astounded and impressed by the quantity of decorations available on the market. I mean, there is just no excuse for an ugly cupcake at this point in civilization. Glitter sugars, colored sugars, every shape and size of sprinkles for every occasion, instant decorator tubes in every color of the rainbow, colored sprays, edible decorations in the form of flowers, clowns, footballs—you name it—plus all the rest including candied, dried, and jellied fruits, nuts, gummy candies, miniature candies, and cookies— and those are just some of the obvious ones. So, in the spirit of that party beast known as the cupcake—free your inner "cupcake decorator"—and have a ball.

GRANDMA'S
FAVORITES

ZUCCHINI PINE NUT
Cupcakes

This is one way of using up some of that extra zucchini and getting your kids to eat it too. They'll never know but they will surely ask for seconds. And it will be a great hit with adults as well.

MAKES: ABOUT 12–14 CUPCAKES

1½ cups shredded zucchini
1⅓ cups all-purpose flour
2 teaspoons baking powder
1 teaspoon salt
1 cup ground almonds
1 egg
⅔ cup sugar
⅔ cup heavy cream
⅓ cup vegetable oil
½ cup pine nuts

CREAM CHEESE FROSTING
1 cup powdered sugar
4 ounces cream cheese, softened
1 egg white, slightly beaten
Pinch of salt
1 teaspoon vanilla extract
½ cup pine nuts for decoration

1. Preheat oven to 350°F.

2. In a large bowl, mix together zucchini, flour, baking powder, salt, and ground almonds.

3. In another bowl, mix the egg, sugar, cream, oil, and pine nuts. Pour this batter into the first one and blend well with a whisk or a wooden spoon.

4. Fill cupcake papers about ¾ full and cook for 20–25 minutes or until a tester inserted into the center comes out clean. Remove from the oven and cool.

5. Beat all the frosting ingredients together until light and of good spreading consistency. Frost the cooled cupcakes and sprinkle a few pine nuts over each cupcake before serving. Alternatively, dust the cooled cupcakes with powdered sugar.

CUPCAKE TIP
If you don't have pine nuts, use either walnuts or hazelnuts.

CHOCOLATE COCONUT
Cupcakes

Instant chocolate pudding was a staple of my childhood. My mother would make it as a special treat, to be eaten slowly, treasuring every mouthful. These cupcakes are a tribute to that time long ago and the coconut is my little personal touch.

MAKES: ABOUT 12–14 CUPCAKES

1²/₃ cups all-purpose flour
2 teaspoons baking powder
1 teaspoon salt, plus pinch for egg
   whites
3 eggs, separated
½ cup brown sugar
½ cup vegetable oil, plus
   2 tablespoons
1 cup shredded coconut, plus
   2 tablespoons for dusting
2 tablespoons unsweetened cocoa
   powder
4 ounces dark chocolate, grated
4 tablespoons milk
Chocolate pudding (instant, ready-
   made or homemade)
Whipped cream, for decoration
Powdered chocolate or cocoa powder,
   for dusting

1. Preheat oven to 350°F.

2. Mix flour, baking powder, and salt and set aside.

3. With a whisk or a wooden spoon, mix egg yolks and sugar together. Add oil and then flour mixture, beating until batter is smooth. Mix in coconut, cocoa powder, grated chocolate, and milk and blend well.

4. Using an electric beater, beat egg whites with a pinch of salt until stiff but not dry. Gently fold into chocolate batter.

5. Spoon batter into cupcake papers, filling about ²/₃ full. Smooth batter with the back of a spoon. Sprinkle a little coconut over each cupcake. Cook for 10 minutes and then lower temperature to 300°F and cook for another 20 minutes or until a tester inserted into the center comes out clean. Remove from oven and cool.

6. When cupcakes are completely cool, cut a circle or cone out of the top with an apple corer and heap chocolate pudding in it. Add a little dollop of whipped cream for decoration. Dust with powdered chocolate or cocoa powder.

BLACK & WHITE
Cupcakes

Native New Yorkers will be familiar with these cupcakes although they are traditionally found in cookie form at delicatessens throughout the U.S.

MAKES: ABOUT 16 CUPCAKES

CHOCOLATE & VANILLA MARBLE CUPCAKE
1½ cups all-purpose flour

2 teaspoons baking powder

1 teaspoon salt, plus pinch for the egg whites

6 tablespoons/¾ stick unsalted butter, room temperature

1 cup sugar

2 eggs, separated

⅓ cup whole milk

1 teaspoon vanilla extract

1 tablespoon unsweetened cocoa powder

BLACK & WHITE ICING
2 cups powdered sugar

¼ cup boiling water (more or less, depending on spreading consistency)

1 ounce dark chocolate

Chocolate buttons for decoration

1. Preheat oven to 350°F. Mix dry ingredients together in a bowl. Set aside.

2. In the large bowl of an electric mixer, cream butter and sugar until light and fluffy. Add egg yolks and beat to blend. Alternately add dry ingredients and milk, beating well after each addition.

3. Divide batter into two separate bowls. Mix the vanilla into one of the batters and cocoa powder into the other.

4. Beat egg whites with a pinch of salt until they form stiff peaks. Divide in half and gently fold half into each of the two batters.

5. Spoon batter into cupcake papers, filling cups about ⅔ full, 1 heaping teaspoon at a time, alternating batters. They will appear not to be mixed but will "marble" when cooked. Bake for 25 minutes or until a tester inserted into the center comes out clean. Remove from oven and cool.

6. To make the icing: place powdered sugar in a medium-size bowl. Gradually mix in boiling water, 1 tablespoon at a time. Mixture should be very thick but easy to spread. Divide mixture into two parts.

7. Put half the icing in a double boiler with the chocolate over simmering (not boiling) water. Stir and remove from heat as soon as the chocolate is melted. While icing is warm to the touch, spread on cupcakes—half white, half chocolate. Place a chocolate button in the center of each cupcake.

BLUE BLUEBERRY 'N' CREAM Cupcakes

The "trick," for these cupcakes is to defrost the blueberries until they became mushy so that they impart their blue color to the batter.

MAKES: ABOUT 18 REGULAR CUPCAKES OR 8 JUMBO CUPCAKES

2¹/₂ cups all-purpose flour

3 teaspoons baking powder

1 teaspoon salt

¹/₂ cup/1 stick unsalted butter, room temperature

1 cup sugar

2 eggs

1 cup milk or light cream

³/₄ cup blueberries (if you are using frozen blueberries, defrost beforehand), plus ¹/₂ cup frozen or fresh blueberries

1 tablespoon water

BLUE BLUEBERRY WHIPPED CREAM

1 cup whipping cream

¹/₄ cup sugar

¹/₄ cup reserved crushed blueberries (see method)

Dried blueberries (optional) for decoration

1. Preheat oven to 350°F. Mix flour, baking powder, and salt together and set aside.

2. In the large bowl of an electric mixer, cream butter and sugar until light and fluffy. Add eggs, one at a time, beating well after each addition. Alternately add dry ingredients and milk or cream.

3. Using a fork, crush ³/₄ cup blueberries with 1 tablespoon water until they are soft. Save ¹/₄ cup for the frosting. Add ¹/₂ cup to the batter and blend thoroughly. Batter will be blue. Gently fold in remaining ¹/₂ cup blueberries.

4. Spoon batter into cupcake papers, filling cups about ²/₃ full. Cook for 20–25 minutes or until a tester inserted into the center comes out clean. Remove from oven and cool.

5. To make the whipped cream: with an electric beater, beat cream until it starts to form soft peaks. Gradually add sugar, beating constantly. Add crushed blueberries and beat until stiff.

6. Frost cupcakes and sprinkle with dried blueberries, if desired. These cupcakes should be frosted just before serving. Alternatively, because of their beautiful color, you can leave them as is and dust them with powdered sugar.

BROWNIE Cupcakes

This recipe is dedicated to Julien, who is my biggest brownie fan, no matter what form they come in!

MAKES: ABOUT 12 CUPCAKES

1 cup all-purpose flour
1 teaspoon baking powder
1 teaspoon salt
6 ounces dark chocolate, broken into pieces
6 tablespoons/¾ stick unsalted butter, room temperature, cut into pieces
¾ cup sugar
2 eggs
1 teaspoon vanilla extract
1 cup chopped walnuts

WALNUT FUDGE FROSTING

3 ounces dark chocolate, cut into pieces
1 cup sugar
⅓ cup milk
3 tablespoons unsalted butter
1 tablespoon corn syrup
Pinch of salt
1 teaspoon vanilla extract

FOR DECORATION

½ cup chopped walnuts (optional) or 12 walnut halves
Chocolate buttons

1. Preheat oven to 350°F.

2. Mix flour, baking powder, and salt together and set aside.

3. Place chocolate, butter, and sugar in a large bowl over simmering water. Heat until just melted, stirring from time to time (do not cook). This will only take a few minutes. Remove from heat. Add eggs, one at a time, blending well after each addition. Add vanilla. Gradually add dry ingredients. When batter is smooth and dry ingredients have been absorbed, fold in chopped walnuts.

4. Divide batter between 12 cupcake papers, smoothing with the back of a spoon. Cook for about 20–25 minutes. Cupcakes should form a crust on top and be a little moist inside. Remove from oven and cool completely before removing from tin.

5. To make the frosting: place all of the ingredients except the vanilla and walnuts in a heavy pan. Bring to a full boil and cook for 1 minute, stirring constantly. Remove from heat and cool (you can set bowl in cold water to speed up the process).

6. Add vanilla and beat until thick, about 10 minutes, until frosting is fluffy and the color has slightly lightened. If you are using chopped walnuts in the frosting, fold them in now. Frost cooled cupcakes. Top each cupcake with a walnut halves and a chocolate button.

CHOCOLATE PEANUT BUTTER Cupcakes

Peanut butter and chocolate are one of those fabulous duos, immortalized in many children's candies and traditional desserts.

MAKES: ABOUT 18 CUPCAKES

2 cups all-purpose flour
2 teaspoons baking powder
1 teaspoon salt
2 ounces good quality dark chocolate
1/4 cup/1/2 stick unsalted butter, room temperature
4 tablespoons smooth peanut butter
1 cup sugar
2 eggs
3/4 cup milk
1 cup peanut chocolate chips (optional)

FROSTING

3 ounces milk chocolate
1/4 cup/1/2 stick unsalted butter, cut into small pieces
1 2/3 cups powdered sugar
Pinch of salt
1/4 cup heavy cream
1 teaspoon vanilla extract
3 tablespoons smooth peanut butter
Peanut-chocolate candies (peanut M&M's, Reese's Pieces etc.)

1. Preheat oven to 350°F.

2. Mix flour, baking powder, and salt together and set aside.

3. Melt chocolate in a double boiler or microwave. Set aside and cool.

4. In the large bowl of an electric mixer, cream butter, peanut butter, and sugar until light and fluffy. Add eggs, one at a time, mixing well after each addition. Add cooled chocolate and blend well. Alternately beat in dry ingredients and milk.

5. Spoon batter into cupcake papers, filling cups about 2/3 full. Sprinkle a few peanut chocolate chips over each cupcake, gently pressing them into the batter with a fork. Bake for 25 minutes or until a tester comes out clean. Remove from oven and cool.

6. To make the frosting: heat chocolate and butter in a double boiler or a microwave until just melted.

7. Remove from heat and cool. Using a whisk or a wooden spoon, beat sugar, salt, cream, and vanilla until smooth. Add cooled chocolate mixture and peanut butter and beat until blended. Put the frosting in the refrigerator until it thickens (about 20–30 minutes).

8. Remove from refrigerator, beat until frosting is of spreading consistency and frost cooled cupcakes. Decorate with peanut-chocolate candies.

LEMON MERINGUE PIE Cupcakes

These lemon meringue cupcakes will add an elegant touch to the end of any meal. Lemon desserts are always a favorite because of their tart flavor. Add this one to your repertory.

MAKES: ABOUT 12 CUPCAKES

1 1/2 cups all-purpose flour
2 teaspoons baking powder
1 teaspoon salt
2 tablespoons grated lemon rind
1/2 cup/1 stick unsalted butter
1 cup sugar
2 eggs
2 tablespoons lemon juice

LEMON CREAM
3/4 cup sugar
3 tablespoons all-purpose flour
Pinch of salt
1/4 cup lemon juice
Grated rind of 1 lemon
1/2 cup water
3 egg yolks, beaten (save whites for meringue)
2 tablespoons/1/4 stick unsalted butter

MERINGUE TOPPING
3 egg whites
Pinch of salt
1/4 cup sugar
A few teaspoons of sugar for dusting

1. Prepare the lemon cream. In the top of a double boiler, mix sugar, flour, and salt together. Add lemon juice and rind. Mix well. Beat in water, egg yolks, and butter (if the butter is still chunky it will melt over the hot water).

2. Place mixture over hot simmering water in a double boiler and cook until smooth and thick, stirring constantly with a whisk (about 20 minutes). Cool and set aside. Preheat oven to 350°F.

3. Mix flour, baking powder, salt, and lemon rind together. Set aside.

4. Cream butter and sugar together until light and fluffy. Add eggs, one at a time, beating after each addition. Add lemon juice and beat until well blended. Add flour mixture and continue beating until batter is smooth.

5. Fill 12 cupcake papers with the batter. Cook for 15 minutes or until cupcakes are golden on top. Remove from oven and cool for 10 minutes.

6. To make the meringue: beat egg whites with a pinch of salt until they start to stiffen. Gradually add sugar, beating until stiff but not dry.

7. Using a sharp knife, carefully remove a little cone from the center of the cooled cupcakes using an apple corer and fill with lemon cream.

8. Place 1 tablespoon meringue on each cupcake, forming peaks with the back of a spoon or a fork. Dust lightly with sugar. Cook cupcakes in the oven for another 5–7 minutes or until meringue is just golden. Let cool.

APPLE-CRANBERRY CRUMBLE Cupcakes

These moist cupcakes will remind you of the homemade crumbles you ate when you were a kid. The cranberries give a slightly tart taste and a beautiful color.

MAKES: ABOUT 18 CUPCAKES

½ cups all-purpose flour

2 teaspoons baking powder

1 teaspoon salt

2 teaspoons cinnamon

½ teaspoon grated nutmeg

¾ cup/1½ sticks unsalted butter, room temperature

1½ cups sugar

2 eggs

1 cup applesauce (you can either use ready-made or recipe on page 132)

1 tablespoon finely grated lemon rind

1 cup cranberries (fresh or frozen)

½ cup walnuts, chopped (optional)

APPLE-WALNUT CRUMBLE TOPPING

2 tablespoons/¼ stick unsalted butter

6 teaspoons sugar

⅓ cup all purpose flour

1 apple, peeled and cut into small pieces

½ cup walnuts, chopped

1. Preheat oven to 350°F.

2. Mix dry ingredients and spices together and set aside.

3. In the large bowl of an electric mixer, cream butter and sugar until light and fluffy. Add eggs, one at a time, beating well after each addition. Alternately add dry ingredients, applesauce, and lemon rind and blend well. Fold in cranberries and walnuts, if desired. If you are using frozen cranberries, don't defrost them beforehand.

4. Spoon batter into cupcake papers, filling cups a little over ½ full. Smooth batter with the back of a spoon.

5. For topping, melt butter in a pan, add sugar, flour, apple, and walnuts. Mix well and stir until mixture just starts to change color. Remove from heat. Place a spoonful of the mixture on top of each cupcake. Cook cupcakes for about 20 minutes or until a tester inserted into the center comes out clean. Remove from oven and cool completely before removing cupcakes from tin.

CUPCAKE TIP
Serve these cupcakes with a dollop of whipped cream on top.

MAPLE WALNUT DELIGHTS

These cupcakes are a true gourmet delight. The icing is a good example of cooked frosting at its best—it is both beautiful to look at and will melt in your mouth.

MAKES: ABOUT 18 CUPCAKES

2$\frac{1}{2}$ cups all-purpose flour
3 teaspoons baking powder
$\frac{1}{2}$ teaspoon salt
$\frac{1}{2}$ cup/1 stick unsalted butter, room
    temperature
$\frac{1}{2}$ cup light brown sugar
2 eggs
1 cup maple syrup
$\frac{1}{2}$ cup milk
$\frac{1}{2}$ cup chopped walnuts
MAPLE MERINGUE ICING
2 egg whites
Pinch of salt
1 cup maple syrup
1 teaspoon vanilla extract
$\frac{1}{2}$ cup chopped walnuts or walnut
    halves (for decoration)

1. Preheat oven to 350°F.

2. Mix flour, baking powder, and salt together and set aside.

3. In the large bowl of an electric mixer, cream butter and sugar until light and fluffy. Add eggs, one at a time, mixing well after each addition. Alternately add dry ingredients and syrup and milk, blending well after each addition. Fold in walnuts.

4. Spoon batter into cupcake papers, filling cups about $\frac{2}{3}$ full. Bake for 25–30 minutes or until a tester inserted into the center comes out clean. Remove from oven and cool.

5. To make the icing: beat egg whites with a pinch of salt until peaks start to form. Set aside.

6. Boil maple syrup until it forms a soft ball when dropped into a glass of water (about 234°F on a candy thermometer). The time will depend on the maple syrup you are using but should be about 5–10 minutes. Remove from heat immediately. Slowly pour the hot syrup into the egg whites, beating constantly. The hot syrup actually cooks the egg whites. Add vanilla and continue beating until mixture is stiff and stands in soft peaks.

7. Ice the cooled cupcakes, forming peaks with the back of a spoon or a fork. Place a walnut half on top of each cupcake or sprinkle with chopped walnuts before icing hardens. It will harden on the outside and remain soft and creamy inside.

THREE-GINGERBREAD
Cupcakes

The fresh and crystallized ginger give these cupcakes a unique and very pronounced flavor. Enjoy with a cup of strong black tea or an espresso.

MAKES: ABOUT 12 CUPCAKES

1½ cups all-purpose flour
2 teaspoons baking powder
1 teaspoon salt
1 teaspoon ground ginger
½ teaspoon cinnamon
½ teaspoon allspice
Dash each of grated nutmeg and
    ground cloves
½ cup/1 stick unsalted butter, room
    temperature
¾ cup brown sugar
2 eggs
1 teaspoon vanilla extract
1 heaping tablespoon grated ginger
½ cup milk
3 tablespoons finely chopped
    crystallized ginger

FROSTING
1 cup whipping cream, chilled
4 tablespoons sugar
½ teaspoon ground ginger
1 teaspoon finely grated fresh ginger
Sliced crystallized ginger for decoration

1. Preheat oven to 350°F.

2. Mix flour, baking powder, salt, and spices together and set aside.

3. In the large bowl of an electric mixer, cream butter and sugar until light and fluffy. Add eggs, one at a time, mixing well after each addition. Add vanilla and grated ginger. Alternately add dry ingredients and milk, beating continually. When batter is smooth, fold in crystallized ginger.

4. Spoon batter into cupcake papers, filling cups about ⅔ full. Bake for 20–25 minutes or until a tester inserted in the center comes out clean. Remove from oven and cool.

5. To make the frosting: whip cream with an electric beater until almost stiff. Gradually add sugar and ground ginger, beating constantly, until stiff peaks form. Fold in grated fresh ginger and frost cooled cupcakes. Sprinkle with ground ginger (go easy!) and decorate with a slice of crystallized ginger. These cupcakes have to be frosted just before serving them. They will not keep for long unless you use some sort of fixative for the whipped cream.

CUPCAKE TIP
Alternatively, make a simple glaze by heating a few tablespoons of ginger preserves.

STRAWBERRY-FILLED OATMEAL Cupcakes

These moist and crunchy cupcakes make a delicious dessert or a welcome snack, and if they aren't all gobbled down immediately, they keep well and can be eaten for breakfast.

MAKES: ABOUT 12 CUPCAKES

1 cup all-purpose flour
1 teaspoon baking powder
1 teaspoon baking soda
1 teaspoon salt
1 teaspoon cinnamon
¾ cup rolled oats
½ cup/1 stick unsalted butter, room temperature
¾ cup sugar
1 egg
1 teaspoon vanilla extract
1 cup sour cream
12 teaspoons strawberry jelly

OATMEAL CRUNCH TOPPING
½ cup rolled oats
¼ cup light brown sugar
2 heaping tablespoons all-purpose flour
1 teaspoon cinnamon
½ teaspoon salt
¼ cup/½ stick unsalted butter, chilled and cut into little pieces

1. Put all of the topping ingredients in a food processor and process until lumps form. Set aside.

2. Preheat oven to 350°F.

3. Mix dry ingredients together and set aside.

4. In the large bowl of an electric mixer, cream butter and sugar until light and fluffy. Add egg and vanilla and mix well. Alternately add dry ingredients and sour cream, blending well after each addition.

5. Spoon half of the batter into 12 cupcake papers. Make an indentation and place 1 teaspoon of jelly in each cupcake. Fill cupcakes with remaining batter. Using your fingers, sprinkle a little topping over each cupcake. Cook for 25–30 minutes or until cupcakes are golden brown on top. Remove from oven and cool.

CUPCAKE TIP
Any type of jelly can be used for the filling.

PERSIMMON NUT HARVEST Treats

These cupcakes are a nice alternative to spice cake and a good way to use persimmons.

MAKES: ABOUT 18 CUPCAKES

1¾ cups all-purpose flour
2 teaspoons baking powder
1 teaspoon salt
1 teaspoon cinnamon
½ teaspoon ground ginger
Dash each of grated nutmeg and
   ground cloves
1 tablespoon grated orange rind
1 cup/2 sticks unsalted butter
¾ cup granulated white sugar
¾ cup light brown sugar
1 egg
1 cup puréed persimmon pulp (about
   3 very ripe persimmons)
1 cup coarsely ground nuts (walnuts,
   pecans, or hazelnuts)

ORANGE CREAM CHEESE FROSTING
1 cup cream cheese
2 tablespoons/¼ stick unsalted butter
1½ cups powdered sugar
1 teaspoon grated orange rind
2 teaspoons orange juice
Dried persimmons for decoration

1. Preheat oven to 350°F.

2. Mix all of the dry ingredients together and stir in the orange rind. Set aside.

3. In the large bowl of an electric mixer, cream butter and sugars until light and fluffy. Add egg and beat well. Alternately add flour mixture and persimmon pulp, beating well after each addition. Fold in nuts.

4. Spoon batter into cupcake papers, filling cups about ⅔ full. Smooth batter with the back of a spoon. Bake for 25 minutes or until a tester inserted into the center comes out clean. Remove from oven and cool completely before unmolding.

5. To make the frosting: in a large bowl, cream together cream cheese and butter until smooth and well blended. Gradually add sugar and beat until the mixture is light and fluffy. Beat in the orange rind and juice and place in the refrigerator for about an hour before frosting cooled cupcakes. Top with a piece of dried persimmon.

CUPCAKE TIP
You can substitute lemon for the orange in both the cupcake and the frosting.

STRAWBERRY RHUBARB CRISP Cupcakes

Strawberries and rhubarb go particularly well together. The strawberries seem to bring out the subtle flavor of the rhubarb as well as its color.

MAKES: ABOUT 16 REGULAR CUPCAKES OR 8 JUMBO CUPCAKES

1 cup chopped rhubarb, fresh or frozen

1 cup sugar, plus 3 tablespoons if you are using fresh rhubarb (see step 1)

2 cups all-purpose flour

2 teaspoons baking powder

1 teaspoon baking soda

1 teaspoon salt

1 teaspoon cinnamon

½ cup/1 stick unsalted butter, room temperature

2 eggs

1 teaspoon vanilla extract

1 cup buttermilk (you can substitute milk, in which case you eliminate the baking soda)

STRAWBERRY GLAZE

½ cup strawberry jelly

1 cup fresh strawberries, washed, cleaned, and cut into quarters lengthwise, for decoration

1. If you are using fresh rhubarb, wash and peel the rhubarb, cut it into small slices (as you would celery) and place it in a colander in the sink or over a bowl. Sprinkle with 3 tablespoons sugar and let drain for half an hour. This will make the rhubarb more tender and will bring out its taste.

2. Preheat oven to 350°F.

3. Mix flour, baking powder, baking soda, salt, and cinnamon together and set aside.

4. In the large bowl of an electric mixer, cream butter and sugar until light and fluffy. Add eggs, one at a time, mixing well after each addition. Add vanilla. Alternately add dry ingredients and buttermilk or milk, beating continually. When batter is smooth, fold in rhubarb.

5. Spoon batter into either regular or jumbo cupcake papers, filling about ⅔ full. Bake for 20–25 minutes or until a tester inserted into the center comes out clean. Remove from oven and cool.

6. Melt strawberry jelly over very low heat. When just melted, spread on cooled cupcakes with a pastry brush. Place sliced strawberries in a circle in the center. Brush a little jelly over them so that they will stay in place and take on a glossy sheen.

YOGURT Cupcakes

These very-easy-to-make cupcakes are both healthy and tasty and will make
a great snack or an elegant dessert, accompanied by a fresh fruit salad.

MAKES: ABOUT 18 CUPCAKES

1 container yogurt (about $\frac{1}{2}$ cup)
2 containers sugar
3 eggs, lightly beaten
$\frac{1}{2}$ container vegetable oil
3 containers all-purpose flour
2 teaspoons baking powder
1 teaspoon salt
Flavoring (vanilla, almond extract,
    etc.—see step 3)

1. Preheat oven to 350°F.

2. In a large bowl, mix the yogurt, sugar, and eggs until completely
blended with a whisk or a wooden spoon. Add oil and stir. Add flour,
baking powder, and salt and beat until smooth.

3. Add the flavoring of your choice—you could add $\frac{1}{2}$ cup fresh, dried, or
candied fruit or nuts. You can also add the flavoring extract of your
choice—vanilla, almond, mint, lemon (with a little grated lemon rind),
orange flower water, etc. Or you can add food coloring to make party or
holiday cupcakes. Divide up the batter and make several different colors.

4. Spoon batter into cupcake papers, filling cups about $\frac{2}{3}$ full. Cook
cupcakes for about 25 minutes or until a tester inserted into the center
comes out clean. Remove from oven and cool.

VARIATION: FRUIT YOGURT CUPCAKES

Use the basic recipe above but instead of plain yogurt, use one with fruit
or other ingredients already added.

★ If you are using a berry yogurt, add $\frac{1}{2}$ cup dried, frozen, or fresh fruit,
cut into small pieces, or a tablespoon of kirsch or fruit liquor.

★ If you are using apricot yogurt, add 2 tablespoons ground almonds, top
the cooked cupcakes with apricot glaze and caramelized almonds.

★ If you are using strawberry or raspberry yogurt, top cooked cupcakes
with whipped cream with added chopped fresh fruit.

CUPCAKE TIP
*The yogurt
container will be your
measuring cup—so
no mess!*

POPPYSEED & LAVENDER HONEY Cupcakes

Cooking the poppyseeds in honey gives the cupcakes a distinctive flavor.

I prefer lavender honey but you can use the honey of your choice.

MAKES: ABOUT 24 REGULAR CUPCAKES OR 12 JUMBO CUPCAKES

1 cup poppyseeds

½ cup honey

¼ cup water

2½ cups all-purpose flour

1 teaspoon baking soda

1 teaspoon salt, plus a good pinch for egg whites

1 cup/2 sticks unsalted butter, room temperature

1½ cups sugar

4 eggs, separated

1 teaspoon vanilla extract

1 cup sour cream (you can use whipping or liquid cream instead)

Powdered sugar for dusting

1. Preheat oven to 350°F. Cook the poppyseeds with honey and water for about 5 minutes. Let cool.

2. Mix flour, baking soda, and salt together and set aside.

3. In the bowl of an electric mixer, cream butter with sugar until light and fluffy. Add cooled poppyseed mixture. Blend well. Add egg yolks, one at a time, beating well after each addition. Blend in vanilla and sour cream. Add dry ingredients to mixture, blending well.

4. Beat egg whites with a good pinch of salt until stiff but not dry. Gently fold into batter.

5. Spoon batter into either regular or jumbo cupcake papers, filling cups just a little over ½ full. Cook for about 15 minutes or until golden brown on top. Cooking time will depend on the size of the cupcakes you are making. Loosely cover cupcakes with a piece of aluminum foil and cook for another 5–10 minutes or until a tester comes out clean. Remove from oven and cool. Dust with powdered sugar.

SUNSHINE & VITAMIN C
Cupcakes

Just what Grandma ordered! Besides being lovely to look at, these cupcakes provide a triple dose of vitamin C with the lemon, orange, and grapefruit juices.

MAKES: ABOUT 16 CUPCAKES

2 cups all-purpose flour

2 teaspoons baking powder

1 teaspoon salt

1 teaspoon each finely grated lemon, orange, and grapefruit rind

½ cup/1 stick unsalted butter, room temperature

1¼ cups sugar

2 eggs

⅔ cup orange and grapefruit juice mixed (preferably in equal parts)

1 tablespoon lemon juice

THREE CITRUS FRUIT CUSTARD

3 tablespoons each of lemon juice, orange juice, and grapefruit juice

⅓ cup water

½ cup sugar

2 tablespoons all purpose flour

Pinch of salt

3 egg yolks (or 1 egg and 1 yolk)

Candied or jellied citrus fruit for decoration

1. Preheat oven to 350°F.

2. Mix flour, baking powder, and salt together in a medium bowl. Add the fruit rinds and set aside.

3. In the large bowl of an electric mixer, cream butter and sugar until light and fluffy. Add eggs, one at a time, mixing well after each addition. Alternately add dry ingredients and fruit juices, blending until smooth.

4. Fill cupcake papers about ⅔ full. Bake for about 25 minutes or until a tester inserted into the center comes out clean. Remove from oven and cool.

5. Mix all the custard ingredients together in a large bowl over simmering water. Stir mixture constantly until it is hot to the touch and thick. It should coat the back of a wooden spoon.

6. Remove from heat and cool, stirring from time to time so that a skin doesn't form. When it has cooled, you can cover it with plastic wrap and put it in the refrigerator until you are ready to use it. Heap onto cooled cupcakes and top with a piece of candied or jellied citrus fruit.

CUPCAKE TIP
You can also cut the center out of the cupcakes and fill it with a heaping portion of custard.

KIDS'
CUPCAKES

YETI Cupcakes

The Yeti, or the Abominable Snowman, is a mythical creature. The only thing that everyone agrees on about Yeti is that he is snow white—and very cool. Thus, the Yeti Cupcake!

MAKES: ABOUT 18 CUPCAKES

WHITE VELVET CUPCAKE

2 cups all-purpose flour

2 teaspoons baking power

1 teaspoon salt, plus a pinch for the egg whites

$\frac{1}{2}$ cup/1 stick unsalted butter, room temperature

$1\frac{1}{4}$ cups sugar

$\frac{2}{3}$ cup milk

1 teaspoon vanilla extract (you can replace with another flavoring if you prefer: lemon, almond extract, etc.)

3 egg whites

1 cup mini-marshmallows

SNOW FROSTING

2 egg whites

$\frac{3}{4}$ cup sugar

$\frac{1}{4}$ cup light corn syrup

Pinch of salt

1 teaspoon vanilla extract

$\frac{1}{2}$ cup sweetened shredded coconut (optional)

Sweetened shredded coconut for decoration

1. Preheat oven to 350°F.

2. Mix flour, baking powder, and salt together and set aside.

3. Cream butter and sugar until light and fluffy. Alternately add flour mixture and milk and beat until batter is smooth. Add flavoring.

4. Beat egg whites with a pinch of salt until stiff but not dry. Gently fold into batter. Fold in mini-marshmallows.

5. Spoon batter into cupcake papers, filling cups about $\frac{2}{3}$ full. Bake for 20–25 minutes or until tester inserted into the center comes out clean. Remove from oven and cool.

6. To make the frosting: in a large bowl, preferably the top of a double boiler, mix egg whites, sugar, corn syrup, and salt until combined. Place the bowl over simmering water and whisk until the sugar dissolves and the mixture is hot. This will take about 3 minutes. Remove from heat and beat for 5–7 minutes until frosting is cool and stiff peaks form. Beat in vanilla and delicately fold in the coconut by hand, if desired. The frosting will be ready to spread. Decorate frosted cupcakes to your taste.

CUPCAKE TIP

This is one version of what is know as a "7-minute frosting." It is light and delicious and has a marshmallow feel to it.

CHOCOLATE HAZELNUT
Cupcakes with Chocolate Hazelnut Spread

Chocolate hazelnut spreads are a great favorite among French children (and adults!) on a fresh baguette or a hot crepe for breakfast or a snack. These light cupcakes will be a big success for any kid's birthday party or a special dessert for the whole family.

MAKES: ABOUT 16 CUPCAKES

1¾ cups all-purpose flour

2 teaspoons baking powder

½ teaspoon salt

½ cup/1 stick unsalted butter, room temperature

½ cup sugar

3 eggs

1½ cups chocolate hazelnut spread (Nutella or similar)

¼ cup milk

½ cup roasted ground hazelnuts or whole hazelnuts for topping (optional)

1. Preheat oven to 350°F.

2. Mix flour, baking powder, and salt together and set aside.

3. Cream butter and sugar until light and fluffy. Add eggs, one at a time, mixing well after each addition. Add half of the chocolate hazelnut spread and blend thoroughly. Alternately add flour mixture and milk, blending well after each addition.

4. Spoon batter into cupcake papers, filling about ⅔ full. Bake for 20–25 minutes or until a tester inserted into the center comes out clean. Remove from oven and cool.

5. When cupcakes are cool, generously frost them with remaining chocolate hazelnut spread. Sprinkle with roasted ground hazelnuts or place a whole or half hazelnut on top of each cupcake.

ROOT BEER Floats

Root beer floats were a staple of my childhood and teenage years and the mere thought brings back memories of hot summers where I grew up. My parents used to take us to the ice cream parlor where we could indulge in what seemed at the time like a mile-high root beer float. Try one of these on a warm summer day and see if it has the same effect on you!

MAKES: ABOUT 16 CUPCAKES

1 cup all-purpose flour
1 cup sugar
1 teaspoon baking powder
1 teaspoon baking soda
1 teaspoon salt
½ cup root beer
½ cup/1 stick unsalted butter, cut into small pieces
1 egg, slightly beaten
⅓ cup buttermilk
1 teaspoon vanilla extract
1 cup mini-marshmallows (optional)

ROOT BEER FROSTING
2 cups powdered sugar
Pinch of salt
¼ cup root beer
½ cup/1 stick unsalted butter, cut into small pieces
1 teaspoon vanilla extract
Whipped cream for topping
Root beer candies (optional) for decoration
Decorative straws

1. Preheat oven to 350°F.

2. In a large bowl, mix flour, sugar, baking powder, baking soda, and salt together and set aside.

3. In a heavy pan, bring root beer and butter to a boil, stirring constantly. Remove from heat and pour into flour mixture, beating well with a wooden spoon. Add egg, buttermilk, and vanilla. When batter is smooth, fold in mini-marshmallows.

4. Spoon batter into cupcake papers, filling cups about ⅔ full. Bake for 20–25 minutes or until a tester inserted into the center comes out clean. Remove from oven and cool.

5. To make the frosting: place powdered sugar and salt in a large bowl.

6. In a heavy pan, bring root beer and butter to a boil, stirring constantly. Remove from heat and slowly add to sugar, stirring continually until mixture is smooth. When frosting has cooled, beat it for a few minutes with an electric beater. Frost cupcakes and top each cupcake with a dab of whipped cream and a root beer candy, if desired. Cut pretty straws in half and stick one into each cupcake.

BIRTHDAY Beauties

You can of course use any recipe for a birthday cake but I have suggested three here that are sure to please the kids – strawberry, lemon, and chocolate. My mother used to make these for my birthday parties when I was little and ice them with lovely pastel-colored frosting.

MAKES: **ABOUT 12 CUPCAKES**

STRAWBERRY CUPCAKE
2½ cups all-purpose flour
¾ cup sugar
2½ teaspoons baking powder
1 teaspoon baking soda
½ teaspoon salt
1 cup buttermilk
6 tablespoons/¾ stick unsalted
   butter, melted and slightly cooled
2 eggs, slightly beaten
1 teaspoon vanilla extract
1 cup fresh strawberries, cleaned and
   cut into small pieces

PASTEL CUPCAKE FROSTING
1 x quantity ready-to-use fondant
   frosting (about 1 cup per
   12 cupcakes)
Food coloring (various colors)

FOR DECORATION
Shredded coconut
Chocolate sprinkles
Candies
Colored sugars
Candied fruits
Nuts

1. Preheat oven to 350°F. In a large bowl, mix flour, sugar, baking powder, baking soda, and salt together and set aside.

2. In another bowl, mix buttermilk, melted butter, eggs, and vanilla. Add liquid ingredients to dry ingredients and beat well with a wooden spoon. Fold in strawberries.

3. Spoon batter into cupcake papers, filling cups about ²⁄₃ full. Bake for 20–25 minutes or until a tester inserted into the center comes out clean. Remove from oven and cool.

4. To make the pastel frosting: put fondant frosting in separate bowls and add several drops of food coloring to each bowl until you obtain the desired color. Frost or dip cupcakes in frosting and decorate with shredded coconut, chocolate sprinkles, candies, colored sugars, candied fruits, nuts, etc.

VARIATION: LEMON CUPCAKES
Follow recipe for Easter Lemon Chiffon Cupcakes (page 124) and top with the pastel cupcake frosting. Decorate as desired.

VARIATION: CHOCOLATE CUPCAKES
Follow any of the chocolate cupcake recipes in this book, such as Chocolate Hazelnut Cupcake (page 42) or Chocolate Malted Milkshake Cupcake (page 56). Decorate as desired.

CHOCOLATE SUNDAE Cupcakes

These one-egg cupcakes will be light and velvety and the vanilla bean will give them an unrivaled flavor.

MAKES: ABOUT 18 CUPCAKES

REAL VANILLA CUPCAKE
³/₄ cup milk
1 vanilla bean, split lengthwise
2 cups all-purpose flour
2 teaspoons baking powder
1 teaspoon salt
¹/₂ cup/1 stick unsalted butter, room temperature
1 cup sugar
1 egg

OLD-FASHIONED FUDGE FROSTING
1¹/₂ cups sugar
³/₄ cup milk
2 tablespoons unsweetened cocoa powder
Pinch of salt
1 tablespoon unsalted butter
1 teaspoon vanilla extract
¹/₂ cup finely ground peanuts (optional)
Maraschino cherries for decoration

1. In a small saucepan, heat milk with vanilla bean. When milk boils, remove from heat immediately and let cool, about an hour. After the milk has cooled, remove the vanilla bean and scrape out the inside into the milk Discard the bean.

2. Preheat oven to 350°F. Mix flour, baking powder, and salt together and set aside.

3. Cream butter and sugar until light and fluffy. Add egg and beat well. Alternately add dry ingredients and milk, mixing well after each addition.

4. Spoon batter into cupcake papers, filling cups about ²/₃ full. Bake for about 15–20 minutes or until a tester inserted into the center comes out clean. Remove from oven and cool.

5. To make the frosting: mix sugar, milk, cocoa, and salt in a medium pan. Cook slowly over medium heat until mixture comes to a boil. Continue cooking until mixture forms a soft ball when dropped into a glass of water (about 234°F on a candy thermometer). This may take 15 minutes. Remove mixture from heat. Add butter and vanilla and blend well.

6. Put pan in cold water and beat until mixture is of spreading consistency. This could take 15 minutes. Spread on cupcakes immediately, sprinkle with peanuts, if desired, and top with a cherry before the frosting hardens.

COOKIES 'N' CREAM
Cupcakes

Remember when you were a kid and you used to dunk those cookies in a tall glass of cold milk? Well, this is the cupcake version. Use any type of sandwich cookie—choose your favorite.

MAKES: ABOUT 18–20 CUPCAKES

1⅔ cups all-purpose flour

2 teaspoons baking powder

1 teaspoon salt

½ cup/1 stick unsalted butter, room temperature

1 cup sugar

2 eggs

1 teaspoon vanilla extract

¾ cup half-and-half or light cream

1 cup coarsely crushed sandwich cookies (Oreo type)

WHITE CHOCOLATE
CREAM CHEESE FROSTING

6 ounces good quality white chocolate, broken into pieces

¾ cup cream cheese, softened, cut into pieces

6 tablespoons/¾ stick unsalted butter, room temperature, cut into pieces

Miniature sandwich cookies or crushed cookies for decoration

1. Preheat oven to 350°F.

2. Mix flour, baking powder, and salt together and set aside.

3. Cream butter and sugar until light and fluffy. Add eggs, one at a time, mixing well after each addition. Add vanilla. Alternately add flour mixture and half-and-half or cream and beat until batter is smooth. Fold in crushed cookies.

4. Spoon batter into cupcake papers, filling cups about ⅔ full. Bake for 20–25 minutes or until a tester inserted into the center comes out clean. Remove from oven and cool.

5. To make the frosting: in a microwave or a double boiler, melt white chocolate until smooth and creamy, just a few minutes. It should be just warm to the touch.

6. Beat the cream cheese and butter until light and fluffy. Add melted chocolate and beat again until smooth. Use the frosting immediately or it will harden. Press in a little cookie or sprinkle with crushed cookies at once, while frosting is still soft. This frosting looks like the cream filling in sandwich cookies.

HOT CHOCOLATE & MARSHMALLOW
Cupcakes

Serve these delicious chocolate cupcakes while they are still warm to get the full effect.

MAKES: ABOUT 12 CUPCAKES

8 ounces dark chocolate

1 cup/2 sticks unsalted butter, room
   temperature

4 eggs

1 cup sugar

¾ cup all-purpose flour

1 teaspoon salt

½ cup mini-chocolate chips or grated
   chocolate

Marshmallows or mini-marshmallows
   for decoration

1. Preheat oven to 350°F. Melt chocolate and butter in a double boiler or microwave until just melted (do not cook). Set aside until just warm.

3. Cream the eggs and sugar together until light and foamy. Add flour and salt and mix. Pour in the chocolate mixture and beat until batter is smooth.

4. Spoon batter into 12 cupcake papers. Sprinkle a scant teaspoon of mini-chocolate chips or grated chocolate over each cupcake and bake for 15 minutes. Remove cupcakes from oven. They will be very moist inside.

5. Place a marshmallow or several mini-marshmallows on each cupcake. Put cupcakes under broiler for a few seconds until marshmallows start to brown. This will take only a second so be very careful. Remove from oven and wait for about 5 minutes before eating since the marshmallows will be very hot. These cupcakes are best eaten while still slightly warm.

CUPCAKE TIP
Alternatively, bake in a silicon mold. Leave off the marshmallow and sprinkle with a few grains of "fleur de sel."

JELLY-FILLED Cupcakes

These cupcakes are perfect for any occasion and can be decorated
accordingly for birthdays or holidays or for a special dessert or snack.

MAKES: **ABOUT 12 CUPCAKES**

BASIC YELLOW CUPCAKE

1 1/2 cups all-purpose flour

2 teaspoons baking powder

1 teaspoon salt

1/2 cup/1 stick unsalted butter, room
    temperature

1 cup sugar

2 eggs

1 teaspoon vanilla extract (or another
    flavoring, such as almond extract,
    orange flower water, etc.)

1/2 cup milk

Jam, jelly, marmalade, or preserves of
    your choice

BASIC WHITE CUPCAKE ICING

3 tbsp hot milk or cream

2 1/2 cups powdered sugar

FOR DECORATION

Colored sugars

Candies

Stencils etc.

1. Preheat oven to 350°F. Mix dry ingredients together and set aside.

2. Cream butter and sugar until light and fluffy. Add eggs, one at a time,
mixing well after each addition. Add vanilla. Alternately add flour mixture
and milk and beat until batter is smooth.

3. Spoon batter into cupcake papers, filling cups about 2/3 full. Bake for
20–25 minutes or until tester inserted into the center comes out clean.
Remove from oven and cool.

4. When cupcakes are cool, scoop out the center and fill with the jam,
jelly, marmalade, or preserves of your choice. Replace the core.

5. Put hot milk or cream in a large bowl. Gradually add sugar until icing is
thick enough to spread. Beat for several minutes until icing is smooth and
creamy. You may need to add more sugar or liquid to get the right
consistency but remember to beat well after each addition.

6. While the icing is still soft, decorate with colored sugars, candies,
stencils, etc.

VARIATION: BASIC CHOCOLATE CUPCAKE

Use the recipe for Basic Yellow Cupcake but replace 1/4 cup flour with
1/4 cup unsweetened cocoa powder.

VARIATION: BASIC CHOCOLATE CUPCAKE ICING

Use the recipe for Basic White Cupcake Icing but replace 1/4 cup powdered
sugar with 1/4 cup unsweetened cocoa powder.

PEANUT BUTTER & JELLY SWIRLS

These cupcakes are definitely a throwback to childhood and those peanut butter and jelly sandwiches of my youth.

MAKES: ABOUT 20 CUPCAKES

2½ cups all-purpose flour
3 teaspoons baking powder
1 teaspoon salt
½ cup/1 stick unsalted butter, room temperature
1½ cups light brown sugar
¾ cup chunky peanut butter
1 teaspoon vanilla extract
3 eggs
1 cup half-and-half or light cream
4 ounces jelly (about 6 heaping tablespoons)

PEANUT BUTTER FROSTING
¼ cup/½ stick unsalted butter, room temperature
½ cup smooth peanut butter
2 cups powdered sugar
2 tablespoons milk

FOR DECORATION
½ cup chopped peanuts
Jelly

1. Preheat oven to 350°F.

2. Mix flour, baking powder, and salt together and set aside.

3. Cream butter and sugar until light and fluffy. Add peanut butter and vanilla and continue beating until thoroughly blended. Add eggs, one at a time, mixing well after each addition. Alternately add half-and-half or cream and dry ingredients, beating well after each addition.

4. Dollop the jelly over the cupcake batter in 6 heaping tablespoons. Swirl jelly into batter with a long knife or spatula. Don't overmix.

5. Spoon batter into cupcake papers, filling cups about ⅔ full. Bake for 25–30 minutes or until a tester inserted in the center comes out clean. Remove from oven and cool.

6. Make the frosting: cream butter, peanut butter, and sugar together until light and fluffy. Gradually add milk and beat until creamy and of spreading consistency. You can add more milk if needed.

7. Ice cupcakes, add a swirl of jelly, and sprinkle with chopped peanuts.

CUPCAKE TIP
You can also fill the cupcake with jelly rather than swirling it in— just take out the center of a cooled cupcake with an apple core, put a teaspoon of jelly in the hole and replace the core.

ROCKY ROAD
Cupcakes

Rocky Road is a big favorite among kids. It is usually a combination of chocolate, walnuts, marshmallows, and chocolate chips, whether it be in an ice cream, a brownie, or a cupcake. You can improvise with this recipe—tailor it to your family's and friends' tastes.

MAKES: ABOUT 18 CUPCAKES

1½ cups all-purpose flour
2 teaspoons baking powder
1 teaspoon salt
⅓ cup unsweetened cocoa powder
4 ounces dark chocolate
¼ cup vegetable oil
1 egg
1 teaspoon vanilla extract
1 cup milk
½ cup mini-marshmallows
½ cup dark chocolate chips,
　plus ½ cup for topping
½ cup coarsely chopped walnuts,
　plus ½ cup for topping
½ cup white chocolate chips for
　topping (optional)

1. Preheat oven to 350°F.

2. Mix flour, baking powder, salt, and cocoa powder together, mix thoroughly, and set aside.

3. Melt chocolate in a microwave or a double boiler (do not cook). Remove from heat as soon as chocolate is just melted. Using either an electric mixer or a wooden spoon, beat in oil, egg, and vanilla. Alternately add flour mixture and milk, beating well after each addition. When batter is smooth and thoroughly blended, fold in ½ cup each mini-marshmallows, chocolate chips, and walnuts.

4. Spoon batter into cupcake papers, filling just over ½ full. Mix remaining walnuts and chocolate chips together and sprinkle over batter. Bake for about 20 minutes or until topping is cooked. If the topping starts to burn before the cupcakes are cooked, cover lightly with a piece of aluminum foil. Remove from oven and cool.

CUPCAKE TIP
Try using different flavor chips (mint, peanut, coffee, etc.)

BANANA SPLIT
Cupcakes

Who doesn't remember banana splits from their childhood, when no one worried about their waistlines or cholesterol level!

MAKES: ABOUT 18 CUPCAKES

2 cups all-purpose flour
2 teaspoons baking powder
1 teaspoon baking soda
1 teaspoon salt
½ cup/1 stick unsalted butter
1½ cups sugar
2 eggs
1 teaspoon vanilla extract
1 cup ripe mashed bananas (about 2 medium bananas)
½ cup buttermilk or sour cream
Strawberry preserves for filling

CHOCOLATE FUDGE ICING
4 tablespoons/¼ stick unsalted butter, cut into little pieces
4 ounces dark chocolate, broken into pieces
3 cups powdered sugar
⅓ cup hot milk
1 teaspoon vanilla extract
Pinch of salt
Maraschino cherries and banana candies for decoration

1. Preheat oven to 350°F.

2. Mix flour, baking powder, baking soda, and salt together and set aside.

3. Cream butter and sugar until light and fluffy. Add eggs, one at a time, mixing well after each addition. Add vanilla and mashed bananas and mix thoroughly. Alternately beat in flour mixture and liquid and blend until smooth.

4. Spoon batter into cupcake papers, filling cups about ⅔ full. Smooth batter with the back of a spoon. Bake for 20 minutes or until a tester inserted in the center comes out clean. Remove from oven and cool.

5. When cupcakes are cool, scoop out the center of each cupcake with an apple corer. Drop in a teaspoon of strawberry preserves.

6. To make the icing: melt butter and chocolate in a double boiler or a microwave. Stir until just melted and set aside until cool to the touch. You can set the bowl in cold water to speed up the process.

7. Put sugar and hot milk in a large bowl and stir until smooth. Add vanilla, salt, and chocolate mixture. Using an electric beater, beat icing until smooth and thickened, about 5 minutes. Ice cooled, filled cupcakes. Decorate with a cherry and banana candies.

S'MORES
Cupcakes

I guess that anyone who grew up in the United States knows what a S'more is—
a sort of graham cracker sandwich with chocolate and marshmallow. Here is my
cupcake version. I hope you will find it to your liking and will ask for s'more!

MAKES: **ABOUT 18 CUPCAKES**

GRAHAM CRACKER AND MILK
CHOCOLATE CUPCAKE
½ cup all-purpose flour
1½ cups finely crushed graham
    crackers (about 20 grahams)
2 teaspoons baking powder
1 teaspoon salt
½ cup/1 stick unsalted butter, room
    temperature
¾ cup sugar
2 eggs
1 teaspoon vanilla extract
¾ cup milk
1 cup milk chocolate chips

NO-COOK MARSHMALLOW ICING
2 egg whites
Pinch of salt or ¼ teaspoon cream of
    tartar
¼ cup sugar
¾ cup corn syrup
Grated milk chocolate or chocolate
    sprinkles for decoration

1. Preheat oven to 350°F.

2. Mix flour, crushed graham crackers, baking powder, and salt together
and set aside.

3. Cream butter and sugar until light and fluffy. Add eggs, one at a time,
mixing well after each addition. Add vanilla. Alternately add flour mixture
and milk and beat until batter is smooth. Fold in chocolate chips.

4. Spoon batter into cupcake papers, filling cups about ⅔ full. Bake for
20–25 minutes or until a tester inserted into the center comes out clean.
Remove from oven and cool.

5. To make the icing: beat egg whites
with salt or cream of tartar until soft
peaks form. Gradually add sugar,
beating continually. Slowly add
corn syrup. Icing will form peaks
and will have a marshmallow
consistency. Ice cooled cupcakes
and sprinkle with milk chocolate or
chocolate sprinkles.

CUPCAKE TIP
*For a cooked version
of this frosting, you can use
the recipe for Snow Frosting,
(page 40). You can also
use ready-made
marshmallow frosting if
you are in a hurry.*

CHOCOLATE MALTED MILK SHAKE Cupcakes

These cupcakes remind me of those fabulous chocolate malted milk shakes we used to drink at the soda fountain of the local drug store when we were kids.

MAKES: ABOUT 18 CUPCAKES

¾ cup chocolate malted milk candies, crushed

½ cup chocolate malted milk powder

2 cups all-purpose flour

3 teaspoons baking powder

1 teaspoon salt

¾ cup/1½ sticks unsalted butter, room temperature

1 cup light brown sugar

2 eggs

1 teaspoon vanilla extract

1 cup half-and-half or light cream

CHOCOLATE MALTED MILK FROSTING

6 tablespoons/¾ stick unsalted butter, room temperature

⅓ cup chocolate malted milk powder

2 cups powdered sugar

Pinch of salt

¼ cup milk

1 teaspoon vanilla extract

Whipped cream (optional)

Chocolate malted milk candies

1. Preheat oven to 350°F.

2. In a small bowl, mix crushed chocolate malted milk candies, malted milk powder, flour, baking powder, and salt together. Set aside.

3. Cream butter and sugar until light and fluffy. Add eggs, one at a time, beating well after each addition. Add vanilla. Alternately add dry ingredients and half-and-half or light cream, beating until smooth after each addition.

4. Fill cupcake papers just a little over ½ full and bake for about 20 minutes or until a tester inserted into the center comes out clean. Remove from oven and cool.

5. To make the frosting: beat butter, malted milk powder, sugar, and salt until light and fluffy. Gradually add milk and vanilla, beating continuously, until frosting is of the desired consistency. You may want to use less milk. Frost cooled cupcakes, top with a dollop of whipped cream, if desired, and place a chocolate malted milk candy on top.

CUPCAKE TIP
Replace cream with low-fat milk for a lighter version.

AFTER DINNER
CUPCAKES

BURGUNDY BLUES
Cupcakes

Burgundy is one of the major wine-producing regions in France and some of the finest and best-known wines in the world are produced there. The combination of chocolate and red wine may seem strange at first but is actually quite delicious.

MAKES: ABOUT 16–18 CUPCAKES

¾ cup all-purpose flour
1 teaspoon baking powder
½ teaspoon salt
2 tablespoons instant cocoa powder
   (the presweetened kind)
1 teaspoon cinnamon
½ cup/1 stick unsalted butter, room
   temperature
½ cup sugar
2 eggs
¼ cup dry red wine
2 ounces grated dark chocolate
CHOCOLATE GLAZE
4 ounces good quality dark chocolate
¼ cup/½ stick unsalted butter
1 tablespoon corn syrup
Red and blue sugar for decoration

1. Preheat oven to 350°F.

2. Mix dry ingredients together and set aside.

3. Cream butter and sugar until light and fluffy. Add eggs, one at a time, mixing well after each addition. Alternately beat in flour mixture and wine. Fold in grated chocolate.

4. Spoon batter into cupcake papers, filling cups about ⅔ full. Bake for 20–25 minutes or until a tester inserted into the center comes out clean. Remove from oven and cool.

5. To make the chocolate glaze: melt chocolate and butter in a double boiler or a microwave. When just melted and barely warm to the touch, remove from heat and stir in corn syrup. Either dip cooled cupcakes in glaze or dribble a little over each cupcake. Sprinkle with red and blue sugar.

CUPCAKE TIP
These cupcakes will go down particularly well with a glass of port wine or a cream sherry.

RUM RAISIN Cupcakes with Butter Rum Frosting

Rum and raisins are a very popular duo, and justifiably so. I think that the rum brings out the flavor of the raisins and vice versa. Make these in mini cupcake molds and serve them with rum and raisin ice cream for a special dessert treat.

MAKES: **ABOUT 16 REGULAR CUPCAKES OR 40 MINI-CUPCAKES**

½ cup raisins

¼ cup dark rum

1 cup, plus 2 tablespoons all-purpose flour

1½ teaspoons baking powder

1 teaspoon salt

½ cup/1 stick, plus 2 tablespoons unsalted butter, cut into small pieces

¾ cup light brown sugar

3 eggs, slightly beaten

BUTTER RUM FROSTING

¼ cup/½ stick unsalted butter, room temperature

2 cups powdered sugar

Pinch of salt

3 tablespoons rum (use raisin-soaking liquid)

Raisins for decoration

1. Soak raisins in rum for about 30 minutes, turning from time to time. Drain and set aside. Save liquid for frosting.

2. Preheat oven to 350°F.

3. In a large bowl, mix flour, baking powder, and salt together and set aside.

4. In a small pan, melt butter and sugar over low heat, stirring constantly. When sugar has dissolved, remove from heat and pour into the center of the flour mixture. Mix well. Add drained raisins and eggs and stir vigorously with a wooden spoon until the batter is smooth.

5. Fill cupcake papers about ⅔ full. Bake for about 25 minutes or until a tester inserted into the center comes out clean. Remove from oven and cool.

6. To make the frosting: cream butter, sugar, and salt until light and fluffy. Add rum and continue beating. If too thick, add more rum; if too thin, add more sugar. Frost cooled cupcakes and decorate with raisins.

BEER & PEANUTS
Cupcakes

These original and spectacular looking cupcakes will almost make you feel like you are sitting in a cosy pub in merry old England, downing a pint of ale and munching on some peanuts.

MAKES: ABOUT 12–14 CUPCAKES

1 cup dark beer
²/₃ cup light brown sugar
6 tablespoons/¾ stick unsalted butter, cut into pieces
½ cup raisins
1²/₃ cups all-purpose flour
2 teaspoons baking powder
1 teaspoon baking soda
1 teaspoon salt
1 teaspoon cinnamon
½ teaspoon ground ginger
Dash of grated nutmeg
2 eggs, slightly beaten

PEANUT BRITTLE TOPPING
6 tablespoons/¾ stick unsalted butter
1 cup light brown sugar
2 tablespoons sugar syrup (ready-made or boil equal amounts of sugar and water)
½ teaspoon lemon juice
1 cup grilled peanuts, lightly salted

1. In a large saucepan, bring beer, sugar, and butter to a boil. Add raisins and cook for 5 minutes over medium heat. Remove from heat and let cool, stirring from time to time so that a crust doesn't form.

2. Preheat oven to 350°F.

3. In a large bowl, mix dry ingredients together. Pour in cooled beer mixture and blend well. Add eggs, a little at a time, and continue mixing until batter is smooth.

4. Spoon batter into cupcake papers, filling cups about ½ full. Bake for about 15–20 minutes or until just starting to brown on top. Remember, they are going to cook for another 5–7 minutes.

5. While the cupcakes are cooking, make the topping. In a heavy pan, mix butter, sugar, syrup, and lemon juice and heat slowly until all of the sugar has dissolved, stirring from time to time. Continue to cook over low heat for another 5 minutes. Stir in peanuts and cook another 2 minutes.

6. Spread a layer of peanut topping over each cupcake. Return to oven and cook for 5–7 minutes. When peanuts start to brown, remove from oven and let cool in pan before removing cupcakes.

KIR Cupcakes

The inspiration for these cupcakes is the "Kir," a cocktail made with white wine and black currant liqueur (Crème de Cassis). It originated in Dijon but is found in bars and on tables throughout France.

MAKES: ABOUT 20 CUPCAKES

1²/₃ cups all-purpose flour
1¹/₄ cups sugar
2 teaspoons baking powder
¹/₂ teaspoon salt, plus pinch for the egg whites
¹/₂ cup vegetable oil
¹/₂ cup white wine
4 eggs, separated
³/₄ cup dried currants

BLACK CURRANT GLAZE
6 ounces black currant jelly (about 8 heaping tablespoons)
2 tablespoons black currant liqueur (optional)

FOR DECORATION
White decorator frosting
Red or black currants (optional)

1. Preheat oven to 350°F.

2. Mix flour, sugar, baking powder, and salt in a bowl. Gradually add liquid, mixing well. Add egg yolks, beating well after each addition. The batter should be smooth and light.

3. Beat egg whites with a pinch of salt until stiff but not dry. Gently fold into batter. Carefully fold in dried currants.

4. Fill cupcake papers about ³/₄ full with the mixture and bake for about 20 minutes or until a tester inserted into the center comes out clean. Remove from oven and cool.

5. To make the glaze: In a small pan, heat blackcurrant jelly with liqueur, if using, and cook for about 2 minutes. With a pastry brush, spread glaze on cooled cupcakes.

6. When glaze has cooled, decorate with a zigzag of white decorator frosting and fresh currants (red or black) if the season permits.

CUPCAKE TIP
If you want to make a "Kir Royale," replace the white wine in the cupcake batter with champagne.

CAPPUCCINO
Cupcakes

This light coffee cupcake with its meringue-like cooked coffee frosting is a delight to the eyes and a wonderful accompaniment to a real cappuccino at any time of the day.

MAKES: ABOUT 12 CUPCAKES

1 cup all-purpose flour
2 teaspoons baking powder
1 teaspoon salt
³/₄ cup/1¹/₂ sticks unsalted butter, room temperature
³/₄ cup brown sugar
2 eggs
1 tablespoon coffee extract
¹/₂ cup half-and-half or light cream

STEAMED COFFEE FROSTING
1¹/₄ cups brown sugar
3 tablespoons extra-strong coffee
2 egg whites
¹/₄ teaspoon baking powder or cream of tartar
Unsweetened cocoa powder or cinnamon for dusting
Chocolate sprinkles or chocolate coffee beans (optional) for decoration

1. Preheat oven to 350°F.

2. Sift flour, baking powder, and salt together and set aside.

3. Cream butter and sugar until light and fluffy. Add eggs, one at a time, blending well after each addition. Add coffee extract. Alternately add dry ingredients and half-and-half or cream, beating until smooth.

4. Divide batter between 12 cupcake papers. Cook for 25 minutes or until a tester inserted into the center comes out clean. Remove from oven and cool.

5. To make the frosting: mix all ingredients in the top of a double boiler. Place over rapidly boiling water and beat for about 7 minutes with an electric or rotary beater until frosting stands in peaks.

6. Remove from heat and spread on cupcakes or apply a generous spoonful to each cupcake. Sprinkle with cocoa powder before frosting hardens. Frosting will be hard on the outside and creamy on the inside. Sprinkle with chocolate sprinkles and put a chocolate coffee bean on top, if using. This is another variation on a 7-minute frosting.

CUBA LIBRE
Cupcakes

A "Cuba Libre" (Free Cuba) is generally a cocktail made with rum and cola and served with a lime wedge. Its origins are widely disputed but lets hope that its metamorphosis into a cupcake will meet with widespread approval!

MAKES: ABOUT 12 CUPCAKES

¹/₂ cup/1 stick unsalted butter, cut into small pieces
¹/₂ cup cola
1 cup all-purpose flour
1 teaspoon baking powder
1 teaspoon baking soda
¹/₂ teaspoon salt
1 cup sugar
¹/₄ cup buttermilk
1 egg, slightly beaten
1 teaspoon vanilla extract

RUM FROSTING
¹/₂ cup/1 stick unsalted butter, room temperature
2 cups powdered sugar
Pinch of salt
2 tablespoons dark rum
Candied or jellied lime slices for decoration

1. In a medium saucepan, heat butter and cola until it boils. Remove from heat and let cool, about 10–15 minutes (you can set it in a pan of cold water to speed up the process).

2. Preheat oven to 350°F.

3. In a large mixing bowl, combine flour, baking powder, baking soda, salt, and sugar. Add cooled liquid to mixture and stir vigorously until batter is smooth and well blended. Beat in buttermilk, egg, and vanilla.

4. Spoon batter into cupcake papers, filling cups about ²/₃ full. Bake for 20–25 minutes or until a tester inserted into the center comes out clean. Remove from oven and cool.

5. To make the frosting: cream butter, sugar, and salt until light and fluffy. Gradually add rum, beating continually until frosting is of spreading consistency. Frost cooled cupcakes. Decorate with candied or jellied lime slices.

IRISH COFFEE
Cupcakes

These cupcakes are a bit reminiscent of Irish soda bread, but with a dose of whiskey for good measure. The Mocha Butter Cream Frosting adds an elegant touch.

MAKES: ABOUT 16 CUPCAKES

1 1/2 cups all-purpose flour
3/4 cup brown sugar
1 teaspoon baking powder
1 teaspoon baking soda
1 teaspoon salt
1 teaspoon cinnamon
1/2 teaspoon ground ginger
Dash of grated nutmeg
1/2 cup dark raisins
1/2 cup coarsely chopped nuts
   (pistachios, walnuts, or hazelnuts)
2 eggs, slightly beaten
1/2 cup vegetable oil
1/2 cup Irish whiskey
1/4 cup light cream or milk

MOCHA BUTTER CREAM FROSTING
1 cup/2 sticks unsalted butter, room
   temperature, cut into small pieces
1 2/3 cups powdered sugar
2 egg yolks
1 tablespoon coffee extract or very
   strong coffee (more or less,
   depending on your taste)

1. Preheat oven to 350°F.

2. In a large bowl, mix all of the dry ingredients together. Add eggs, oil, whiskey, and cream or milk to dry ingredients and mix until thoroughly blended with a wooden spoon.

3. Fill cupcake papers about 2/3 full. Bake for 25–30 minutes or until a tester inserted into the center comes out clean. Remove from oven and cool.

4. To make the frosting: cream butter and sugar together until light and fluffy. Add egg yolks and coffee extract to taste and beat until mixture is light, shiny, and of good spreading consistency (at least 10 minutes).
Frost cooled cupcakes.

CUPCAKE TIP
If you don't have the time or are otherwise inclined, frost these cupcakes with coffee-flavored whipped cream or use the Irish Whiskey Frosting (page 124).

MINT JULEP
Cupcakes

A mint julep is a cocktail composed of fresh mint, bourbon, and crushed ice. It is traditionally served in an iced pewter or silver mug during the Kentucky Derby.

MAKES: ABOUT 18 CUPCAKES

1 cup all-purpose flour
1 teaspoon baking powder
1 teaspoon salt
¾ cup/1½ sticks unsalted butter, room temperature
1 cup sugar
3 eggs
½ cup bourbon
¼ cup fresh finely chopped mint

WHITE CHOCOLATE MINT FROSTING
½ cup whipping cream
1 tablespoon unsalted butter
8 ounces white chocolate
2 tablespoons crème de menthe (or any other mint liqueur)
Green food coloring (optional)
Several sprigs of fresh mint for decoration
Green sugar (optional) for decoration
Decorative straws

1. Preheat oven to 350°F.

2. Mix flour, baking powder, and salt together and set aside.

3. Cream butter and sugar until light and fluffy. Add eggs, one at a time, mixing well after each addition. Alternately beat in flour mixture and bourbon. Fold in fresh mint.

4. Spoon batter into cupcake papers, filling cups about ⅔ full. Bake for 20–25 minutes or until a tester inserted into the center comes out clean. Remove from oven and cool.

5. To make the frosting: heat cream and butter in a pan over medium heat, stirring until butter melts. Remove from heat and add white chocolate. Stir until melted. Add mint liqueur and food coloring, if desired. Transfer frosting to a bowl and let cool, stirring from time to time, until it is of spreading consistency. This will probably take about 2 hours. You can speed up the process by putting the bowl in cold water.

6. Frost cooled cupcakes and decorate with a sprig of mint. Alternatively, you can dip the cupcakes in the frosting once the mixture has cooled a bit. Decorate immediately with green sugar and a mint sprig before frosting hardens. Stick in a little straw for good measure.

MEZZO-MEZZO Cupcakes

Chocolate and coffee are an irresistible duo. These sour cream cupcakes will be a gourmet ending to any gourmet meal.

MAKES: ABOUT 16 REGULAR CUPCAKES, 8 JUMBO CUPCAKES, OR 40 MINI-CUPCAKES

1⅓ cups all-purpose flour
2 teaspoons baking powder
1 teaspoon baking soda
1 teaspoon salt
½ cup unsweetened cocoa powder
1 cup light brown sugar
3 tablespoons instant cappuccino powder (you can use espresso or even decaffeinated coffee powder)
½ cup/1 stick unsalted butter, melted and cooled
2 eggs, slightly beaten
1 cup sour cream

CHOCOLATE WHIPPED CREAM FROSTING
1 cup heavy whipping cream, chilled
3 tablespoons sugar
1 tablespoon unsweetened cocoa powder, plus more for dusting
1 tablespoon instant cappuccino powder (you can use espresso or decaffeinated coffee powder)
Chocolate coffee beans for decoration

1. Preheat oven to 350°F.

2. In a large bowl, mix all of the dry ingredients together and set aside.

3. In another bowl, mix butter, eggs, and sour cream together. Pour into dry ingredients, rapidly mixing with a wooden spoon until batter is smooth.

4. Spoon batter into cupcake papers, filling cups about ⅔ full. Cook for 15–20 minutes or until a tester inserted into the center comes out clean. Remove from oven and cool.

5. To make the frosting: put cream, sugar, cocoa, and coffee powder in a large bowl. Stir, cover, and let sit in the refrigerator for about an hour, until chocolate and coffee have dissolved. Remove from refrigerator and beat with an electric beater until stiff.

6. Frost cooled cupcakes just before serving. Dust with cocoa powder and top each cupcake with a chocolate coffee bean.

CUPCAKE TIP
*Serve with
a little cup of
espresso
on the side.*

MARGARITA
Cupcakes with Lime Glaze

For this cupcake version of a margarita cocktail, I have recommended using coarse sugar to imitate the salt but if you are particularly daring you could put a few grains of "fleur de sel" on top. The contrast of the very sweet lime glaze and the salt would certainly take one back to this cupcake's origins.

MAKES: ABOUT 18 CUPCAKES

1 cup all-purpose flour
1 teaspoon baking powder
½ teaspoon salt, plus pinch for the egg whites
½ cup/1 stick unsalted butter, room temperature
¾ cup sugar
3 eggs, separated
1 tablespoon finely grated lime rind
2 tablespoons tequila

LIME GLAZE
2 tablespoons fresh lime juice
1 cup powdered sugar
1 tablespoon tequila
Green food coloring (optional)
Coarse sugar (or salt, see step 6)
Jellied lime slices for decoration

1. Preheat oven to 350°F.

2. Mix flour, baking powder, and salt together and set aside.

3. Cream butter and sugar until light and fluffy. Add egg yolks, one at a time, mixing well after each addition. Add lime rind and tequila. Gradually stir in dry ingredients until all of the flour is absorbed and the batter is smooth.

4. Beat egg whites with a pinch of salt until stiff but not dry. Gently fold whites into batter.

5. Fill cupcake papers a little over ½ full. Bake for about 20–25 minutes or until a tester inserted into the center comes out clean. Remove from oven and cool.

6. To make the glaze: in a medium bowl, mix the lime juice, powdered sugar, and tequila and beat until smooth and blended. Stir in green food coloring, if desired. Brush cooled cupcakes with glaze and sprinkle with coarse sugar (or a few grains of "fleur de sel"). Decorate with a jellied lime slice.

MIDNIGHT MADNESS
Cupcakes

Wait until midnight and surprise your guests
with these indulgent little black gems.

MAKES: ABOUT 20 CUPCAKES

1¼ cups all-purpose flour
¾ cup light brown sugar
¼ cup unsweetened cocoa powder
2 teaspoons baking powder
½ teaspoon salt
¾ cup water
¼ cup vegetable oil
1 egg, lightly beaten
1 teaspoon vanilla extract

FILLING

1 cup/8 ounces cream cheese
⅓ cup sugar
1 egg
½ teaspoon salt
1 tablespoon rum or brandy (optional)
3 ounces chocolate chips

MIDNIGHT SKY FROSTING

2½ cups powdered sugar
2 egg whites
Pinch of salt or cream of tartar
Black food coloring

FOR DECORATION

Glitter sugar for dusting
Silver balls and candy banana shape

1. Preheat oven to 350°F.

2. To make the filling: beat cream cheese, sugar, egg, salt, and rum until smooth. Fold in chocolate chips and set aside.

3. Mix flour, sugar, cocoa powder, baking powder, and salt in a large bowl. Add water, oil, egg, and vanilla and beat with a wooden spoon until smooth.

4. Fill cupcake papers ½ full with chocolate batter. Place a heaping teaspoon of the cream cheese mixture on each. Bake for about 15–25 minutes or until firm to the touch. The cream cheese filling will be a bit soft. Remove from oven and cool.

5. To make the frosting: using an electric beater, beat sugar with egg whites and salt or cream of tartar until mixed. Increase speed to high and beat for about 5 minutes or until very thick and fluffy. Add black food coloring. Frost cooled cupcakes and dust with glitter sugar, silver balls and candy banana shape for the moon.

CUPCAKE TIP
Alternatively, instead of making Midnight Sky Frosting you could top with ready-to-use black cake frosting.

PINA COLADA
Cupcakes

The main ingredients in a Piña Colada cocktail, just like in this cupcake, are pineapple, coconut, and rum. Sit back, enjoy, and listen to the palm trees swaying in the ocean breeze.

MAKES: ABOUT 16–18 CUPCAKES

2 cups all-purpose flour
2 teaspoons baking powder
1 teaspoon salt, plus pinch for the
   egg whites
½ cup/1 stick unsalted butter, room
   temperature
1¼ cups sugar
2 eggs, separated
½ cup pineapple juice
¼ cup light rum (or coconut cream or
   more pineapple juice)
½ cup shredded coconut

COCONUT ICING
2 egg whites
Pinch of salt
2 cups powdered sugar
½ cup shredded coconut

FOR DECORATION
Toasted shredded coconut
Dried or crystallized pineapple

1. Preheat oven to 350°F.

2. Mix together flour, baking powder, and salt together in a bowl and set aside.

3. Cream butter and sugar until light and fluffy. Add egg yolks, one at a time, mixing well after each addition. Alternately beat in flour mixture and liquid and blend until smooth. Stir in coconut. Beat egg whites with pinch of salt until stiff but not dry and gently fold into mixture.

4. Spoon batter into cupcake papers, filling cups about ⅔ full, smoothing with the back of a spoon. Bake for 20–25 minutes or until a tester inserted into the center comes out clean. Remove from oven and cool.

5. To make the icing: beat egg whites with a pinch of salt until stiff but not dry. Add sugar by heaping tablespoons, beating continually. Fold in shredded coconut. Add additional powdered sugar if necessary so that icing holds its shape. Ice cooled cupcakes and sprinkle with toasted coconut and a piece of dried or crystallized pineapple.

PASTIS Cupcakes with Anise Frosting

"Pastis" is an anise-based liqueur, diluted with water, and extremely popular in the south of France as an aperitif. Any brand will do. The result is surprising and extraordinary—a delicate anise-flavored batter, topped with creamy anise-flavored butter cream frosting.

MAKES: ABOUT 18 CUPCAKES

1½ cups all-purpose flour
2 teaspoons baking powder
1 teaspoon salt
¾ cups/1½ sticks unsalted butter, room temperature
¾ cup sugar
3 eggs
¼ cup pastis

ANISE BUTTER CREAM FROSTING
1 cup/2 sticks unsalted butter, room temperature, cut into small pieces
1⅔ cups powdered sugar
Pinch of salt
2 tablespoons pastis (or anise syrup or licorice essence to taste)
Liqcorice strands, licorice candies, or black decorator frosting for decoration

1. Preheat oven to 350°F.

2. Mix flour, baking powder, and salt together and set aside.

3. Cream butter and sugar until light and fluffy. Add eggs, one at a time, mixing well after each addition. Alternately beat in flour mixture and pastis.

4. Spoon batter into cupcake papers, filling cups about ⅔ full. Bake for 25 minutes or until a tester inserted into the center comes out clean. Remove from oven and cool.

5. To make the frosting: in the large bowl of an electric mixer, beat butter, sugar, and salt until light and fluffy. Add pastis and continue beating until of good spreading consistency. Frost cooled cupcakes. Decorate with a strand of licorice (arranged in a spiral shape over the icing), licorice candies, or black decorator frosting.

CUPCAKE TIP
If you prefer, use anise syrup for a non-alcoholic version.

AFTER EIGHT Cupcakes

These cupcakes will dazzle the eyes as well as the taste buds. When you bite into them—crispy on the outside and creamy on the inside—chocolate mint heaven, beyond a doubt!

MAKES: ABOUT 12 CUPCAKES

1⅓ cups all-purpose flour

⅓ cup unsweetened cocoa powder

2 teaspoons baking powder

1 teaspoon salt

6 tablespoons/¾ stick unsalted butter, room temperature

½ cup sugar

2 eggs

⅔ cup half-and-half or light cream

Few drops of mint extract

½ cup miniature chocolate mint chips

MINT BUTTER CREAM FROSTING

¾ cup/1½ sticks unsalted butter, room temperature, cut into small pieces

2 cups powdered sugar

2 tablespoons milk

Few drops of mint extract

Food coloring (optional)

CHOCOLATE GANACHE

5 ounces dark chocolate, broken into little pieces

⅔ cup heavy cream

12 little chocolate-covered mint patties (optional) for decoration

1. Preheat oven to 350°F.

2. Mix flour, cocoa, baking powder, and salt together and set aside.

3. Cream butter and sugar until light and fluffy. Add eggs, one at a time, mixing after each addition. Alternately beat in flour mixture and half-and-half or cream. Add a few drops of mint extract to batter and mix well.

4. Spoon batter into 12 cupcake papers. Sprinkle chocolate mint chips over cupcakes and bake for 20–25 minutes or until a tester inserted into the center comes out clean. Remove from oven and cool.

5. To make the frosting: cream butter and sugar until light and fluffy. Add milk and mint extract and mix well. You may want to add more or less milk. Add food coloring if you are using it. Spread over cooled cupcakes and set in a cool place until frosting has hardened.

6. To make the ganache: place chocolate and cream in a double boiler or a microwave and heat until cream is warm to the touch and the chocolate starts to melt. Remove from heat and stir until all of the chocolate has melted and the mixture is homogeneous. Remember—you don't want to cook the chocolate, you just want to melt it. You can always put it back over the warm water or in the microwave for a few seconds if you need to. Cool slightly and dip cupcakes in chocolate ganache, leaving a little of the butter cream showing around the edges. Place a little chocolate-covered mint patty on top, if desired.

GOURMET
CUPCAKES

TARTE TATIN Cupcakes with Caramelized Apples

A Tarte Tatin is a French upside-down apple tart, one of the simplest and most delicious of traditional French desserts and very popular in my family, especially in the fall when the apples are at their finest. This is my cupcake version.

MAKES: **ABOUT 16 CUPCAKES**

1²/₃ cups all-purpose flour
2 teaspoons baking powder
1 teaspoon salt
1 cup packed brown sugar
¹/₂ cup/1 stick unsalted butter, room
    temperature
2 eggs, slightly beaten
¹/₂ cup milk
1 teaspoon vanilla extract

CARAMELIZED APPLES
¹/₄ cup/¹/₂ stick unsalted butter
4 apples, peeled, cored, and cut into
    16 (cut each quarter into four
    parts, lengthwise)
4 tablespoons sugar

CARAMEL GLAZE
¹/₄ cup/¹/₂ stick butter
¹/₄ cup firmly packed brown sugar
1¹/₂ cups powdered sugar
1 teaspoon vanilla extract
1 tablespoon milk

1. Preheat oven to 350°F.

2. In a large bowl, mix flour, baking powder, salt, and sugar. Add remaining cupcake ingredients and beat with a wooden spoon or whisk for 3 minutes.

3. Spoon batter into cupcake papers, filling about ²/₃ full. Bake for about 20 minutes or until a tester inserted into the center comes out clean. Remove from oven and cool.

4. To caramelize the apples: in a large pan, melt the butter and lay out the pieces of apple, cooking them on both sides. When they are golden, sprinkle them with sugar and remove from heat. Arrange them attractively on the cupcakes, four apple sections per cupcake. You may want to cook the apples in two batches.

5. To make the glaze (or use ready-made caramel if you prefer): melt butter in a heavy pan over low heat. Add brown sugar and stir for about 3 minutes until sugar is melted. Remove from heat. Add powdered sugar, vanilla, and milk and blend with a whisk. Dribble about a tablespoon of caramel over each cupcake.

BOURDALOUE Cupcakes with Caramelized Almonds

Any preparation with the adjective "Bourdaloue" attached to it means that it is prepared with some combination of pears and almonds. A cupcake "à la Bourdaloue"—you guessed it—has pears and almonds as its main ingredients! These cupcakes are made in jumbo cupcake molds and are not only delicious but are impressive to behold.

MAKES: ABOUT 6–8 JUMBO CUPCAKES

¾ cup/1½ sticks unsalted butter, room temperature

½ cup sugar

3 eggs

2 teaspoons vanilla extract

1½ cups ground almonds

¼ cup all-purpose flour

1 teaspoon salt

6–8 pear halves, (fresh or canned), cut lengthwise into quarters

CARAMELIZED ALMONDS

1 cup slivered almonds

¼ cup sugar

1. Preheat oven to 350°F.

2. Cream butter and sugar together until light and fluffy. Add eggs, one at a time, blending well after each addition. Add vanilla. Add ground almonds, flour, and salt and mix until batter is smooth.

3. Divide batter between 6–8 jumbo cupcake papers. Place a pear quarters in the center, pressing in just slightly. Cook for 30 minutes or until cupcakes are golden brown and spring back to the touch. Remove from oven and cool before unmolding.

4. Mix almonds and sugar in a cold nonstick pan. Turn heat to high, stirring constantly. When almonds start to brown (this will take only a few minutes), pour them immediately into a heat-proof dish. When they are completely cool, gently break them loose with a fork or your fingers. Sprinkle them over cupcakes just before serving.

CUPCAKE TIP
Bake these in a silicon mold and serve with custard sauce (see page 164)

CEVENOL Cupcakes with Crème de Marron icing

The Cevennes mountains in the south of France are known for their rustic landscapes and the chestnut trees that grow on their gentle slopes. Robert Louis Stevenson immortalized the Cevennes in a book that he wrote about a trip he took through these mountains with a donkey. The area is also known for its many local specialties made from chestnuts.

MAKES: ABOUT 16 CUPCAKES

²/₃ cup all-purpose flour

2 teaspoons baking powder

1 teaspoon salt

5 tablespoons unsalted butter

2 cups "crème de marron" chestnut spread (can be found in most gourmet food stores)

¹/₂ cup sugar

2 eggs

2 tablespoons rum

8 glazed chestnuts (can be found in most gourmet food stores) for decoration

1. Preheat oven to 350°F.

2. Mix flour, baking powder, and salt together and set aside.

3. In the large bowl of an electric mixer, cream butter and 1 cup chestnut spread until smooth and creamy. Add sugar, eggs, and rum and beat until thoroughly blended. Mix in dry ingredients.

4. Spoon batter into cupcake papers, filling about ²/₃ full. Bake for about 25 minutes or until a tester inserted into the center comes out clean. Remove from oven and cool.

5. Ice cooled cupcakes with remaining chestnut spread and top each cupcake with half a glazed chestnut.

CRÈPE SUZETTE Cupcakes

A "Crèpe Suzette" is a crepe that is filled with a butter cream made with orange liqueur (Grand Marnier, Cointreau, Triple Sec, Curaçao, etc.) and flambéed before being eaten. This is the cupcake version, frosted with the same cream I use for my Crèpes Suzettes.

MAKES: ABOUT 12 CUPCAKES

2 cups all-purpose flour
2 teaspoons baking powder
1 teaspoon salt
½ cup/1 stick unsalted butter, room
    temperature
¾ cup sugar
2 eggs
Juice and finely grated rind of
    1 medium-sized orange
2 tablespoons orange liqueur (Grand
    Marnier, Cointreau, Triple Sec,
    Curaçao, etc.)
Water, if necessary

SUZETTE FROSTING
⅔ cup/1¼ sticks unsalted butter,
    room temperature
¾ cup sugar
Juice and finely grated rind of
    1 medium orange or two small
    tangerines
¼ cup orange liqueur
Candied orange peel for decoration

1. Preheat oven to 350°F.

2. Mix flour, baking powder, and salt together. Set aside.

3. Cream butter and sugar until light and fluffy. Add eggs, one at a time, beating thoroughly after each addition. Add orange rind. Combine orange juice and orange liqueur and add water, if necessary, to make ½ cup. Alternately add dry ingredients and liquid to butter mixture, blending until batter is smooth.

4. Fill cupcake papers about ⅔ full and bake for about 20–25 minutes or until a tester inserted into the center comes out clean. Remove from oven and cool.

5. To make the frosting: cream butter with sugar until it is light and fluffy. Slowly add the juice and rind of the orange or tangerines, beating continually. Carefully add the liqueur, little by little, making sure that the mixture doesn't curdle. Keep beating until mixture is of spreading consistency. Frost cooled cupcakes and decorate with a piece of candied orange peel. The butter will harden when it sets so make sure to frost the cupcakes while the frosting is still creamy.

CUPCAKE TIP
Suzette frosting is a challenge. You can replace it with any other orange frosting (see page 137)

CHOCOLATE MOUSSE Cupcakes

The chocolate mousse cake that inspired this recipe was and still is my son's preferred birthday cake recipe. This 2-in-1 recipe includes both the batter and the frosting for these light and very moist cupcakes. For chocoholics only!

MAKES: ABOUT 12 CUPCAKES

4 heaping tablespoons all-purpose flour
2$\frac{1}{2}$ teaspoons baking powder
$\frac{1}{2}$ teaspoon salt, plus good pinch for the egg whites
10 ounces dark chocolate
1 cup/2 sticks unsalted butter, room temperature
6 eggs, separated
1 cup sugar
Grated chocolate for decoration

CUPCAKE TIP
You might want to double this recipe— you will never have too many.

1. Preheat oven to 350°F.

2. Mix flour, baking powder, and salt together and set aside.

3. Melt the chocolate and butter in a double boiler or microwave. Don't cook—the chocolate and butter should be just melted. Stir and set aside.

4. Beat egg yolks and sugar until light yellow and foamy. Beat in the melted chocolate until totally blended.

5. Beat egg whites with a pinch of salt until stiff but not dry. Gently fold into chocolate mixture. Divide mixture into two parts and put one of them in the refrigerator to be used later to frost cupcakes. Gently whisk flour mixture into other half until it is completely absorbed.

6. Fill cupcake papers about $\frac{2}{3}$ full with batter and bake for 15–20 minutes. Don't overcook. Cupcakes should be just cooked and moist in the center. Remove from oven and cool.

7. When cupcakes are cool, frost with remaining chocolate mousse. Decorate with grated chocolate.

EARL GREY Cupcakes

The distinctive taste of Earl Grey tea is due to bergamot, a small tree in the orange family. The rind of the bergamot orange yields an aromatic oil, used in the tea and perfume industries.

MAKES: 12 CUPCAKES

⅔ cup whole milk

2 teaspoons loose or 2 tea bags
   Earl Grey tea

1½ cups all-purpose flour

2 teaspoons baking powder

1 teaspoons salt

½ cup/1 stick unsalted butter, room
   temperature

1 cup sugar

2 eggs

3 tablespoons candied orange rind,
   chopped into little pieces
   (optional)

CHOCOLATE EARL GREY GANACHE

6 ounces good quality dark chocolate,
   broken into pieces

1 tablespoon unsalted butter, room
   temperature

½ cup heavy cream

2 teaspoons loose or 2 tea bags
   Earl Grey tea

1. In a small pan, heat milk with tea. Bring to a boil and then remove from heat and let steep until milk is cool to the touch, about 30 minutes. Filter the tea or remove tea bags and set liquid aside.

2. Preheat oven to 350°F.

3. Mix flour, baking powder, and salt together and set aside.

4. Cream butter and sugar together until light and fluffy. Add eggs, one at a time, mixing well after each addition. Alternately beat in dry ingredients and liquid. Fold in candied orange rind, if desired.

5. Spoon batter into cupcake papers, filling cups about ⅔ full. Bake for about 25 minutes or until a tester inserted into the center comes out clean. Remove from oven and cool.

6. To make the ganache: put chocolate and butter in a large mixing bowl and set aside. Combine cream and tea in a small pan and slowly bring to a boil. Remove from heat, cover, and let tea steep in cream for at least 30 minutes.

7. Boil mixture once again and strain over the bowl with chocolate and butter. Let sit for about 2 minutes until chocolate and butter have started to melt and then whisk until smooth. Put ganache in the refrigerator until it is thick enough (but not too thick!) to spread over cupcakes. You can also wait until it cools and beat it with an electric beater for about 5–10 minutes for a lighter, creamier chocolate frosting.

CRÈME BRULÉE Cupcakes

Crème Brulée literally means "burnt cream." Basically, it is a vanilla custard that is chilled, sprinkled with sugar just before serving, and placed under a broiler so that the sugar burns and forms a crust. There are many variations on the theme. Here is a cupcake one.

MAKES: **ABOUT 16 CUPCAKES**

2½ cups all-purpose flour

3 teaspoons baking powder

½ teaspoon salt, plus pinch for the egg whites

½ cup/1 stick unsalted butter, room temperature

1½ cups sugar

2 eggs, separated

1 cup milk

3 tablespoons caramel syrup (the kind used for ice cream sundaes)

1 teaspoon vanilla extract

BROWN SUGAR FROSTING

1½ cups dark brown sugar

¾ cup granulated sugar

Pinch of salt

½ cup milk

3 tablespoons unsalted butter, cut into pieces

2 tablespoons corn syrup

2 teaspoons vanilla extract

Brown sugar for sprinkling

1. Preheat oven to 350°F.

2. Mix flour, baking powder, and salt together and set aside.

3. Cream butter and sugar together until light and fluffy. Add egg yolks, one at a time, mixing well after each addition. Alternately beat in dry ingredients and milk. Add caramel syrup and vanilla. Beat until smooth.

4. Beat egg whites with a pinch of salt until stiff but not dry. Gently fold whites into batter.

5. Spoon batter into cupcake papers, filling cups about ⅔ full. Bake for about 20 minutes or until a tester inserted into the center comes out clean. Remove from oven and cool.

6. Mix all the frosting ingredients except the vanilla in a heavy pan over low heat. Slowly bring mixture to a boil, stirring constantly, and boil for 1 minute. Remove from heat and cool until just warm to the touch. Add vanilla and beat until thick enough to spread. Frost cooled cupcakes and sprinkle with brown sugar.

CUPCAKE TIP
You can substitute the vanilla in the cupcake batter with lavender extract, orange flower water, or rose water to add your own individual touch.

THE ARLÉSIENNE

When I had my restaurant in the south of France, one of my most popular summer desserts was a tart made with fresh apricots, almonds, and raspberry jelly, known as the "Arlésienne." Arles is a lovely little city, located in Provence, on the banks of the Rhone river and in the middle of the Camargue, home to wild horses and pink flamingos. Provence abounds with apricot trees, almond trees, whose lovely pink blossoms announce the arrival of spring, and raspberries. The combination is definitely a winner.

MAKES: ABOUT 12 CUPCAKES

1½ cups all-purpose flour
2 teaspoons baking powder
1 teaspoon salt
½ cup/1 stick unsalted butter, room
   temperature
½ cup sugar
2 eggs
5 tablespoons milk
Few drops of almond extract
   (optional)
½ cup dried apricots, or dried
   raspberries (or a combination of
   both), cut into little cubes
½ cup coarsely ground almonds
6 small apricots, halved
12 teaspoons raspberry jelly

1. Preheat oven to 350°F.

2. Mix flour, baking powder, and salt together and set aside.

3. Cream butter and sugar until light and fluffy. Add eggs, one at a time, mixing well after each addition. Alternately beat in flour mixture and milk. Add almond extract to taste. Fold in dried apricots and almonds.

4. Spoon batter into cupcake papers, filling a little over ½ full. Place an apricot half in the top of each cupcake, hollow side up, pressing gently into batter. Put a teaspoon of raspberry jelly in each hollow. Bake for 20–25 minutes or until a tester inserted into the center comes out clean and the tops are golden brown. Remove from oven and cool.

CUPCAKE TIP
The picture opposite depicts the cupcakes before they are baked. They should be a lovely golden color when cooked.

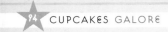

PECHE MELBA Cupcakes

Try this very easy one-bowl cupcake version of the popular dessert. If you prefer you could bake the cupcakes in silicon molds and serve with Raspberry Sauce and whipped cream.

MAKES: ABOUT 16 CUPCAKES

3 eggs, slightly beaten

1½ cups sugar

½ cup vegetable oil

2 cups all-purpose flour

2 teaspoons baking powder

1 teaspoon salt

1 teaspoon cinnamon (optional)

2 cups fresh, canned, or frozen peaches, cut into pieces (set aside enough thin slices to decorate cupcakes)

RASPBERRY CREAM FROSTING

1 cup heavy whipping cream, chilled

3 tablespoons sugar

½ cup slightly sweetened raspberry purée (if you are using fresh raspberries, purée them with a fork or in a food processor with 1 tablespoon sugar)

RASPBERRY SAUCE

2 cups raspberries (set a few aside to decorate cupcakes)

½ cup sugar

¼ cup water

Few drops lemon juice

Whipped cream for decoration

1. Preheat oven to 350°F.

2. In a large bowl, mix all of the cupcake ingredients apart from the peaches with a wooden spoon. Gently fold in peaches.

3. Spoon batter into cupcake papers, filling about ⅔ full. Bake for about 25 minutes or until a tester inserted into the center comes out clean. Remove from oven and cool.

4. Make either Raspberry Whipped Cream Frosting or Raspberry Sauce. For frosting: beat cream with sugar until soft peaks form. Gradually add raspberry purée, beating continually. Beat until stiff peaks form. Add more sugar, if necessary. Frost cupcakes just before serving and decorate with a peach slice.

5. To make the sauce: wash and clean raspberries. Slowly heat raspberries and sugar in a medium pan with water. When mixture starts to boil, cook for 1 minute and remove from heat. Purée by hand or in a food processor with a few drops lemon juice. Spoon raspberry sauce over cupcakes. Serve with a dollop of whipped cream and a fresh raspberry.

CUPCAKE TIP
The Raspberry Sauce can be kept in the refrigerator or frozen for later use.

THE LANGUEDOCIENNE

Languedoc is a region in southern France known for its abundant sunshine, fields of lavender, figs, goat cheese, honey, and great wines. These cupcakes embody the spirit of the region. Enjoy them after a meal with a glass of sweet Muscat wine.

MAKES: ABOUT 16 CUPCAKES

¾ cup honey

½ cup brown sugar

¼ cup/½ stick unsalted butter, cut into pieces

3 tablespoons milk

1⅔ cups all-purpose flour

2 teaspoons baking powder

1 teaspoon salt

1 tablespoon dried lavender (optional)

2 eggs

1 cup dried figs, cut into little pieces (save a few pieces for the decoration)

GOAT CHEESE FROSTING

¾ cup very fresh goat cheese or creamy goat's cheese such as Chavroux (can be found in most supermarkets)

2 tablespoons/¼ stick unsalted butter, softened

1½ cups powdered sugar

1. In a medium pan, heat honey, sugar, butter, and milk over very low heat. Stir until the sugar has dissolved and remove from heat. Let cool.

2. Preheat oven to 350°F.

3. Mix flour, baking powder, salt, and lavender together. Add to cooled honey mixture and beat well with a wooden spoon. Add eggs, one by one, beating well after each addition. Fold figs into batter.

4. Fill cupcake papers about ⅔ full. Bake for about 25 minutes or until a tester inserted into the center comes out clean.

5. To make the frosting: cream goat cheese, butter, and sugar until smooth and well blended. If frosting is too soft or liquid, place it in the refrigerator until it is of good spreading consistency. Put a dollop of frosting on each cupcake and decorate with a piece of dried fig.

CUPCAKE TIP
If you can't get goat cheese, use cream cheese instead.

RICOTTA LIME
Cupcakes with Lime Glaze

These light and airy cupcakes will be as welcome as a lime cooler on a hot summer's day. You can dust them with powdered sugar or use a lime glaze that will look very cool with a dollop of whipped cream, sprinkled with green sugar, and topped with a candied or jellied lime section.

MAKES: ABOUT 16 CUPCAKES

1¼ cups all-purpose flour
1½ teaspoons baking powder
1 teaspoon salt, plus pinch for the
   egg whites
Juice (about 3 tablespoons) and
   finely grated rind of 1 lime
5 tablespoons unsalted butter, room
   temperature
¾ cup sugar
⅓ cup ricotta cheese
3 eggs, separated

LIME GLAZE
2 tablespoons freshly squeezed lime
   juice
½ cup powdered sugar

FOR DECORATION
Whipped cream (optional)
Green sugar
Candied or jellied lime sections

1. Preheat oven to 350°F.

2. Mix flour, baking powder, salt, and lime rind together and set aside.

3. Cream butter and sugar together until light and fluffy. Add ricotta, beating until smooth. Add egg yolks, one at a time, blending well after each addition. Add flour mixture and lime juice and mix well.

4. Beat egg whites with a pinch of salt until stiff but not dry. Gently fold whites into batter.

5. Spoon batter into cupcake papers, filling cups about ⅔ full. Bake for about 20–25 minutes or until a tester inserted into the center comes out clean. Remove from oven and cool.

6. To make the frosting: in a small bowl, combine lime juice and sugar and whisk until smooth. Spread over cooled cupcakes with a pastry brush. Decorate whipped cream with green sugar and a candied or jellied lime section.

TIRAMISU Cupcakes with Mascarpone Cream

Tiramisu is an Italian cake usually made with sponge cake or ladyfingers soaked in a mixture of coffee and Marsala, filled with mascarpone cream and topped with grated chocolate. Here is one cupcake version.

MAKES: ABOUT 12 CUPCAKES

1 cup all-purpose flour
1 teaspoon baking powder
$\frac{1}{2}$ teaspoon salt
2 eggs, separated
$\frac{1}{4}$ cup very strong coffee
1 tablespoon Marsala or 1 tablespoon
   Kahlua or 1 teaspoon vanilla
   extract
$\frac{3}{4}$ cup sugar
Pinch of salt
Extra Marsala for sprinkling (optional)

MASCARPONE CREAM
2 egg yolks
3 teaspoons sugar
1 tablespoon Kahlua (optional)
1 cup mascarpone
Kahlua for drizzling
Grated chocolate for decoration

1. Preheat oven to 350°F.

2. Mix flour, baking powder, and salt together and set aside.

3. Beat egg yolks with coffee and Marsala until very thick and creamy. Gradually add $\frac{1}{2}$ cup of the sugar, beating continually. Set aside.

4. Beat egg whites with salt until they start to form moist peaks and gradually beat in remaining $\frac{1}{4}$ cup sugar. Continue beating until egg whites are stiff but not dry. Stir 3 tablespoons of the whites into yolk mixture. Gradually fold dry ingredients into mixture, using a whisk. When the dry ingredients have been absorbed, gently fold in remaining whites.

5. Spoon batter into 12 cupcake papers, filling about $\frac{2}{3}$ full. Bake for about 20 minutes or until a tester inserted into the center comes out clean. Remove from oven and cool.

6. When cupcakes are cool, you can poke tops with a fork a few times and sprinkle a tablespoon of Marsala over each cupcake, if desired.

7. To make the mascarpone cream: beat egg yolks with sugar until they are light and fluffy. Beat in Kahlua, if desired. Gradually add mascarpone, beating continually. Pile cream on cupcakes, drizzle with kahlua, and sprinkle with chocolate.

LINZERTORTE
Cupcakes

These cupcakes are an adaptation of a recipe from my friend Hannelore, who grew up on her Austrian mother's linzertortes, to which she added a touch of chocolate to give them more body.

MAKES: ABOUT 12 CUPCAKES

³/₄ cups/1½ sticks unsalted butter, room temperature

1 cup all-purpose flour

½ teaspoon salt, plus good pinch for the egg whites

3 tablespoons unsweetened cocoa powder

1½ cups powdered sugar

³/₄ cup ground almonds

³/₄ cup ground hazelnuts

6 egg whites

Good pinch of salt

Raspberry jelly, (see method)

Whipped cream or decorator frosting

Hazelnuts or almonds, halved, for decoration

Powdered sugar for dusting

1. Preheat oven to 350°F.

2. In a small pan, melt butter, letting it brown just slightly. Remove from heat and cool.

3. In a large bowl, mix flour, salt, cocoa powder, powdered sugar, ground almonds, and hazelnuts together. Set aside.

4. Beat egg whites with a pinch of salt until they are foamy but not stiff.

5. Make a well in the middle of the dry ingredients and add egg whites and cooled butter. Mix well.

6. Spoon batter into cupcake papers, filling about ²/₃ full. Bake for about 20–25 minutes or until a tester inserted into the center comes out clean. Remove from oven and cool.

7. When cupcakes are cool, take out the centers with an apple corer and fill each cupcake with a teaspoon of raspberry jelly. Replace core.

8. To glaze, heat ½ cup raspberry jelly in a small pan over low heat. Brush on cooled and filled cupcakes with a pastry brush. Make criss-cross patterns on top of each cupcake with either whipped cream or a decorator tube. Put a half hazelnut or almond in each square and dust with a little powdered sugar.

MENDIANT Cupcakes with Fig Topping

The term "mendiant" generally means beggar in French, but in the kitchen it refers to preparations made with dried fruits and nuts. Use your favorite one.

MAKES: ABOUT 16 REGULAR CUPCAKES OR 8 JUMBO CUPCAKES

$\frac{1}{2}$ cup hazelnuts

$\frac{1}{2}$ cup almonds

2 cups all-purpose flour

2 teaspoons baking powder

1 teaspoon baking soda

1 teaspoon salt

1 teaspoon cinnamon

$\frac{1}{2}$ teaspoon allspice

$\frac{1}{2}$ cup/1 stick unsalted butter, room temperature

1 cup dark brown sugar, firmly packed

2 eggs

4 teaspoons white vinegar

$\frac{2}{3}$ cup milk

$\frac{1}{2}$ cup raisins

FIG TOPPING

2 cups dried figs

1$\frac{1}{2}$ cups water

1 cinnamon stick

$\frac{3}{4}$ cup sugar

1. Place all of the topping ingredients in a heavy pan and bring to a boil. Lower heat and simmer for about 20 minutes or until the figs are tender and about half of the water has evaporated. Remove cinnamon stick and discard. Purée the fig mixture in a food processor. Set aside.

2. Preheat oven to 350°F. Put hazelnuts and almonds in a dish in the oven and cook them until they are browned, about 10 minutes, stirring from time to time. Keep a close eye on them as you don't want them to burn. You can do the same thing in a heavy pan on a burner. Coarsely grind the nuts in a food processor and set aside.

3. Mix flour, baking powder, baking soda, salt, and spices and set aside.

4. Cream butter and sugar until light and fluffy. Add eggs, one at a time, mixing well after each addition. Combine vinegar and milk. Alternately add dry ingredients and liquid, beating until smooth after each addition. Fold in raisins and ground nuts.

5. Spoon batter into regular or jumbo cupcake papers, filling cups just a little over $\frac{1}{2}$ full. Cook for about 20 minutes, until just barely cooked. Remove from oven and spread fig mixture over each cupcake. Return to oven and cook for another 10 minutes or until cooked. Remove from oven and cool completely before unmolding.

MARRAKECH Moments

I remember arriving in Marrakech at Christmas time with the orange trees heavy with fruit and the smell of orange flower blossom in the air. Thus, my inspiration for this dazzling duo.

MAKES: **ABOUT 12 CUPCAKES**

³/₄ cup cream cheese, softened

¹/₄ cup sugar

2 tablespoons finely grated orange rind

1 tablespoon orange juice

CHOCOLATE BATTER

1¹/₂ cups all-purpose flour

2 teaspoons baking powder

1 teaspoon salt

1 cup sugar

¹/₃ cup unsweetened cocoa powder

¹/₂ cup milk

¹/₃ cup vegetable oil

1 egg

1 teaspoon vanilla extract

CHOCOLATE ORANGE GANACHE

6 ounces dark chocolate, broken into little pieces

³/₄ cup heavy cream

3 tablespoons orange liqueur (Cointreau, Grand Marnier, etc.)

FOR DECORATION

Orange sugar or grated orange rind

Candied orange

1. Preheat oven to 350°F. Mix the cream cheese, sugar, orange rind, and orange juice in a bowl and set aside.

2. In a large bowl, mix flour, baking powder, salt, sugar, and cocoa powder.

3. In a small bowl, mix milk, oil, egg, and vanilla. Pour liquid into flour mixture and beat well with a wooden spoon.

4. Put a heaping tablespoon of the chocolate batter in the bottom of 12 cupcake papers. Divide up the orange cream cheese batter among the cupcakes (about a heaping teaspoon per cupcake).

5. Spoon over the remaining chocolate batter. Gently swirl batter with a knife (don't overdo it). Bake for 25–30 minutes or until a tester inserted into the center comes out clean. Remove from oven and cool.

6. To make the ganache: place chocolate and cream in a double boiler or a microwave and heat until cream is warm to the touch and chocolate starts to melt. Remove from heat and stir until all of the chocolate has melted and the mixture is homogeneous. Remember, you don't want to cook the chocolate, you just want to melt it. You can always put it back over warm water or in the microwave for a few seconds if you need to. Stir in orange liqueur. Cool slightly then dip cupcakes in chocolate. The ganache will be smooth and shiny. Decorate with orange sugar or a piece of candied orange rind.

PINEAPPLE Surprises

The origin of this cupcake is a dessert that we used to serve at our restaurant. We were looking for something easy to put together and discovered this one on a trip to Spain and then adapted it to our taste. It actually consists of a regular size cupcake, topped with a mini-cupcake (with a brandied cherry hidden inside) and decorated to look like a pineapple.

MAKES: ABOUT 12 CUPCAKES

1½ cups all-purpose flour
2 teaspoons baking powder
1 teaspoon salt
¾ cup/1½ sticks unsalted butter
1½ cups sugar
3 eggs
½ cup juice (drained from pineapple)
1 small can crushed pineapple, drained (about ½ cup)
½ cup shredded coconut
12 pitted brandied cherries or maraschino cherries

PINEAPPLE FONDANT GLAZE
1½ cups powdered sugar
2 tablespoons juice drained from pineapple
Yellow food coloring
Brown decorator frosting or caramel for decoration
Candied pineapple or pineapple candy for decoration

1. Preheat oven to 350°F.

2. Mix flour, baking powder, and salt together and set aside.

3. Cream butter and sugar until light and fluffy. Add eggs, one at a time, mixing well after each addition. Alternately add dry ingredients and pineapple juice. When batter is well blended, fold in pineapple and shredded coconut.

4. Spoon batter into 12 regular cupcake papers and 12 mini silicon molds, filling cups about ½ full. Bake regular cupcakes for about 20–25 minutes and mini-cupcakes for a shorter time, or until a tester inserted into the center comes out clean. Remove from oven and cool.

5. Turn cooled mini-cupcakes over and remove a little bit of the center. Replace it with a brandied cherry.

6. To make the glaze: mix powdered sugar and pineapple juice together until you obtain a smooth paste. Add yellow food coloring. Frost top of regular cupcakes. Place a mini-cupcake (with the cherry inside) on top while glaze is still soft. Ice. Decorate with brown decorator frosting or caramel to make the cupcake look like a pineapple. Place a piece of candied pineapple or a pineapple candy on top.

MACADAMIA & WHITE CHOCOLATE Cupcakes

This cupcake recipe combines two ingredients with a unique flavor and texture—macadamia nuts and white chocolate.

MAKES: ABOUT 12–14 CUPCAKES

1½ cups all-purpose flour

2 teaspoons baking powder

1 teaspoon baking soda

1 teaspoon salt

½ cup/1 stick unsalted butter

¾ cup sugar

2 eggs

½ cup buttermilk

½ cup white chocolate chips

½ cup chopped macadamia nuts

WHITE CHOCOLATE FROSTING

4 ounces good quality white
    chocolate

¼ cup heavy cream

¾ cup cream cheese, room
    temperature

⅓ cup powdered sugar

FOR DECORATION

Macadamia nuts, whole

Grated white chocolate

1. Preheat oven to 350°F.

2. Mix flour, baking powder, baking soda, and salt together and set aside.

3. Cream butter and sugar until light and fluffy. Add eggs, one at a time, mixing well after each addition. Alternately add the dry ingredients and the liquid, beating until smooth after each addition. Fold in chocolate chips and macadamia nuts.

4. Spoon batter into cupcake papers, filling cups about ⅔ full. Bake for about 20–25 minutes or until a tester inserted into the center comes out clean. Remove from oven and cool.

5. To make the frosting: melt chocolate and cream in a double boiler or a microwave. Remove from heat when chocolate is just melted, stir and let cool. When mixture is cool to the touch, add cream cheese and powdered sugar. Beat until mixture is thick and creamy. Frost cooled cupcakes and decorate with macadamia nuts and grated white chocolate.

ORIENT EXPRESS Cupcakes
with Yin-Yang Frosting

East meets West in these lovely little green tea cupcakes. Enjoy them with a cup of green tea in the afternoon or for dessert after an Oriental-inspired meal.

MAKES: ABOUT 12 CUPCAKES

GREEN TEA CUPCAKE

1 cup all-purpose flour

1 teaspoon baking powder

½ teaspoon salt, plus pinch for the egg whites

2 teaspoons powdered Japanese green tea

2 eggs, separated

⅔ cup powdered sugar

½ cup ground almonds

6 tablespoons/¾ stick unsalted butter, room temperature, cut into little pieces

YIN-YANG FROSTING

See Midnight Sky Frosting (page 74)

1. Preheat oven to 350°F.

2. Mix flour, baking powder, salt, and tea together and set aside.

3. In a large bowl, beat egg yolks with powdered sugar until light in color. Add ground almonds and beat well. Add butter and blend until mixture is smooth. Add dry ingredients and mix well. Beat egg whites with a pinch of salt until stiff but not dry and gently fold into batter.

4. Spoon batter into cupcake papers, filling about ⅔ full. Bake for about 20 minutes or until a tester inserted into the center comes out clean. Remove from oven and cool.

5. Make the frosting according to the Midnight Sky Frosting recipe but before adding the black food coloring, divide the frosting into two bowls. Add black food coloring to one bowl and leave the other one white. Frost cooled cupcakes with a yin-yang design.

CUPCAKE TIP
You can also frost the cupcakes with ready-made fondant or one of the fondant recipes on page 140. Another possibility would be to decorate the cupcakes with a Chinese character.

MINI-FINANCIER
Cupcakes

A "financier," which literally means exactly that in French, is a small cake that is made with ground nuts and whipped egg whites. A dab of apricot jelly with some ground pistachios sprinkled on top and you will have a perfect accompaniment to a fruit salad or ice cream for dessert or a delicate finger cake for a 5 o'clock tea.

MAKES: ABOUT 24–30 MINI-CUPCAKES

1 cup all-purpose flour
1 teaspoon baking powder
½ teaspoon salt, plus pinch for the
    egg whites
½ cup finely ground almonds
1 cup light brown sugar
5 egg whites
½ cup/1 stick unsalted butter, melted
    and cooled
Several drops of almond extract
½ cup apricot jelly
½ cup ground pistachio nuts

1. Preheat oven to 350°F.

2. In a large bowl, combine the first five ingredients and set aside.

3. Beat egg whites with a pinch of salt until stiff but not dry. Fold into dry ingredients. Gradually add melted butter with a few drops of almond extract, gently folding it in with a whisk or a rubber spatula.

4. Spoon batter into mini-cupcake papers or silicon molds, filling just a little over ½ full. Bake for about 20 minutes or until a tester inserted in the center comes out clean. Remove from oven and cool.

5. In a small pan, melt apricot jelly until just warm. Add a few drops of water, if necessary. Brush the jelly on the cooled cupcakes with a pastry brush and sprinkle with ground pistachio nuts.

CUPCAKE TIP
You can bake them either in mini-cupcake papers or in a silicon mini-cupcake mold.

POIRE Belle Helene

Here is another elegant French dessert transformed into a cupcake. A Poire Belle Hélène is usually vanilla ice cream served with a poached or ripe pear half and doused in chocolate sauce.

MAKES: ABOUT 12 REGULAR CUPCAKES OR 6 JUMBO CUPCAKES

1 cup all-purpose flour

1 teaspoon baking powder

½ teaspoon salt, plus pinch for the egg whites

7 ounces good quality dark chocolate (at least 55% cocoa solids)

½ cup/1 stick unsalted butter

⅔ cup sugar

3 eggs, separated

3 pears (fresh or canned), drained and cut into small pieces, plus 1 pear cut into lengthwise slices for decoration

CREAMY CHOCOLATE SAUCE

½ cup sugar

1 tablespoon all-purpose flour

Pinch of salt

1½ cups whole milk

3 ounces good quality dark chocolate (at least 55% cocoa solids), broken into pieces

2 tablespoons/¼ stick unsalted butter, cut into little pieces

1 teaspoon vanilla extract

1. Preheat oven to 350°F.

2. Mix flour, baking powder, and salt together and set aside.

3. Melt chocolate with butter in a double boiler or microwave. When just melted, remove from heat, stir well, and add sugar to chocolate mixture. Mix thoroughly. Add egg yolks, one by one, mixing well after each addition, followed by dry ingredients. Beat batter until smooth and all of the flour has disappeared.

4. Beat egg whites with pinch of salt until stiff but not dry. Gently fold into batter. Chop 2 pears into small pieces and carefully add to batter.

5. Spoon batter into cupcake papers, filling cups about ⅔ full. Bake for about 25 minutes or until a tester inserted into the center comes out clean. Remove from oven and cool.

6. To make the chocolate sauce (or use ready-made): in a small bowl, mix sugar, flour, and salt together and set aside.

7. Heat milk and chocolate in a heavy pan over low heat until just melted. Stir with a wooden spoon until smooth. Add dry ingredients to chocolate mixture, mixing well. Simmer for 5 minutes, stirring constantly. Remove from heat and stir in butter and vanilla.

8. Spoon warm chocolate sauce over cupcakes or dribble a little over the top of each cupcake and decorate with a slice of the remaining pear.

WHITE CHOCOLATE & RASPBERRY Cupcakes

These easy and elegant cupcakes were inspired by a pie that a friend of mine once made with white chocolate, fresh raspberries, and decorated with real chocolate leaves.

MAKES: ABOUT 12–14 CUPCAKES

1$\frac{1}{3}$ cups all-purpose flour

1$\frac{1}{2}$ teaspoons baking powder

1 teaspoon salt

6 ounces white chocolate, broken up into little pieces

$\frac{1}{2}$ cup/1 stick unsalted butter, cut into little pieces

1 cup sugar

6 eggs

$\frac{3}{4}$ cup dried raspberries

RASPBERRY BUTTER CREAM FROSTING

1$\frac{2}{3}$ cups powdered sugar

1 cup/2 sticks unsalted butter, room temperature, cut into small pieces

Pinch of salt

2 tablespoons crème de framboise, raspberry liqueur or raspberry syrup

Chocolate leaves for decoration (see step 6)

Fresh or frozen raspberries for decoration

1. Preheat oven to 350°F.

2. Mix flour, baking powder, and salt together and set aside.

3. Melt chocolate and butter in a double boiler or a microwave. Remove from heat. Add sugar and mix well. Add eggs, one at a time, mixing well after each addition. Add dry ingredients. Fold in raspberries.

4. Spoon batter into cupcake papers, filling about $\frac{2}{3}$ full. Bake for about 20–25 minutes or until a tester inserted into the center comes out clean. Remove from oven and cool.

5. To make the frosting: sift sugar into the large bowl of an electric mixer. Add butter and a pinch of salt. Beat on medium speed until frosting is light and fluffy. Add raspberry flavoring and continue beating until frosting is of good spreading consistency. Frost cooled cupcakes.

6. To make the chocolate leaves: melt about 8 ounces dark chocolate in a double boiler or microwave. Using a pastry brush, paint the undersides of leaves with the chocolate. You can use any nontoxic leaf (lemon or orange tree leaves). Place leaves on a piece of wax paper on a tray and put them in the refrigerator until chocolate has hardened (this will take only a few minutes). Very carefully peel off leaves.

7. Decorate frosted cupcakes with a few raspberries and chocolate leaves.

GATEAU DE SAVOIE
(Savoy Cake)

This cupcake is actually a very simple and basic sponge cake, that originated in the Savoy region of France, in the French Alps. The beauty of these cupcakes lies in their simplicity. You can add ½ cup of your favorite nuts or dried fruits, a few spoonfuls of coconut, a teaspoon of strong powdered espresso, etc. A very versatile cupcake, to say the least!

MAKES: **ABOUT 12 REGULAR CUPCAKES AND 24–30 MINI-CUPCAKES**

1 cup all-purpose flour
1 teaspoon baking powder
½ teaspoon salt, plus pinch for the egg whites
½ cup/1 stick unsalted butter, room temperature
¾ cup sugar
4 eggs, separated
1 teaspoon vanilla extract
Powdered sugar for dusting (optional)
Glaze or frosting of your choice

1. Preheat oven to 350°F.

2. Mix flour, baking powder, and salt together and set aside.

3. Cream butter with sugar until light and fluffy. Add egg yolks, one at a time, mixing well after each addition. Add the dry ingredients.

4. Beat egg whites with a pinch of salt until stiff but not dry. Gently fold into batter.

5. Spoon batter into cupcake papers, filling cups about ⅔ full. Bake for 20–25 minutes or until a tester inserted into the center comes out clean. Cupcakes should be elastic to the touch. Remove from oven and cool.

6. Dust the cooled cupcakes with powdered sugar, or glaze or frost them with the icing of your choice.

CUPCAKE TIP
You can either frost them, glaze them, or dust them with powdered sugar and serve with a fruit salad.

SAFFRON & ORANGE
Cupcakes

These gourmet cupcakes with their delicate saffron threads and subtle flavors of orange and almond will be the perfect accompaniment to a 5 o'clock cream tea. Serve them with a bowl of fresh cream and a mug of black tea and enjoy. You won't be hungry for dinner.

MAKES: ABOUT 16–18 CUPCAKES

2 cups freshly squeezed orange juice

1 tablespoon finely grated orange rind

¼ teaspoon saffron threads (not powder)

3 eggs

1 cup powdered sugar, plus more for dusting

1⅔ cups all-purpose flour

2 teaspoons baking powder

1 teaspoon salt

1½ cups ground almonds

½ cup/1 stick unsalted butter, melted

1. Preheat oven to 350°F.

2. In a medium pan, bring orange juice, orange rind, and saffron to the boil. Lower the heat and simmer for 1 minute. Remove from heat and cool.

3. In a large bowl, cream eggs and sugar until they are light and foamy. Add flour, baking powder, salt, almonds, orange juice mixture, and butter, mixing ingredients in rapidly with a wooden spoon. The mixture may be a little lumpy.

4. Spoon batter into cupcake papers, filling ⅔ full, and smoothing over with a spoon. Bake for about 25 minutes or until a tester inserted into the center comes out clean. Remove from oven and cool.

5. Dust with powdered sugar and serve with a bowl of thick fresh cream.

CUPCAKE TIP

You can also frost these cupcakes if you prefer. Try one of the orange frostings (Fresh Orange Juice Frosting, page 135, for example) and decorate with Caramelized Slivered Almonds (page 85).

STRAWBERRY Cheesecakes

A cheesecake in a cupcake! Is it possible? Not really, but a little imagination will go a long way and no one will be disappointed after they have tasted these scrumptious, delectable morsels with a surprise inside and strawberries and cream on top. Let them eat cupcakes!

MAKES: ABOUT 12 CUPCAKES

3 tablespoons cream cheese
³/₄ cup sugar
2¹/₃ cups all-purpose flour
2¹/₂ teaspoons baking powder
1 teaspoon salt
2 eggs, lightly beaten
1 cup milk
2 tablespoons/¹/₄ stick unsalted
    butter, melted
1 tablespoon finely grated orange
    rind
12 small strawberries, hulled and
    cleaned, for the filling

STRAWBERRIES AND CREAM
FROSTING
1 egg white
Pinch of salt
1 cup heavy whipping cream
³/₄ cup powdered sugar
2 tablespoons strawberry liqueur or
    strawberry syrup
¹/₂ cup strawberry purée

1. Preheat oven to 350°F.

2. Mix cream cheese with ¹/₄ cup sugar and set aside.

3. In a large bowl, mix flour, baking powder, salt, and the remaining ¹/₂ cup sugar.

4. In a separate bowl, beat eggs with milk and melted butter. Pour liquid into flour mixture and mix together rapidly with a wooden spoon. Blend in orange rind.

5. Put a heaping spoonful of the mixture into 12 cupcake papers (half the mixture). Place a strawberry and a teaspoonfull of the cream cheese in the center and cover with remaining mixture. Cook for 20 minutes in the oven. Remove and let cool before unmolding.

6. To make the frosting: beat egg white with salt until stiff but not dry. Beat whipping cream separately until it forms soft peaks, then slowly beat in the sugar and strawberry flavoring. Fold two mixtures together. Gently fold in puréed strawberries. Just before serving, heap the cream on the cupcakes and decorate to your taste.

HOLIDAY
CUPCAKES

VALENTINE'S DAY Cupcakes

These filled cupcakes bring together one of the most divine duos known to chocolate lovers—chocolate and cherry—with a little cream thrown in for good measure.

MAKES: **ABOUT 16 CUPCAKES**

1½ cups all-purpose flour
½ cup unsweetened cocoa powder
2 teaspoons baking powder
1 teaspoon baking soda
1 teaspoon salt
½ cup/1 stick unsalted butter
1¼ cups sugar
2 eggs
1 teaspoon vanilla extract
⅔ cup sour cream

CHERRY CREAM CHEESE FILLING
¾ cup cream cheese
3 tablespoons sugar
4 tablespoons Maraschino cherry syrup
Maraschino cherries or pitted brandied cherries

CHERRY JUBILEE FROSTING
¼ cup/½ stick unsalted butter
2 cups powdered sugar
3 tablespoons Maraschino cherry syrup
Several drops red food coloring (optional)
Unsweetened cocoa powder (about 2 tablespoons) for dusting
Maraschino cherries for decoration

1. Preheat oven to 350°F.

2. Mix flour with cocoa, baking powder, baking soda, and salt. Set aside.

3. Cream butter and sugar until light and fluffy. Add eggs, one at a time, mixing well after each addition. Add vanilla. Alternately beat in flour mixture and sour cream.

4. Fill cupcake papers about ⅔ full. Bake for 25 minutes or until a tester inserted into the center comes out clean. Remove from oven and cool.

5. To make the filling: using a fork or in a blender or mixer, mix cream cheese, sugar, and cherry syrup together until smooth. You can use more syrup if necessary. Scoop out the center of each cupcake with an apple corer. Drop in a teaspoon of filling and a cherry. Replace core. Save leftover filling for frosting.

6. To make the frosting: cream butter with any leftover filling until light and fluffy. Add powdered sugar, cherry syrup, and food coloring and beat until smooth and creamy. Add more cherry syrup if necessary. Frost filled cupcakes. Lightly dust with cocoa and place a cherry on the top of each cupcake.

CUPCAKE TIP
For a simpler alternative, use the Chocolate Fudge Icing for the Banana Split Cupcake (page 54).

EPIPHANY Cupcakes

The Feast of the Epiphany (also known as King's Day) celebrates the visit of the Three Wise Men to Bethlehem. In France today it is the unofficial ending of the holiday season.

MAKES: **ABOUT 12 CUPCAKES**

1³/₄ cups all-purpose flour

2 teaspoons baking powder

1 teaspoon salt

½ cup/1 stick unsalted butter

1¹/₈ cups sugar

3 eggs

½ cup milk

1 cup blanched almonds, finely chopped

ALMOND FILLING

½ cup almond paste, softened and cut into little pieces

¹/₃ cup cream cheese, room temperature

½ cup powdered sugar

12 jelly beans or Jordan almonds

ALMOND BUTTER CREAM FROSTING

6 tablespoons/³/₄ stick unsalted butter, room temperature

½ cup almond paste, softened and cut into little pieces

2¹/₂ cups powdered sugar

2 tablespoons milk

¹/₈ teaspoon almond extract

Jelly beans or Jordan almonds

1. To make filling: mix first three ingredients together (you can use a food processor, if necessary) and set aside. Preheat oven to 350°F.

2. Mix together flour, baking powder, and salt and set aside.

3. Cream butter and sugar together until light and fluffy. Add eggs, one at a time, mixing well after each addition. Alternately add dry ingredients and milk, beating until smooth. Fold in chopped almonds.

4. Fill 12 cupcake papers with half of the batter. Place a spoonful of filling in the center of the batter with a jelly bean or Jordan almond. Cover with remaining batter. Bake for about 20 minutes or until a tester inserted into the center comes out clean. Remove from oven and cool.

5. To make the frosting: cream butter and almond paste together until smooth (you can use a food processor, if necessary). Transfer to a large bowl, add sugar and beat until creamy. Gradually add milk and almond extract and continue beating. You can add a little extra milk for a softer frosting and more extract, if necessary.

6. Frost cooled cupcakes. Decorate with either jelly beans or Jordan almonds, three to a cupcake (for the Three Wise Men!). Alternatively, you can sprinkle the frosted cupcakes with caramelized slivered almonds (page 85). If you are using almond charms, be sure to warn your guests!

ST. PATRICK'S DAY
Pistachio Yogurt Cupcakes

St. Patrick's Day is marked by parades and fireworks, and symbolized by the shamrock, a three-leaved clover. So paint the town green with this little green gem of a cupcake.

MAKES: ABOUT 18 CUPCAKES

1 cup all-purpose flour
1 teaspoon baking powder
1 teaspoon baking soda
1 teaspoon salt
1 teaspoon ground cardamom
 (optional)
¾ cup/1½ sticks unsalted butter,
 room temperature
¾ cup brown sugar
3 eggs
1 teaspoon vanilla extract
½ cup whole yogurt
⅔ cup unsalted pistachios, coarsely
 chopped (they can be roasted for
 more flavor)
Green food coloring (optional)

GREEN ICING
1 tablespoon unsalted butter, melted
2 tablespoons hot milk
1½ cups powdered sugar
Flavoring (optional)
Green food coloring

1. Preheat oven to 350°F.

2. Mix flour, baking powder, baking soda, salt, and ground cardamom together and set aside.

3. Cream butter and sugar until light and fluffy. Add eggs, one at a time, mixing well after each addition. Add vanilla and green food coloring, if using. Alternately beat in flour mixture and yogurt. Fold in pistachios.

4. Spoon batter into cupcake papers, filling cups about ⅔ full. Bake for 25 minutes or until a tester comes out clean. Remove from oven and cool.

5. To make the icing: mix butter with hot milk in a large bowl. Slowly beat in sugar until the icing is of good spreading consistency. If you are using flavoring (almond, vanilla, etc.), add it now. Add green food coloring, drop by drop, until you obtain the desired color. Ice the cooled cupcakes and decorate to your taste.

CUPCAKE TIP
You could decorate white iced cupcakes with orange sugar (for Northern Ireland) and green sugar (for the Republic of Ireland), with a white stripe down the middle representing hope for peace between them.

ST. PATRICK'S DAY IRISH SODA BREAD Cupcakes

The oatmeal, caraway seeds, and dried currants are typical of the traditional Irish recipe but this lighter version will definitely get you in the mood. Wash it down with a glass of Irish Whiskey or Bailey's Irish Cream and you may even see some leprechauns!

MAKES: ABOUT 16 CUPCAKES

2 cups all-purpose flour
1 tablespoon oatmeal
2 teaspoons baking powder
2 teaspoons baking soda
1 teaspoon salt
½ cup/1 stick unsalted butter, room temperature
1 cup sugar
2 eggs
¾ cup buttermilk
½ cup dried currants or raisins
1 tablespon caraway seeds (optional)

IRISH WHISKEY FROSTING
¼ cup/½ stick unsalted butter, room temperature
2 cups powdered sugar
Pinch of salt
2 tablespoons Irish whiskey (or Bailey's Irish Cream)
Green food coloring (optional)
Green sugar for sprinkling

1. Preheat oven to 350°F.

2. Mix dry ingredients together and set aside.

3. Cream butter and sugar until light and fluffy. Add eggs, one at a time, beating well after each addition. Alternately beat in flour mixture and buttermilk. Fold in currants or raisins and caraway seeds.

4. Spoon batter into cupcake papers, filling cups about ⅔ full. Bake for 25 minutes or until a tester inserted into the center comes out clean. Remove from oven and cool.

5. To make the frosting: cream butter, sugar, and salt until light and fluffy. Slowly add whiskey or Irish Cream (and food coloring, if you are using it) and beat until frosting is of good spreading consistency. Frost cooled cupcakes and sprinkle with green sugar.

CUPCAKE TIP
For a simpler non-alcoholic version, just dust with powdered and green sugars.

MOTHER'S DAY FILLED ROSE Cupcakes

Say it with roses when you offer her these exquisitely delicate cupcakes made with rose water, filled with rose jelly, petals, and all, and topped with rose syrup frosting.

MAKES: ABOUT 18 CUPCAKES

$2\frac{2}{3}$ cups all-purpose flour

3 teaspoons baking powder

1 teaspoon salt

$\frac{1}{2}$ cup /1 stick unsalted butter, room temperature

$\frac{1}{4}$ cup sugar

2 eggs

$\frac{1}{4}$ cup rose syrup

1 cup milk

Rose jelly

ROSE SYRUP FROSTING

6 tablespoons/$\frac{3}{4}$ stick unsalted butter, room temperature

2 cups powdered sugar

3 tablespoons rose syrup

$\frac{1}{2}$ teaspoon rose water (optional)

Red food coloring (optional)

1. Preheat oven to 350°F.

2. Mix flour, baking powder, and salt together and set aside.

3. Cream butter and sugar until light and fluffy. Add eggs, one at a time, mixing well after each addition. Alternately add dry ingredients and syrup and milk to butter mixture, blending well after each addition.

4. Spoon batter into cupcake papers, filling cups about $\frac{2}{3}$ full. Bake for 25–30 minutes or until a tester inserted into the center comes out clean. Remove from oven and cool.

5. When cupcakes are cool, take the center out of each cupcake, using an apple corer. Drop a scant teaspoon of rose jelly into the center and replace cupcake core.

6. To make the frosting: cream butter with sugar until it is light and fluffy. Gradually add rose syrup, rose water, and food coloring, beating continually until frosting is of good spreading consistency. Frost cooled cupcakes and decorate to your taste.

EASTER LEMON CHIFFON Cupcakes

Use bright Easter colors and decorate these cupcakes as if they were Easter eggs, using colored sugars, little candies, stencils etc. Have the kids pitch in and decorate their own.

MAKES: ABOUT 18 CUPCAKES

½ cup all-purpose flour, sifted
Finely grated rind of 1 small lemon
6 egg whites
Pinch of salt or ½ teaspoon cream of tartar
1 cup sugar

EASTER EGG ICING

1 pound ready-to-use fondant or use one of the Fondant recipes (page 140)—if using the white meringue fondant, thin it with a little milk or sugar syrup
Sugar syrup (if required)
Food coloring

FOR DECORATION

Colored sugars
Easter motifs

1. Preheat oven to 350°F. Mix flour and lemon rind and set aside.

2. Put the egg whites, salt, or cream of tartar in a large bowl. Beat egg whites until stiff but not dry. You want them to be a little moist. Beat in sugar, little by little. Gradually fold in flour with a whisk. This is the only time I ever sift flour. It allows me to add it slowly and not to deflate the egg whites. Do not overmix. The batter will be just gorgeous —like a meringue.

3. Spoon batter into cupcake papers using two soup spoons, filling a little over halfway. Cook for about 15–20 minutes until cupcakes are golden on top and spring back to the touch. Remove from oven and cool.

4. Prepare ready-to-use fondant, according to manufacturer's instructions, or one of the fondant recipes. This will probably require heating the fondant, either in a microwave or in a double boiler, until just melted. Overheating will spoil the glossy appearance and change the texture. Add enough sugar syrup to achieve the desired consistency. Pour the fondant into separate bowls, depending on the number of colors you wish to use. Add food coloring until you have obtained the desired color. Either dip cupcakes into the fondant or ice using a knife. Decorate with colored sugars and Easter motifs.

EASTER LAVENDER BUTTERFLY Cupcakes

A bouquet of flowers in a cupcake—lavender, poppy, rose, and, with a little bit of luck, violet! Easter is the holiday that we all associate with the beginning of spring, so offer your friends and family a bouquet of flowers—with a butterfly on top.

MAKES: **ABOUT 24–30 CUPCAKES**

1⅓ cups all-purpose flour
2 teaspoons baking powder
1 teaspoon salt
½ cup/1 stick unsalted butter, room temperature
¾ cup sugar
2 eggs
1 teaspoon vanilla extract
½ cup light cream
2 tablespoons dried lavender flowers
2 tablespoons poppyseeds for decoration
Several teaspoons of your favorite jelly (strawberry, raspberry, etc.)

FILLING

1 cup heavy whipping cream, chilled
4 tablespoons sugar
½ teaspoon lemon extract or another flavoring
1 tablespoon grated lemon rind (if using lemon extract)

1. Preheat oven to 350°F.

2. Mix flour, baking powder, and salt together and set aside.

3. Cream butter and sugar until light and fluffy. Add eggs, one at a time, mixing well after each addition, followed by vanilla. Alternately beat in flour mixture and cream. Fold in lavender flowers.

4. Fill cupcake papers about ⅔ full. Bake for about 25 minutes or until a tester inserted into the center comes out clean. Remove from oven and cool.

5. To make the filling: in a large bowl, beat whipping cream. When it starts to stiffen, gradually add sugar and beat until stiff peaks form. Add flavoring and lemon rind.

6. Cut off the top of each cupcake and set aside—this will be the butterfly. Using a sharp knife, carefully remove a little cone from the center of each cupcake and fill with cream. Sprinkle with a few poppyseeds. Cut the top in half and place the halves on top of the cream to look like the wings of a butterfly. Put a little jelly in between the two halves to look like the butterfly's body.

JULY 4TH RED VELVET
Cupcakes

It is hard to imagine why anyone would have thought of adding red food coloring to chocolate cake, but the final effect is quite dazzling—especially with a Red, White, and Blue theme.

MAKES: ABOUT 18 REGULAR CUPCAKES OR 9 JUMBO CUPCAKES

2 cups all-purpose flour

2 tablespoons unsweetened cocoa powder

2 teaspoons baking powder

1 teaspoon baking soda

1 teaspoon salt

$\frac{1}{2}$ cup/1 stick unsalted butter, room temperature

$1\frac{1}{2}$ cups sugar

2 eggs

1 teaspoon vanilla extract

1 teaspoon distilled white vinegar

1 tablespoon red food coloring

1 cup buttermilk

AMERICAN PARFAIT ICING

4 ounces white vegetable shortening (you can replace the shortening with butter but the icing won't be quite as "white")

1 tablespoon milk

$\frac{1}{2}$ teaspoon vanilla extract

$1\frac{2}{3}$ cups powdered sugar

1. Preheat oven to 350°F.

2. Mix flour, cocoa, baking powder, baking soda, and salt together and set aside.

3. Cream butter and sugar together until light and fluffy. Add eggs, one at a time, mixing well after each addition. Blend in vanilla, vinegar, and food coloring. Alternately add flour mixture and buttermilk and beat until batter is smooth.

4. Spoon batter into cupcake papers, filling about $\frac{2}{3}$ full, and cook for 20–30 minutes or until a tester inserted into the center comes out clean. Remove from oven and cool.

5. To make the icing: cream shortening with milk until it is creamy. Add vanilla. Gradually add sugar to shortening. Beat with an electric mixer until icing is pale, light, and fluffy. You may need to add a little more milk to reach the desired consistency. Ice cooled cupcakes and decorate with colored sugars, stencils, sparklers, etc.

CUPCAKE TIP
This icing is perfect for stencils and colored sugars.

JULY 4TH BLUEBERRY & RASPBERRY Cupcakes

These red, white, and blue cupcakes will warm a patriot's heart and a gourmet's stomach! Decorate them with fresh blueberries and raspberries, covered with a raspberry glaze, on a background of white fondant.

MAKES: ABOUT 12 REGULAR CUPCAKES OR 6 JUMBO

1^2/$_3$ cups all-purpose flour
2 teaspoons baking powder
1 teaspoon baking soda
1 teaspoon salt
½ cup/1 stick unsalted butter, room temperature
^{2}/$_3$ cup sugar
1 egg
1 cup buttermilk
1 teaspoon vanilla extract
½ cup blueberries (fresh or frozen)
½ cup raspberries (fresh or frozen)
Powdered sugar or white fondant glaze (see method)
½ cup raspberry jelly for glaze
Raspberries and blueberries for decoration

1. Preheat oven to 350°F.

2. Mix flour, baking powder, baking soda, and salt together and set aside.

3. Cream butter and sugar until light and fluffy. Add egg, buttermilk, and vanilla and mix well. Stir in dry ingredients. Gently fold in the blueberries and raspberries. If you are using frozen fruit, don't defrost before using.

4. Spoon batter into cupcake papers, filling about ²/₃ full. Bake for about 25 minutes or until the top of the cupcakes are golden brown. Remove cupcakes from oven. Cool completely before unmoulding.

5. Dust cooled cupcakes with powdered sugar or frost cooled cupcakes with White Fondant Glaze (page 140) or ready-to-use fondant.

6. After cupcakes are frosted, heat raspberry jelly in a small pan until it is just liquid (do not cook). Remove from heat immediately. Place a few raspberries in the center of the cupcakes (preferably while the fondant is still soft). Surround with blueberries. Using a pastry brush, apply raspberry jelly to fruits. This will make them shiny and will hold them in place after glaze has cooled.

THANKSGIVING CARROT & CRANBERRY Cupcakes

These can be served as a dessert, as an alternative to pumpkin pie, after a Thanksgiving feast, and will be a welcome treat to kids and adults alike throughout the harvest season.

MAKES: ABOUT 12 CUPCAKES

1 cup all-purpose flour
1 teaspoon baking powder
1 teaspoon salt
2 teaspoons cinnamon
$\frac{1}{2}$ teaspoon grated nutmeg
$\frac{1}{2}$ cup vegetable oil
$\frac{1}{2}$ cup sugar
$\frac{1}{4}$ cup brown sugar, packed
2 eggs
1 cup grated carrots
$\frac{1}{2}$ cup walnuts, chopped
$\frac{1}{2}$ cup dried cranberries

CINNAMON AND SPICE FROSTING
$\frac{1}{4}$ cup/$\frac{1}{2}$ stick unsalted butter
$\frac{3}{4}$ cup/9 oz cream cheese
1 cup powdered sugar
1 teaspoon vanilla extract
1 teaspoon cinnamon
$\frac{1}{2}$ teaspoon ground ginger
$\frac{1}{2}$ teaspoon grated nutmeg
$\frac{1}{4}$ teaspoon ground cloves
Cinnamon for dusting
Candy corn for decoration

1. Preheat oven to 350°F.

2. Mix flour, baking powder, salt, and spices together and set aside.

3. Using an electric mixer or a wooden spoon, beat oil and both sugars until blended. Add eggs, one at a time, and beat until smooth. Add flour mixture and blend thoroughly. Fold in carrots, walnuts, and cranberries.

4. Fill cupcake papers about $\frac{2}{3}$ full. Bake for 25–30 minutes or until a tester inserted into the center comes out clean. Remove from oven and cool.

5. To make the frosting: cream butter and cream cheese together until light and fluffy. Gradually add powdered sugar, beating until smooth. Add vanilla and spices and continue beating until frosting is of good spreading consistency. Frost cooled cupcakes, dust with cinnamon, and decorate with candy corn.

CUPCAKE TIP
Fresh or frozen cranberries could be used as well.

THANKSGIVING APPLE CIDER Cupcakes

This cupcake is a perfect fall dessert or snack. The cider gives the batter a certain lightness but if you prefer a non-alcoholic version, just use apple juice.

MAKES: ABOUT 12 CUPCAKES

1½ cups all purpose flour
2 teaspoons baking powder
1 teaspoon salt
1 teaspoon cinnamon
½ cup/1 stick unsalted butter, room temperature
⅔ cup sugar
2 eggs
¾ cup sweet cider
1 cup dried apples, cut into little pieces

APPLE FILLING
2½ cups apples peeled, cored, and chopped into small pieces (about 3–4 apples)
1 cup light brown sugar
6 tablespoons/¾ stick unsalted butter, cut into small pieces
⅛ cup water
1 teaspoon cinnamon
½ teaspoon salt
Cinnamon for dusting
Apple wedges (either dried or fresh)

1. Preheat oven to 350°F.

2. Mix flour, baking powder, salt, and cinnamon together and set aside.

3. Cream butter and sugar together until light and fluffy. Add eggs, one at a time, blending well after each addition. Alternately add cider and dry ingredients. When batter is thoroughly blended, fold in dried apples.

4. Spoon batter into cupcake papers, filling cups about ⅔ full. Bake for about 25 minutes or until a tester inserted into the center comes out clean. Remove from oven and cool.

5. When cupcakes are cool, scoop out the center and heap full with Apple Filling or apple sauce. You can make your own or use the store-bought version. To make your own: combine all filling ingredients in a heavy pan and cook over low heat for about 5–10 minutes or until apples are soft. Remove from heat and crush apples with a fork. Cool before filling cupcakes.

6. Dust each cupcake with a little cinnamon and top with an apple wedges and walnut halves.

CUPCAKE TIP
Save the cupcake centers and freeze them. They will make wonderful Lamingtons (see recipe on page 176).

HALLOWEEN ORANGE JUICE Cupcakes

Orange juice is one of the main ingredients in both the cupcake and the frosting, so it will be both beautiful and healthy! The lovely orange glaze lends itself marvelously well to Halloween decorations—colored sugars, stencils, etc.

MAKES: ABOUT 16 CUPCAKES

2 cups all-purpose flour

2 teaspoons baking powder

1 teaspoon salt

½ cup/1 stick unsalted butter, room temperature

1 cup sugar

2 eggs

Juice and finely grated rind of 1 orange

1 tablespoon lemon juice

A few drops orange food coloring (optional)

ORANGE DECORATOR GLAZE

1 cup sugar

¼ cup cornstarch

1 cup orange juice (fresh, if possible)

1 teaspoon lemon juice

Pinch of salt

2 tablespoons/¼ stick unsalted butter

Orange food coloring (optional)

1. Preheat oven to 350°F. Mix flour, baking powder, and salt and set aside.

2. Cream butter and sugar until light and fluffy. Add eggs, one at a time, mixing well after each addition.

3. Combine orange juice and lemon juice and add enough water to make ⅔ cup. Alternately add flour mixture and liquid. Add orange rind and beat batter until smooth. Add food coloring if you are using it.

4. Spoon batter into cupcake papers, filling cups about ⅔ full. Bake for 25 minutes or until a tester inserted into the center comes out clean. Remove from oven and cool.

5. To make the glaze: combine sugar and cornstarch in a pan over low heat. Gradually add orange and lemon juices and stir until well blended. Add salt and butter. Cook over low heat, stirring constantly until the mixture is thick and glossy. Remove from heat and cool. Add food coloring, if desired. Glaze the cooled cupcakes. Decorate with Halloween colors and themes.

HALLOWEEN PUMPKIN PECAN Cupcakes

This is a pumpkin pie in a cupcake. Offer them to trick-or-treaters when they come to your door or serve them at a Halloween party.

MAKES: ABOUT 16 CUPCAKES

1²/₃ cups all-purpose flour

2 teaspoons baking powder

1 teaspoon salt

1 teaspoon cinnamon

¹/₂ teaspoon ground ginger

¹/₂ teaspoon grated nutmeg

¹/₄ teaspoon ground cloves

¹/₂ cup/1 stick unsalted butter, room temperature

³/₄ cup brown sugar

2 eggs

2 teaspoons vanilla extract

1 cup cooked or canned pumpkin

1 cup chopped pecans (or any type of nut, raisins, or mini-marshmallows)

FRESH ORANGE JUICE FROSTING

¹/₄ cup/¹/₂ stick unsalted butter, room temperature

2 cups powdered sugar

1 tablespoon fresh orange juice

1 tablespoon grated orange rind

1 egg white

Pinch of salt

1. Preheat oven to 350°F.

2. Mix flour, baking powder, salt, and spices together and set aside.

3. Cream butter and sugar until light and fluffy. Add eggs, one at a time, mixing well after each addition. Add vanilla and pumpkin and beat until smooth. Add dry ingredients. Fold in pecans.

4. Spoon batter into cupcake papers, filling cups about ²/₃ full. Smooth batter with the back of a spoon. Bake for 30 minutes or until a tester inserted into the center comes out clean. Remove from oven and cool completely before unmolding.

5. To make the frosting: cream butter and sugar until light and fluffy. Add orange juice and rind and continue beating. Beat egg white with a pinch of salt until stiff but not dry. Gently fold into mixture. Spread on cooled cupcakes and decorate to your taste.

CUPCAKE TIP

The orange frosting can be left as is or decorated for the occasion with a piece of candied orange peel or pumpkin seeds, colored sugars, black decorator frosting, etc.

DAY OF THE DEAD CHOC CINNAMON Cupcakes

"Dia de los Muertos" is a festive Mexican event to honor the dead, celebrated in November. This recipe calls for typical Mexican chocolate (mixed with cinnamon and raw sugar).

MAKES: **ABOUT 16 CUPCAKES**

1¾ cups all-purpose flour
2 teaspoons baking powder
1 teaspoon salt, plus pinch for the
    egg whites
1 teaspoon cinnamon
6 ounces/2 disks Mexican chocolate
½ cup milk
½ cup/1 stick unsalted butter, room
    temperature
¾ cup brown sugar
4 eggs, separated
1 teaspoon vanilla extract (Mexican,
    if possible)

CINNAMON BUTTER FROSTING
½ cup/1 stick unsalted butter
2 cups powdered sugar
1 tablespoon milk
1 teaspoon vanilla extract (Mexican,
    if possible)
1 teaspoon cinnamon

FOR DECORATION
Cinnamon or green and red sugars
Skulls and crossbones
Cinnamon candies

1. Preheat oven to 350°F. Mix dry ingredients together and set aside.

2. Melt chocolate and milk together in a double boiler or a microwave. As soon as the chocolate is melted, remove from heat, stir to blend, set aside, and cool.

3. Cream butter and brown sugar until light and fluffy. Add egg yolks, one at a time, mixing well after each addition. Add chocolate mixture and vanilla and mix until completely blended. Add flour mixture in three parts, blending well until flour disappears.

4. Beat egg whites with a pinch of salt until they are stiff but not dry. Gently fold whites into batter. Spoon batter into cupcake papers, filling cups about ⅔ full. Cook for about 20–25 minutes or until a tester inserted into the center comes out clean.

5. To make the frosting: cream butter and sugar until light and fluffy. Add milk, vanilla, and cinnamon and continue beating until frosting is of a good spreading consistency. Spread over cooled cupcakes and decorate.

6. To decorate: sprinkle with cinnamon or green and red sugars (the color of the Mexican flag), skulls and crossbones, marigolds, little cinnamon candies, etc. Day of the Dead sugar heads can be found in Mexican specialty stores and are a great item besides being a beautiful decoration.

CHANUKAH HONEY HAZELNUT Cupcakes

Chanukah is the Jewish Festival of Lights and one of the most joyous holidays of the Jewish calender. These delicate hazelnut cupcakes will add a gourmet touch to that very ungourmet but oh-so-delicious traditional Chanukah meal of potato latkes with sour cream and applesauce.

MAKES: ABOUT 12 CUPCAKES

10 tablespoons/1¼ sticks unsalted butter, cut into pieces
½ cup honey
¼ cup all-purpose flour
¾ cup sugar
½ cup powdered or ground hazelnuts
1 teaspoon salt, plus pinch for the egg whites
4 eggs, separated

HONEY GLAZE
2 tablespoons honey
1 tablespoon fresh lemon juice
½ cup powdered sugar, plus more for dusting (optional)
Candies (optional) for decoration

1. Preheat oven to 350°F.

2. Melt butter and honey together in a pan and set aside.

3. Mix flour, sugar, hazelnuts, and salt in a bowl and set aside.

4. Beat egg whites with a pinch of salt until stiff but not dry. Set aside.

5. Pour butter and honey into dry ingredients and stir vigorously with a wooden spoon. Add egg yolks and mix well. Gently fold in egg whites. Batter will be light and airy.

6. Spoon batter into 12 cupcake papers, filling a little over ½ full. Cook for 20–25 minutes or until a tester inserted into the center comes out clean. Remove from oven and cool.

7. To make the glaze: heat honey in a small pan until it is just warm. Gradually add honey and lemon juice to sugar, stirring to blend. Spread on cooled cupcakes and let cool. Place a candle in the center of each cupcake before serving. Alternatively, dust the cooled cupcakes with powdered sugar.

CHRISTMAS PEPPERMINT CHOCOLATE Cupcakes

These Christmas cupcakes will definitely evoke unforgettable visions of candy canes. Serve them as part of a Christmas buffet and throughout the holiday season.

MAKES: ABOUT 18 CUPCAKES

1 cup water

4 peppermint tea bags

2 cups all-purpose flour

2 teaspoons baking powder

1 teaspoon baking soda

1 teaspoon salt, plus pinch for the egg whites

3 ounces dark chocolate

1½ cups sugar

½ cup/1 stick unsalted butter, cut into small pieces

2 eggs, separated

½ cup sour cream or buttermilk

PEPPERMINT CANDY FROSTING

½ cup cream cheese, softened

1 tablespoon milk

Pinch of salt

A few drops of mint extract

2½ cups powdered sugar

¼ cup crushed peppermint candies or sticks

Miniature peppermint candy canes or green and red sugar for decoration

1. Preheat oven to 350°F.

2. Boil water in a small pan and add tea bags. Let steep for about 10 minutes. Remove tea bags and discard.

3. While tea is steeping, mix flour, baking powder, baking soda, and salt together and set aside.

4. In the top of a double boiler, over simmering water, place mint tea, chocolate, sugar, and butter. Stir until chocolate and butter have melted and mixture is smooth (you can use a microwave, if you prefer). Remove from heat and whisk in egg yolks, beating well. Alternately add flour mixture and sour cream or buttermilk and beat until batter is smooth.

5. Beat egg whites with a pinch of salt until they are stiff but not dry and gently fold into batter.

6. Spoon batter into cupcake papers, filling cups about ⅔ full. Bake for 25 minutes or until a tester inserted into the center comes out clean. Remove from oven and cool.

7. To make the frosting: in a large bowl, blend cream cheese, milk, salt, and mint extract and beat well. Gradually blend in powdered sugar until smooth and creamy. Fold in crushed candy. Spread on cooled cupcakes and decorate with a miniature candy cane and green and red sugar.

CHRISTMAS FRUIT
Cupcakes with White Fondant

These cupcakes are a cross between a Christmas pudding and a fruit cake, with a dash of brandy to warm your heart on a cold Christmas Eve.

MAKES: ABOUT 12 REGULAR CUPCAKES OR 6 JUMBO CUPCAKES

1 cup candied fruits

1/3 cup brandy

2 cups all-purpose flour

2/3 cup light brown sugar

2 teaspoons baking powder

1 teaspoon salt

1 teaspoon allspice

1 teaspoon ground cinnamon

1/2 teaspoon ground ginger

1/2 teaspoon grated nutmeg

1/2 cup milk

1 egg, slightly beaten

2 tablespoons apricot jelly

1 teaspoon finely grated orange rind

1 teaspoon finely grated lemon rind

1/2 cup/1 stick unsalted butter, melted and cooled

WHITE FONDANT GLAZE

1 cup powdered sugar

1 teaspoon finely grated lemon rind

1 tablespoon lemon juice

1. In a bowl, mix fruits and brandy and let stand for about 2 hours, stirring from time to time.

2. Preheat oven to 350°F.

3. In a large bowl, mix flour, sugar, baking powder, salt, and spices together and set aside.

4. Lightly beat the milk with the egg, apricot jelly, orange and lemon rinds, and melted butter. Add to flour mixture and mix well. Stir in fruits and brandy.

5. Spoon batter into cupcake papers, filling about 2/3 full, and cook for 20–30 minutes, or until a tester inserted into the center comes out clean. Remove from oven and cool.

6. To make the fondant glaze: mix powdered sugar and lemon rind together and gradually add lemon juice until you obtain a smooth paste, easy to spread. You may not need all of the lemon juice. Glaze and decorate cupcakes to your taste.

CUPCAKE TIP
You can use either the fondant glaze recipe or ready-to use fondant.

NEW YEAR'S EVE PINK CHAMPAGNE Cupcakes

There's nothing like champagne to usher out the old year and bring in the new one! Top these light and delicious cupcakes with a champagne popper and welcome in the New Year in style.

MAKES: ABOUT 16 CUPCAKES

2 cups all-purpose flour
2 teaspoons baking powder
½ teaspoon salt
½ cup/1 stick unsalted butter, room temperature
1½ cups sugar
¾ cup pink champagne
Red food coloring (optional)
6 egg whites
Pinch of salt or cream of tartar

CHAMPAGNE FROSTING
¾ cup/1½ sticks unsalted butter, room temperature
2 cups powdered sugar
2 tablespoons champagne
Red food coloring (optional)
Mini champagne poppers for decoration

1. Preheat oven to 350°F.

2. Mix dry ingredients together and set aside.

3. Cream butter and sugar until light and fluffy. Alternately beat in flour mixture and champagne, blending well after each addition. Add food coloring, if desired.

4. Beat egg whites with a pinch of salt or cream of tartar until stiff but not dry and gently fold into batter.

5. Fill cupcake papers about ⅔ full. Bake for 25–30 minutes or until a tester inserted into the center comes out clean. Remove from oven and cool.

6. To make the frosting: beat butter and sugar until soft and creamy. Slowly add champagne and red food coloring, if desired and continue beating until frosting is of good spreading consistency. You can add more champagne for a softer frosting. Frost cooled cupcakes and decorate with a champagne popper.

CUPCAKE TIP
If you prefer not to use alcohol, you can use cherry or strawberry soda instead of champagne to obtain the same effect.

NEW YEAR'S EVE CONFETTI Cupcakes

Welcome the New Year in with confetti. The crushed candies in the cupcakes will look like confetti when you bite in to them.

MAKES: ABOUT 12 REGULAR CUPCAKES OR 24 MINI-CUPCAKES

1 cup all-purpose flour

1 teaspoon baking powder

1 teaspoon salt

6 tablespoons/¾ stick unsalted butter, room temperature

½ cup sugar

3 eggs

1 tablespoon brandy or 1 teaspoon vanilla extract

⅓ cup light cream or half-and-half

½ cup crushed mints or hard candies of different colors

4-MINUTE CONFETTI FROSTING

1 egg white

¾ cup sugar

Pinch of salt

3 tablespoons water

1 teaspoon light corn syrup

1 teaspoon vanilla extract or 1 tablespoon brandy

Candy confetti (can be found in the baking section of grocery stores)

1. Preheat oven to 350°F.

2. Mix flour, baking powder, and salt together and set aside.

3. Cream butter and sugar until light and fluffy. Add eggs, one at a time, mixing well after each addition, followed by brandy or vanilla. Alternately beat in flour mixture and cream or half-and-half. Fold in crushed candies.

4. Fill cupcake papers about ⅔ full. Bake for about 20 minutes or until a tester inserted into the center comes out clean. Remove from oven and cool.

5. To make the frosting: place egg white, sugar, salt, water, and corn syrup in a double boiler. Beat for about 1 minute until thoroughly mixed. Place over boiling water and beat at high speed for about 4 minutes or until frosting forms stiff peaks. Remove from heat and transfer to a large bowl. Add vanilla or brandy and beat for another minute or until of good spreading consistency. Frost cooled cupcakes and sprinkle candy confetti over cupcakes before frosting hardens.

CUPCAKES
PLUS

DESSERT ROSE
Cupcakes

I originally put this "cupcake" in the Kids section since it will certainly be a great favorite with them. But after writing the introduction to this book, I realized that it really doesn't fit my "strict" definition of a cupcake so I moved it here. It doesn't require any cooking and can be made with little or no help from an adult. It is perfect for a party or just a snack and can be whipped up in the blink of an eye. The kids will love this one!

MAKES: ABOUT 12 REGULAR CUPCAKES OR 24 MINI-CUPCAKES

8 ounces milk or dark chocolate, broken into pieces
³/₄ cup/1¹/₂ sticks unsalted butter, room temperature, cut into pieces
1¹/₃ cups powdered sugar
2 cups corn flakes

1. Melt chocolate and butter in a double boiler or a microwave oven. Mix well.

2. Stir in powdered sugar. Add corn flakes and mix gently until all of the corn flakes are coated with chocolate.

3. Spoon mixture into mini- or regular cupcake papers and set in the refrigerator for a few hours. Remove from refrigerator and enjoy.

CUPCAKE TIP
You can replace the milk or dark chocolate with white chocolate and the corn flakes with Rice Krispies, Special K, or similar types of breakfast cereals.

ALMOND & HAZELNUT
Mini-Meringues

These mini-meringues are made in mini-silicon cupcake molds. They can be eaten as is, served with fruit salad or ice cream or used with other desserts. They are easy to make and versatile in addition to being absolutely delicious.

MAKES: ABOUT 30 MINI-MERINGUES CUPCAKES

$\frac{1}{2}$ cup ground almonds
$\frac{1}{2}$ cup ground hazelnuts
$\frac{3}{4}$ cup sugar
5 egg whites
Pinch of salt
$\frac{3}{4}$ cup hazelnuts or almonds, toasted and coarsely chopped
Powdered sugar for dusting

CUPCAKE TIP
They can be kept at room temperature for several days in a sealed container or frozen for future use.

1. Preheat oven to 325°F.

2. Mix ground almonds, ground hazelnuts, and $\frac{1}{4}$ cup of the sugar together. Set aside. If you prefer, you can use just almonds, just hazelnuts, or any combination of either.

3. Beat egg whites with salt until they turn opaque. Gradually add remaining sugar and continue to beat whites until they are stiff and form glossy peaks. Gently fold in ground nut mixture, using a whisk or a rubber spatula. I start with the whisk and finish with the spatula. Take care not to overmix.

4. Fill the mini-cupcake molds with the mixture. You can use a pastry bag to do this if you wish but if not, just heap the mixture into the molds. Sprinkle the toasted nuts over the mini-meringues, pressing them in gently. Lightly dust with powdered sugar. Let the meringues rest for 10 minutes and then dust them again with powdered sugar and let them rest another 10 minutes.

5. Bake for about 25–30 minutes or until they are golden brown and firm to the touch. Cool before unmolding.

DEEP-DISH APPLE PIE
Cupcakes

Deep-Dish Apple Pie is an all-American favorite and for good reason. These cupcakes work particularly well in silicon molds, either the regular or jumbo version. Serve them on individual plates with a wedge of sharp cheddar cheese or a dollop of whipped cream.

MAKES: ABOUT 8 REGULAR CUPCAKES OR 4 JUMBO CUPCAKES

PIE DOUGH
See Chocolate Cupcake Pie
  (page 150)

APPLE PIE FILLING
3 cups apples, peeled, cored, and
  cut into pieces
1 tablespoon lemon juice
$^1/_2$ cup, plus 2 tablespoons sugar
Pinch of salt
Dash of grated nutmeg
1 teaspoon cinnamon
2 tablespoons all-purpose flour
2 tablespoons/$^1/_4$ stick unsalted
  butter, room temperature

1. Preheat oven to 450°F.

2. See Chocolate Cupcake Pie (page 150) for instructions on rolling out pie dough and lining molds. Serve enough dough to cut circles to cover the cupcakes.

3. In a large bowl, toss apples with lemon juice, $^1/_2$ cup sugar, salt, nutmeg, cinnamon, and flour, coating evenly. Scoop mixture into pie shells and dot with butter. Cover each cupcake with a circle of dough, crimping the edges for a pretty effect. Cut two vents into the top of each cupcake so that the steam can escape and sprinkle with remaining sugar.

4. Bake in the oven for 10 minutes and then turn down heat to 350°F. Cook for another 15–20 minutes or until pie crust is golden brown. Cool cupcakes completely before removing from molds.

VARIATION: DEEP-DISH PEACH PIE CUPCAKE

Substitute peaches for apples and cut into slices. Use just a pinch of cinnamon.

VARIATION: DEEP-DISH BLUEBERRY PIE CUPCAKE

Substitute blueberries for apples. Leave out cinnamon.

CHOCOLATE
Cupcake Pies

The inspiration for this cupcake was a pie that I used to make for my restaurant, itself inspired by a recipe from Bernachon, the great "chocolatier" from Lyon. When I was testing the recipe, I just naturally assumed that I would have to use silicon molds but my experiments proved that it was possible to make the cupcakes in cupcake papers as well.

MAKES: ABOUT 14–16 CUPCAKES

PIE DOUGH

Enough pie dough (any type—basic, flaky, etc.), homemade or ready-made to make two 9-inch pies.

All-purpose flour for dusting

CHOCOLATE FILLING

4 ounces good quality dark chocolate, broken into small pieces

2 cups liquid whole cream

$^2/_3$ cup sugar

5 eggs

FOR DECORATION

Walnut halves (optional)

Whipped cream (optional)

1. Preheat oven to 350°F.

2. Roll out the pie doughon a lightly floured surface and cut out circles measuring 4 inches in diameter. Line silicon cupcake molds or cupcake papers, folding the edge of the dough back under so that it will look pretty. Make a few holes in the bottom of the dough so that it doesn't buckle when cooked. Be gentle!

3. Melt chocolate in a double boiler or a microwave. Remove from heat as soon as it is melted (do not cook). Add cream, sugar, and eggs and beat until all of the ingredients are totally blended.

4. Carefully pour chocolate mixture into pie shells, filling about $^3/_4$ full. Bake for about 25 minutes or until chocolate is cooked. The filling will rise while cooking but will fall when it cools. Cool cupcakes completely before removing from molds.

5. Decorate with a walnut half or a dollop of whipped cream, or both. If you are making the cupcakes in the silicon molds, serve them in pretty cupcake papers.

CHERRY ALMOND PIE Cupcakes

Although you can use just about any filling for pie cupcakes, this is one of my favorites. I had it for the first time when I was visiting my cousin Iris in Monkton, Maryland, after a dinner of steamed Chesapeake Bay crabs and homemade coleslaw.

MAKES: ABOUT 14–16 CUPCAKES

PIE DOUGH
See Chocolate Cupcake Pie (page 150).

CHERRY ALMOND FILLING
1/2 cup/1 stick unsalted butter, room temperature
1/2 cup sugar
2 large eggs
1 cup ground almonds
Finely grated rind of 1 lemon
2 1/2 cups pitted morello cherries (canned cherries work wonderfully well but you can use fresh or frozen, depending on the season)
Powdered sugar for dusting
Slivered almonds for decoration

1. Preheat oven to 350°F.

2. See Chocolate Cupcake Pie (page 150) for instructions on rolling out pie dough and lining molds.

3. Beat butter and sugar together until light and fluffy. Add eggs, one by one, beating well after each addition. Add ground almonds and lemon rind and mix well. Spoon mixture into pie shells, filling them about 1/2 full. Press the cherries into the mixture, pushing them under the almond paste with your fingers.

4. Bake for 25–30 minutes until the surface is golden brown, puffed up, and springy to the touch. Turn off oven and leave cupcakes with door open for about 10 minutes. Remove from oven and let cool. Dust with powdered sugar and decorate with slivered almonds before serving.

BAKLAVA Cups

The inspiration for these cupcakes is a wonderful and elegant dessert, found throughout North Africa and in every country around the Mediterranean basin.

MAKES: ABOUT 12 CUPCAKES

1 cup nuts (either walnuts, pistachios, or almonds, or a combination)
¼ cup toasted sesame seeds
1 teaspoon cinnamon
½ teaspoon cardamom
½ cup honey
1 tablespoon lemon juice
1 teaspoon orange blossom or rose water
8 ounces phyllo dough
½ cup/1 stick unsalted butter, melted and slightly cooled

1. Preheat oven to 350°F.

2. Coarsely chop nuts in a food processor. Transfer to a medium bowl and add sesame seeds, cinnamon, and cardamom. Mix well.

3. In a small pan, heat honey with lemon juice and orange blossom or rose water until just liquid and luke warm to the touch (do not cook). Pour mixture over nuts and stir well.

4. Cut phyllo dough into 5-inch squares. Put a square into each regular-size silicon cupcake mold. Brush with melted butter. Repeat five more times for each cupcake, staggering the corners of the square so that the sides of the molds are entirely covered. Flatten dough with the pastry brush as you go along. Put a heaping tablespoon of the nut and honey mixture in the center of each cupcake. Using a scissors or a very sharp knife, trim off excess dough to edge of cupcake molds or leave as is.

5. Bake for about 15–20 minutes until mixture is brown on top and dough is cooked. Remove from oven and cool. Carefully unmold Baklava Cups. They will harden as they cool in the mold. Serve in pretty cupcake papers.

CUPCAKE TIP
Enjoy them with a cup of espresso or a glass of sweet mint tea after a meal or at tea time.

WHITE CHOCOLATE PANNA COTTA Cupcakes With Passion Fruit Sauce

Panna Cotta is an Italian egg cream that literally means "cooked cream." Technically, this recipe is not a real panna cotta since it calls for gelatin instead of egg yolks to set the cream. But this is a "no fail" recipe, easy to make and delicious served with Passion Fruit Sauce or a simple fruit sauce of your choice. If you have any fancy silicon cupcake molds with a design on top (sunflowers, roses, etc.), they would work particularly well.

MAKES: **ABOUT 8–10 CUPCAKES**

PANNA COTTA
1¼ cups heavy cream
¾ cup whole milk
5 ounces white chocolate, broken
   into pieces
¼ cup sugar
2 teaspoons unflavored gelatin
1 tablespoon water
PASSION FRUIT SAUCE
½ cup passion fruit pulp
1 cup sweet white wine (Sauternes or
   Muscat, for example)
¼ cup sugar

1. In a medium pan, mix the cream, milk, chocolate, and sugar. Gently heat mixture, stirring constantly, until it is smooth (do not boil).

2. Heat gelatin and water in a double boiler (over simmering but not boiling water) or a microwave. Stir until gelatin has dissolved and add to chocolate mixture.

3. Divide mixture between 8–10 silicon cupcake molds. Place in the refrigerator for about 3 hours until cream has set.

4. While cream is setting, mix the passion fruit pulp, wine, and sugar in a small pan. Bring to a boil, lower heat, and simmer for about 10 minutes without stirring, until mixture is reduced by about a third. Remove from heat and cool.

5. Unmold the panna cotta on individual plates and serve with Passion Fruit Sauce.

BABA AU RHUM
Cupcakes

These individual rum cakes are delicious with tea and make an elegant dessert, served with whipped cream or custard sauce. Use any size mold, depending on the desired effect. Mini-molds can be used to make bite-size baba that may be a bit messy to eat, but your guests will go away licking their fingers—and complimenting the chef!

MAKES: ABOUT 12 CUPCAKES

3/4 cup, plus 1 tablespoon all-purpose flour

2 teaspoons baking powder

1/2 teaspoon salt, plus pinch for the egg whites

3 eggs, separated

1 1/4 cups sugar

6 tablespoons hot milk

1/4 cup/1/2 stick unsalted butter, room temperature

1 teaspoon vanilla extract

SYRUP

2 cups water

2/3 cup sugar

6 tablespoons rum

1 teaspoon vanilla extract

1. Preheat oven to 350°F.

2. Mix flour, baking powder, and salt together and set aside.

3. Using a mixer, cream egg yolks with sugar until the mixture is creamy and light in color. While the mixer is running, add hot milk, flour mixture, and butter and mix well. Add vanilla.

4. In a separate bowl, beat egg whites with a pinch of salt until stiff but not dry. Gently fold whites into batter. Pour batter into cupcake molds immediately, filling just 1/2 full. Cook for about 20 minutes or until brown on top. Leave babas in molds.

5. To make the syrup: in a medium pan, bring water and sugar to a boil and cook for 2 minutes. Remove from heat and add rum and vanilla. Slowly pour over babas, until all of the liquid is absorbed. Keep babas in their molds until they are to be served so that they soak up a maximum of syrup. You can keep them in the refrigerator for a few days after they have cooled but serve them at room temperature with a dollop of whipped cream or on a bed of custard sauce.

BLUEBERRY TART
Cupcakes

Once again, this pie was a great favorite at my restaurant. I usually made it in the fall with the fresh blueberries from the mountains nearby that inundated the village market at that time of the year. But frozen blueberries work at any time of the year.

MAKES: ABOUT 14–16 REGULAR CUPCAKES OR 7–8 JUMBO CUPCAKES

PIE DOUGH
See Chocolate Cupcake Pie (page 150).

BLUEBERRY FILLING
2 cups blueberries (if you are using frozen blueberries, don't defrost them)
1 cup heavy whipping cream
$^1/_2$ cup sugar
3 eggs
1 teaspoon vanilla extract
Whipped cream (optional)

1. Preheat oven to 350°F.

2. See Chocolate Cupcake Pie (page 150) for instructions on rolling out pie dough and lining molds. For jumbo molds cut out circles measuring 5 inches in diameter.

3. Divide blueberries up among pie shells, filling shells no more than $^1/_2$ full.

4. Beat cream, sugar, eggs, and vanilla together. Pour mixture over blueberries, filling shells about $^2/_3$ full. Bake for about 25 minutes or until cream has set. Cool cupcakes completely before removing from molds.

5. Serve with a dollop of whipped cream. If you are making the cupcakes in the silicon molds, serve them in pretty cupcake papers.

CUPCAKE TIP
You can either use silicon molds or cupcake papers. Either work well.

STRUDEL Cups

Strudel is said to be a Viennese speciality but can be found throughout Eastern Europe. I personally believe that it is the first cousin of baklava, probably brought to Europe by the Turks during the reign of the Ottoman Empire. It is generally made with apples but works well with cherries, ricotta cheese, apricots, or poppyseeds, just to name a few possible ingredients. Here are a few different recipes that you can try.

MAKES: ABOUT 12 CUPCAKES

STRUDEL DOUGH
½ pound phyllo dough
½ cup/1 stick melted butter and
   slightly cooled

APPLE FILLING
2 cups peeled, cored, and chopped
   apple (about 4 medium apples)
2 tablespoons lemon juice
½ cup sugar (more or less to taste)
½ cup walnuts, chopped
¼ cup raisins
1 teaspoon cinnamon
¼ cup browned bread crumbs or
   ground almonds
Whipped cream (optional)

1. Preheat oven to 350°F.

2. Line regular silicon molds with the phyllo pastry according to the directions for Baklava Cups (page 153).

3. To make the filling: place apple pieces in a large bowl. Add lemon juice and coat apples well so that they don't turn brown. Add remaining filling ingredients and mix well. The purpose of the bread crumbs or ground almonds is to absorb the liquid. Proceed as with Baklava Cups using this filling.

4. Serve individually on a plate with a dollop of whipped cream.

VARIATION: CHERRY FILLING

2 cups pitted sour cherries, fresh or frozen and defrosted (you can use any type of cherry but the sour ones work the best), ½ cup sugar (more or less to taste), ⅔ cup ground almonds, 1 teaspoon cinnamon.

VARIATION: RICOTTA FILLING

1½ cups ricotta cheese (you can substitute with cottage cheese), ¼ cup sugar, 1 egg, slightly beaten, 3–5 tablespoons raisins, 2 teaspoons finely grated lemon or orange rind.

BOSTON CREAM
Cupcakes

This cupcake is a variation of a Boston Cream Cake. The principle is two layers of a basic white cake, filled with custard, open on the sides (and a bit oozy!), and frosted on top.

MAKES: ABOUT 18 REGULAR CUPCAKES OR 9 JUMBO CUPCAKES

2 cups all-purpose cake flour
2 teaspoons baking powder
1 teaspoon salt
½ cup/1 stick unsalted butter, room temperature
1 cup sugar
3 egg yolks, well beaten
¾ cup milk
1 teaspoon vanilla extract

VANILLA CUSTARD FILLING
(CRÈME PATISSIÈRE)
1½ cups milk
1 vanilla bean (or 1 teaspoon vanilla extract)
½ cup sugar
¼ cup all-purpose flour
2 eggs, plus 2 yolks
Chocolate Ganache (page 79)

1. Preheat oven to 350°F.

2. Mix flour, baking powder, and salt together and set aside.

3. Cream butter and sugar until light and fluffy. Add egg yolks all at once and blend well. Alternately beat in dry ingredients and milk. Add vanilla.

4. Spoon batter directly into silicon cupcake molds, filling about ⅔ full. Bake for 20–25 minutes or until a tester inserted in the center comes out clean. Remove from oven and cool.

5. To make the filling: in a small pan, heat milk with vanilla. When milk boils, remove from heat. Just before you are ready to use the milk, remove the vanilla bean, split it in half lengthwise and scrape out the seeds inside into the milk. Discard the pod.

6. In the top of a double boiler, combine sugar, flour, eggs, and yolks and whisk until light and creamy. Slowly add milk, stirring continually, and cook until mixture just starts to boil. Remove from heat and continue stirring for a few minutes to release steam and prevent mixture from continuing to cook. Cool completely before using.

7. Cut cupcakes in half. If you are using jumbo cupcakes, you can even cut them in thirds. Fill with Vanilla Custard Filling and ice the tops of the cupcakes with Chocolate Ganache.

CARAMEL VERMICELLI
Cupcake Flans

No, it isn't your imagination! You heard right. Cupcake flans made with vermicelli, the same pasta you put in your soup. Imagine the look on your guests' faces when you tell them what the main ingredient is!

MAKES: ABOUT 16 CUPCAKES

½ cup raisins
2 tablespoons rum
4 cups whole milk
1 cup sugar
1 cup vermicelli
4 eggs, separated
Pinch of salt
Caramel (either ready-made or
   homemade)
Crème Anglaise (page 162)
FOR DECORATION
Candied cherries
Walnuts, coarsely ground

1. Soak raisins in rum for 1 hour. Preheat oven to 350°F.

2. In a large pan, heat the milk with the sugar. When it starts to boil, add vermicelli and cook for 8–10 minutes, stirring continually. Remove pan from heat and let cool.

3. Add raisins, followed by egg yolks, one at a time, beating well after each addition.

4. Beat egg whites with salt until stiff but not dry. Gently fold into vermicelli mixture.

5. Put a little caramel into the bottom of each regular-size silicon cupcake mold (about ½ inch). Pour batter over caramel, filling cups ¾ full, and bake for about 15 minutes or until batter has set. Cool completely before unmolding.

6. Cover cupcakes with Crème Anglaise, decorate with candied cherries and ground walnuts and serve individually.

CUPCAKE TIP
If you are making your own caramel, use sugared cubes instead of loose sugar.

CLAFOUTIS WITH
Crème Anglaise

A clafoutis is a very rustic French dessert, somewhere between a flan and a cake.
It can be made with any fruit but a "real" clafoutis is always made with cherries.

MAKES: ABOUT 16 REGULAR CUPCAKES OR 8 JUMBO CUPCAKES

¾ cup ground almonds

1¼ cups all-purpose flour

1½ teaspoons baking powder

1 teaspoon salt

½ cup/1 stick unsalted butter, room temperature

1 cup sugar

2 eggs, slightly beaten

½ cup milk

1 small shot glass cherry brandy (optional)

2 cups pitted cherries (if you are using frozen cherries don't defrost them)

Maraschino cherries for decoration

CRÈME ANGLAISE (VANILLA CUSTARD)

4 cups whole milk

1 vanilla bean or 1 teaspoon vanilla extract

6 egg yolks

½ cup sugar

1. Preheat oven to 350°F.

2. Mix almonds, flour, baking powder, and salt together and set aside.

3. Cream butter and sugar until light in color and fluffy. Add eggs, one at a time, mixing well after each addition. Alternately beat in dry ingredients and milk. Add cherry brandy. Beat batter until smooth. Fold in cherries.

4. Spoon batter into silicon cupcake molds, filling cups about ⅔ full. Bake for 20–25 minutes or until a tester inserted into the center comes out clean. Remove from oven, top with a maraschino cherry, and cool.

5. To make Crème Angaise: bring milk and vanilla to a boil in a medium pan and remove from heat. Just before you are ready to use the milk, remove the vanilla bean, split it in half lengthwise, and scrape out the inside into the milk. Discard the bean.

6. In a large bowl, combine egg yolks and sugar and mix well. Gradually add hot milk, stirring constinually. When all of the milk is used up and the mixture is smooth, return to pan and cook over very low heat, stirring continually. I always use a wooden spoon. The cream will thicken, little by little (do not boil). When the cream coats the back of the spoon, remove from heat and pour into another container. Stir for a few minutes to release the steam. Cool completely before serving.

CHARLOTTE À LA FRAISE Cupcakes

These are the French equivalent of Strawberry Shortcake and delicious, especially when strawberries are in season. Many variations exist but the following is one of my favorites since the gelatin holds the cream together and it won't fall apart when unmolded.

MAKES: ABOUT 12 JUMBO CHARLOTTES À LA FRAISE

Flavoring (vanilla, kirsch, strawberry liqueur, etc.)
Sugar syrup (made by boiling 1 cup sugar with 1 cup water)
3 cups strawberries, hulled and chopped into little pieces or coarsely crushed
1 cup sugar
2 teaspoons gelatin (or equivalent)
3 tablespoons cold water
3 tablespoons boiling water
1 tablespoon lemon juice
1½ cups whipped cream
1 package ladyfingers (I prefer the spongy ones to the dry ones because they soak up the liquid better)
Strawberry Sauce (page 166) to serve

1. Add flavoring to sugar syrup. Set aside and cool.

2. In a large bowl, mix chopped or crushed strawberries and sugar.

3. In a small bowl, soak gelatin in 3 tablespoons cold water until it is soft. Add 3 tablespoons boiling water and stir until the gelatin is dissolved. Add to strawberries and mix well. Add lemon juice. When mixture starts to set, gently fold in whipped cream.

4. To assemble, quickly dip ladyfingers in cooled sugar syrup (you don't want them to be soggy) and line jumbo silicon cupcake molds, bottom and sides, cutting to fit tightly. Fill lined molds with strawberry cream and put in the refrigerator overnight.

5. Carefully run a dull knife around the edges and unmold on individual plates. Serve with Strawberry Sauce (page 166).

CUPCAKE TIP
You can replace the lemon juice with orange juice. Or the sugar syrup with orange juice, as for Chocolate Charlotte (page 180). This will cut the sweetness a little and the orange flavor will go well with the strawberries.

BLACK FOREST Cupcakes

The inspiration for these cupcakes, a traditional German cake, *Schwarzwälderkirschtorte*, are a mouthwatering combination of chocolate, cherries, and whipped cream.

MAKES: **ABOUT 16–18 REGULAR CUPCAKES OR 8 JUMBO CUPCAKES**

1²/₃ cups all-purpose flour

2 teaspoons baking powder

1 teaspoon salt

²/₃ cup unsweetened cocoa powder

¹/₂ cup/1 stick unsalted butter, room temperature

1¹/₂ cups sugar

2 eggs

1¹/₂ cups milk

1 teaspoon vanilla extract

¹/₂ cup kirsch or cherry brandy (optional but highly recommended!)

FILLING AND FROSTING

1 cup heavy whipping cream

1 cup powdered sugar

¹/₂ teaspoon vanilla extract

1 tablespoon kirsch or cherry brandy (optional)

1 can pitted cherries, drained

Grated dark chocolate for sprinkling

1. Preheat oven to 350°F.

2. Mix flour, baking powder, salt, and cocoa together and set aside.

3. Cream butter and sugar until light and fluffy. Add eggs, one at a time, mixing well after each addition. Alternately add flour mixture and milk. Add vanilla and beat well.

4. Spoon batter into cupcake papers, filling cups about ²/₃ full. Bake for 25 minutes or until a tester inserted into the center comes out clean. Remove from oven and cool.

5. When cupcakes are cool, unmold, cut in half or in thirds, and sprinkle with cherry liqueur.

6. To make the filling and frosting: in a large bowl, whip the cream until it forms soft peaks. Add sugar, vanilla, and kirsch. Beat until stiff. Spread layer(s) of cake with half the filling. Press cherries into whipped cream before adding next layer. Save enough cherries to decorate cupcakes. Frost top and sides of cupcakes with whipped cream. Decorate with remaining cherries. Sprinkle grated chocolate over cupcakes and serve individually in a pretty cupcake paper.

CUPCAKE TIP
You can replace the canned cherries with Maraschino cherries if preferred.

CUPCAKE KEBABS

This variation on the cupcake theme is perfect for a party or for an elegant dessert, depending on the desired effect. Just about any cupcake recipe that you can use for making mini-cupcakes will do. Following are two different variations on the theme.

MAKES: ABOUT 12 KEBABS

MINI-CUPCAKES
White Fondant Glaze (page 140) or
    ready-made fondant
Food coloring (3 different ones)
Gummy candies or fresh fruit
Bamboo skewers

STRAWBERRY SAUCE
2 cups strawberries
½ cup sugar
¼ cup water
A few drops lemon juice
Whipped cream for decoration

CUPCAKE TIP
*This strawberry sauce
can be kept in the
refrigerator or frozen
for later use.*

1. Follow the recipe for Lamingtons (page 176), Mini-financiers (page 108) or Genoise (page 173).

2. Either make your own fondant (see recipe for Christmas Cupcake, page 140) or use ready-made fondant, following manufacturer's instructions. Divide fondant into three bowls and put a different food coloring in each. Dip cupcakes in fondant and drain on a rack.

3. Assemble cupcakes, three to a skewer (one of each color), alternating with the following decorations:

VARIATION: PARTY CUPCAKE KEBABS

Alternate the cupcakes with gummy candies. Arrange the skewers attractively on a plate, surrounded by gummy candies. These Cupcakes-on-a-Stick will be a great addition to any child's party.

VARIATION: DESSERT CUPCAKE KEBABS

Alternating the cupcakes with fresh fruit. Wash and clean the strawberries. Slowly heat the strawberries and sugar in a medium pan with water. When mixture starts to boil, cook for 1 minute and remove from heat. Purée by hand or in a food processor with a few drops of lemon juice. Cool before serving. Ladle a little Strawberry Sauce in a plate and lay a skewer over the sauce. Put remaining Strawberry Sauce in a bowl so that your guests can serve themselves. The idea is similar to a fondue.

ROSEMARY'S SUMMER PUDDING Cupcakes

This recipe was passed on to me by Rosemary, an Irish woman living in the south of France, who made it for me for lunch one beautiful sunny day in her village, perched between the Mediterranean and the Cevennes mountains.

MAKES: **ABOUT 8 JUMBO CUPCAKES**

4 cups summer fruits (black and red currants, cherries, strawberries, raspberries, blackberries, rhubarb, etc.)

½ cup sugar (to taste, depending on the sweetness of the fruit used)

5–6 tablespoons water

About 8–10 thin slices of white bread, crusts removed

Whipped or liquid cream

Mint sprigs for decoration (optional)

1. In a large pan, gently cook fruit, sugar, and water until sugar is just melted. Fruits should hold their shape so don't overcook. Remove from heat and cool slightly.

2. Cut rounds of white bread to fit the bottom of jumbo silicon cupcake molds. Cut bread to line the sides. You want the entire inside of the mold to be covered, fitting the bread neatly together. Carefully scoop fruit into lined cupcakes, saving a little of the juice. Cut the remaining bread to form a lid and cover the fruit, pressing the bread into the fruit so that it absorbs the liquid. Cover with aluminum foil and place in the refrigerator overnight.

3. When ready to serve, invert onto a serving dish and pour a little of the reserved liquid over each cupcake. The fruit will have completely saturated the bread and it will be a wonderful dark purple color. Serve with whipped or liquid cream and a sprig of mint.

CUPCAKE TIP
I have found that frozen berry mixtures work particularly well

CHOC & NUT Dacquoise

A "Dacquoise" is a classic French pastry of baked nut meringues layered with butter cream. Here, the meringue is made with almonds and hazelnuts with a chocolate ganache filling.

1. Make the meringues following Almond and Hazelnut Mini-Meringues (page 148), using regular silicon molds instead of mini-cupcake molds. Put about ½ inch of the uncooked meringue in the bottom of a mold. (You can also trace circles the diameter of a cupcake on a piece of wax paper. Turn the paper over, place it on a rigid ovenproof dish and pipe or spread meringue over the circle, about ½ inch thick.)

2. Bake until meringue is golden brown and firm to the touch. Wait until it has entirely cooled to unmold.

3. To make the ganache: place chocolate and cream in a double boiler and heat until cream is warm to the touch and the chocolate starts to melt. Remove from heat and stir until all of the chocolate has melted and the mixture is homogeneous. Remember—you don't want to cook the chocolate, you just want to melt it. Place bowl in cold water. When chocolate is cool to the touch, beat ganache for about 10 minutes with an electric beater until the color lightens and soft shiny peaks form.

4. To assemble: when the disks are cool, line a cupcake mold with pretty cupcake papers. Place a disk in the bottom of each cupcake paper. Spread or pipe a layer of ganache over the disk and place a second disk on top, lightly pressing it into the ganache. Cover the cupcake tin with plastic and put it in the refrigerator for at least 2 hours until the ganache has set. Dust with powdered sugar before serving.

MAKES: **ABOUT 10 CUPCAKES**

Almond and Hazelnut Mini-Meringues
   (page 148)
WHIPPED CHOCOLATE GANACHE
6 ounces dark chocolate, broken into
   little pieces
¾ cup heavy cream
Powdered sugar for dusting

CUPCAKE TIP
You can also assemble these cupcakes in silicon molds without cupcake papers or in no mold at all.

GELÉE OF FRUIT WITH WHITE WINE IN A Cupcake

This surprising dessert lends itself well to a cupcake format. Basically, it is a fruit salad in white wine jelly, an ideal and elegant dessert for any season, depending on the fruit that is available. It will be a perfect and light ending to a gourmet meal.

MAKES: ABOUT 12 REGULAR CUPCAKES OR 6 JUMBO CUPCAKES

3 cups of fresh fruit, washed and cut into small pieces (pears, cherries, strawberries, bananas, pineapple, peaches, apricots, oranges, apples, etc.)

1 heaping tablespoon unflavored gelatin (or equivalent)

1 cup water

½ cup sugar

1 cup dry white wine

1 tablespoon lemon juice

Whipped cream

1. Prepare fruits. Place fruits on a paper towel or a clean dish towel to absorb extra moisture.

2. Dissolve gelatin in ½ cup water in a double boiler. After it has dissolved, remove it from the heat but keep it over hot water.

3. In a large bowl, mix remaining water, sugar, wine, and lemon juice. Stir with a whisk until all of the sugar has dissolved. Add gelatin and continue stirring. Pour ¼ inch of the liquid into each cup of a silicon cupcake mold (either regular or jumbo). Put mold in refrigerator until gelatin has set (about 1 hour).

4. Remove from refrigerator and fill cups with mixed fruits. Pour remaining gelatin mixture over fruits, covering them with ¼ inch of the liquid. Put mold back in the refrigerator for at least 6 hours.

5. To unmold, run a dull knife (very carefully!) around the edges of the mold and unmold onto a serving platter. Keep in the refrigerator until you are ready to serve. Serve on individual plates with whipped cream.

DESSERT
Cups

Dessert Cups are hard chocolate cups made in a cupcake paper. They can be made with dark chocolate, milk chocolate, or white chocolate. The white chocolate cups are wonderful filled with fresh berries and the dark cups are delicious with raspberries. Fill any of them with candy for a party and set them in pretty cupcake papers.

MAKES: ABOUT 12 CUPS

15 ounces white chocolate
2 cups fresh or defrosted frozen
   berries (raspberries, strawberries,
   etc.)
Sugar to taste
Raspberry sauce (see page 94)
Whipped cream (optional)

1. Melt the chocolate over a double boiler or in a microwave.

2. Using a pastry brush, coat inside of a cupcake paper set in a muffin tin with melted chocolate (chocolate should be cool to the touch but of good spreading consistency). Put muffin tin in the refrigerator for about 20 minutes or until chocolate has hardened. Take it out of the refrigerator and add another coat. You may need to set chocolate over warm water or put it back in the microwave again to get it to the right consistency. Put cups back in refrigerator again so that the chocolate can harden. If you want sturdier cups, add a third coat.

3. When the cups are hard, peel off paper very carefully. You can keep these cups in a cool dry place or freeze them for future use.

4. Fill cups with berries, sprinkle with sugar, and drizzle with raspberry sauce. Add a dollop of whipped cream, if desired.

SPECIAL OCCASION
Cupcakes

These cupcakes are perfect for special occasions such as birthdays, weddings, graduations, or showers. The principle is that they are made of two cupcakes made in a silicon mold—a regular size and a mini-size—assembled, frosted with fondant, and decorated for the occasion, whatever it may be.

MAKES: **10 REGULAR AND 10 MINI-CUPCAKES**

GENOISE CUPCAKE
1¼ cups sugar
6 eggs
1⅔ cups all-purpose flour
½ cup/1 stick unsalted butter, melted and slightly cooled (but still warm to the touch)
Flavoring (vanilla, almond extract, etc.)
FOOD COLORING (OPTIONAL)
White Fondant Glaze (page 140)

1. Preheat oven to 350°F.

2. Put sugar and eggs in a double boiler over simmering water. Using a whisk or a hand-held beater (electric or otherwise), beat mixture constantly as it heats until it is lemony in color and forms soft peaks. The whole procedure should take about 10–15 minutes. Remove from heat and very gently fold in the flour, butter, and flavoring with a whisk.

3. Carefully spoon batter into regular and mini-silicon molds (you will need the same number of each), filling about ⅔ full. Bake for about 20 minutes, a shorter time for the mini-cupcakes, or until a tester inserted into the center comes out clean and cupcakes are just slightly golden on top. Remove from oven and cool.

4. Add food coloring to the fondant, depending on occasion. (For instance, you can use red and/or blue food coloring for a baby shower.) Set some of the fondant aside for dipping the mini-cupcakes.

5. To assemble: frost cooled regular-size cupcakes with fondant. Dip mini-cupcakes in the fondant and place on top of regular cupcakes. Decorate.

FAR BRETON
Cupcakes

A Far Breton is a speciality from Brittany, in the Celtic northwest corner of France. It is a rather rustic flan, made with prunes, a perfect dessert for winter when fresh fruits are rare. I suggest making these cupcakes in a silicon cupcake mold so that they can be easily unmolded and served luke warm with Vanilla Custard flavoured with a little rum.

MAKES: ABOUT 12 CUPCAKES

12 pitted prunes
1 small glass of rum for soaking
   prunes (about ¼ cup)
¾ cup all-purpose flour
Pinch of salt
½ cup sugar
2 eggs, slightly beaten
1½ cups whole milk
2 tablespoons/¼ stick unsalted
   butter, melted and cooled
Powdered sugar for dusting
Vanilla custard (page 162) to serve

1. In a bowl, soak prunes in rum for about an hour, turning from time to time. Drain liquid and save. Set prunes aside.

2. Preheat oven to 350°F.

3. In a large bowl, mix the flour, salt, and sugar. Beat eggs with milk and butter and add liquid to dry ingredients, mixing well with a wooden spoon or an electric mixer. Batter will be liquid. Stir in 2 tablespoons of the liquid from the prunes.

4. Place a prune in each cup of a regular silicon cupcake mold and fill just ½ full. Cook for about 35 minutes or until brown on top. Batter will rise and then deflate when it cools. Remove from oven and cool.

5. Sprinkle with powdered sugar and serve on a plate with Vanilla Custard (page 162) to which you have added a little of the rum used for soaking the prunes.

CUPCAKE TIP
*Alternatively,
just serve them in a
pretty cupcake paper
dusted with
powdered sugar.*

LAMINGTON
Mini-Cupcakes

A Lamington is a small square of plain white cake or sponge cake, dipped in melted chocolate and sugar and coated with shredded coconut. It is a specialty of Australia.

MAKES: ABOUT 40 MINI-CUPCAKES

2 cups all-purpose flour

2 teaspoons baking powder

1 teaspoon salt

¼ cup/½ stick unsalted butter, room temperature

¾ cup sugar

2 eggs

1 teaspoon vanilla extract

½ cup milk

2 cups shredded coconut, toasted for extra flavor

CHOCOLATE ICING

3 tablespoons boiling water

1 tablespoon unsalted butter

¼ cup unsweetened cocoa powder

2 cups powdered sugar

1. Preheat oven to 350°F. Mix flour, baking powder, and salt and set aside.

2. Cream butter and sugar together until light and fluffy. Add eggs, one at a time, mixing well after each addition. Blend in vanilla. Alternately add flour mixture and milk and beat until batter is smooth.

3. Spoon batter into silicon mini-cupcake molds, a heaping teaspoon of batter per mini-cupcake. Cook for about 15 minutes or until brown on top. Remove from oven and cool.

4. Spread out coconut on a piece of wax paper or in a large shallow bowl and set aside.

5. To make the icing: pour boiling water over butter. Add cocoa and mix well. Gradually add sugar and beat until mixture is smooth with a whisk or a wooden spoon. The chocolate should be smooth and glossy (it should also be thin enough to easily cover the cupcakes—add extra boiling water if necessary).

6. Using two forks or prongs, dip the cupcakes into the chocolate and roll in the coconut. Set cupcakes on a cake rack until they have cooled. These cupcakes freeze well.

PARTY SUNDAE
Cupcakes

Serve these cupcakes as you would a sundae, in an ice cream dish, with all the trimmings. I have given a recipe for Hot Fudge Sauce but you can use any sauce you wish.

MAKES: 16 CUPCAKES

VANILLA PEANUT CUPCAKE

2 cups all-purpose flour

2 teaspoons baking powder

$\frac{1}{2}$ cup/1 stick unsalted butter, room temperature

$\frac{2}{3}$ cup light brown sugar

2 eggs

1 teaspoon vanilla extract

$\frac{3}{4}$ cup milk

$\frac{1}{2}$ cup coarsely chopped salted peanuts

HOT FUDGE SAUCE

1 cup whipping cream

$\frac{1}{4}$ cup light corn syrup

12 ounces good quality chocolate (at least 55% cocoa solids)

2 tablespoons/$\frac{1}{4}$ stick unsalted butter, room temperature

1 teaspoon vanilla extract

Ice cream of your choice

Chopped peanuts, Whipped cream, Maraschino cherries for decoration

1. Preheat oven to 350°F.

2. Mix flour and baking powder together and set aside.

3. Cream butter and sugar until light and fluffy. Add eggs, one at a time, mixing well after each addition. Alternately beat in flour mixture, milk, and vanilla extract. Fold in peanuts.

4. Spoon batter into regular silicon cupcake molds, filling about $\frac{2}{3}$ full. Bake for 20–25 minutes or until a tester inserted in the center comes out clean. Remove from oven and cool.

5. To make the sauce: in a pan, slowly heat cream, corn syrup, and chocolate, stirring constantly. Simmer for 5–10 minutes or until mixture starts to thicken. Remove from heat and stir in butter and vanilla. Cool slightly before using. You can keep this sauce in the refrigerator and gently reheat it before using.

6. Using a sharp knife, cut a wide shallow hole in the top of each cupcake, the width of a scoop of ice cream, and just deep enough to hold it. Put cupcake in an ice cream dish, fill with a scoop of ice cream and pour the fudge sauce over the cupcake. Top with chopped peanuts, whipped cream, and a maraschino cherry.

OPERA Cupcakes

An "Opera" is a traditional French pastry found in the finest pastry shops across France. It is not difficult to make but requires a bit of time and patience. The traditional cake usually comes in the form of a layered sheet cake cut into rectangles. A true "Opera" will have a little piece of gold leaf (edible, of course) on top. This is a somewhat simplified version.

MAKES: ABOUT 12 REGULAR CUPCAKES OR 6 JUMBO CUPCAKES

GIOCONDA BISCUIT (BISCUIT JOCONDE)—THE TRADITIONAL CAKE RECIPE USED TO MAKE THE PASTRY):

2 tablespoons/¼ stick unsalted butter
½ cup finely ground almonds
⅔ cup, plus 2 tablespoons sugar
¼ cup all-purpose flour
4 eggs, separated
Pinch of salt
Chocolate Ganache (page 169) made using 4 ounces chocolate and ½ cup heavy cream
½ quantity Mocha Butter Cream Frosting (page 68)
Edible gold leaf or glitter sugar for decoration

1. Preheat oven to 250°F.

2. Melt butter and set aside until cool.

3. Beat almonds, ⅔ cup sugar, flour, and egg yolks until the mixture is light and foamy (at least 10 minutes).

4. In a separate bowl, beat egg whites with salt and remaining sugar until they are stiff but not dry. Gently fold into almond mixture. Delicately add cooled melted butter, using a spatula or a whisk.

5. Fill silicon cupcake molds just a little over half way. Bake for about 10 minutes or until brown on top. Be careful not to burn these cupcakes—they will cook quickly.

6. Unmold when cupcakes are cool and cut into three equal layers.

7. Beat half of the ganache with an electric beater for about 5–10 minutes until it is light and fluffy. If the other half hardens before you can use it, set it over warm water until it is of the right consistency.

8. To assemble, spread Mocha Butter Cream Frosting on the first layer. Add second layer and spread beaten Chocolate Ganache. Add third layer and ice with liquid ganache. Decorate with a piece of edible gold leaf or glitter sugar and serve in pretty cupcake papers.

CHOCOLATE CHARLOTTE Cupcakes

When I had my restaurant in the south of France, Chocolate Charlotte was by far the most popular dessert we made and I had to make one every day or my customers would go away disappointed. This is the cupcake version of that very charlotte.

MAKES: **ABOUT 8–10 JUMBO CUPCAKES**

8 ounces dark chocolate
½ cup/1 stick unsalted butter, cut into small pieces
½ cup sugar
3 eggs, separated
½ cup whipping cream
Pinch of salt
1 package ladyfingers (I prefer the spongy ones to the dry ones because they soak up the liquid better)
Orange juice

FOR DECORATION
Custard or Raspberry Sauce (page 94)
Roses and extra chocolate sauce

1. Melt chocolate, butter, and sugar in a double boiler until chocolate is just melted. Remove from heat immediately and add egg yolks, one at a time, beating well after each addition. Set mixture aside and let cool. When mixture is cool, pour in cream. The mixture will seize up a bit and thicken.

2. Beat egg whites with a pinch of salt until stiff but not dry. Gently fold into chocolate mixture.

3. To assemble, briefly dip ladyfingers in orange juice—you don't want them to be soggy. Line the sides of the jumbo silicon cupcake molds, cutting ladyfingers to size and squeezing them together tightly. Fill lined molds with chocolate mixture to just a little below the top. Cover cupcakes with more ladyfingers dipped in orange juice, fitting them well to cover all of the chocolate. Place mold in refrigerator overnight.

4. Unmold onto a serving dish and serve upside down, either in a pretty cupcake paper or on a plate with custard and/or Raspberry Sauce (page 94).

AUNT FLORENCE'S FROZEN LEMON Cupcakes

This recipe comes to me from my cousin Deborah (via her cousin Jocelyn) whose mother (my Aunt Florence) used to make them for her for as a special treat. Deborah tells me that she used to make them as well until she realized how bad whipping cream was for the health. So throw caution to the wind and make these very easy and elegant cupcakes for that special occasion.

MAKES: ABOUT 12 CUPCAKES

LEMON CREAM

1 cup sugar

Juice and finely grated rind of 1 lemon

2 cups whipping cream

CRUST

¼ cup/½ stick unsalted butter, room temperature

½ cup crushed graham crackers

½ cup crushed corn flakes

2 tablespoons sugar

Jellied lemon slices for decoration

1. To make the lemon cream: combine sugar and lemon juice and rind in a large bowl. Gradually beat in cream.

2. To make the crust: melt butter in a pan over low heat and stir in crushed graham crackers, corn flakes, and sugar.

3. Place crust mixture in the bottom of cupcake molds. Pour lemon cream on top. Freeze for at least 3 hours. Unmold, top with a jellied lemon slice, and serve.

CUPCAKE TIP
You can use cupcake papers or make these frozen cupcakes in either a rigid or a silicon mold.

INTRODUCTION

Nothing can beat the aroma of a freshly baked cookie. Homemade cookies make a wonderful gift to brighten someone's day and they are great fun to make with children.

★ ORIGINS ★

The word cookie has become commonplace all over the world but in Britain the word biscuit is also used. Cookie comes from the Dutch word *koekje* and it means little cake. Biscuit on the other hand comes from the French *bis cuit* and it means twice cooked. This harks back to the days when bakers put slices of fresh baked bread back in the oven to dry out and they became hard like rusks. This of course improved the keeping qualities, and was especially important when such foods were taken on long sea voyages and had to keep for a long length of time. Nowadays, soft cake-like confections are known as cookies (choc chip cookies for example) whereas crisper versions, such as shortbread are known as biscuits.

Apart from the obvious satisfaction which comes from making your own cookies, there is the added advantage that you can use the best ingredients and know exactly what they contain. Cookies are easy to make and many in this book are of the free-form kind, which you either spoon onto a tray or shape with your hands, so no extra equipment is needed. Homemade cookies are always popular so if you refrain from making them because they will all disappear in a flash, then make the refrigerator type where you slice off the raw dough as you need them or make sure you have some freezer bags handy to pop some in the deep freeze. Cookies are not only great as a midmorning treat, they are also good in lunchboxes and make a great quick dessert when accompanied by ice cream or thick fruity yogurt.

★ GET BAKING ★

There is something very therapeutic about baking cookies—it is to do with allowing ourselves to play again. Children love baking and you can have such fun with them, so don't just look at the wonderful pictures in this book—get baking and bring pleasure to yourself and those you love.

EQUIPMENT

To bake good cookies you don't need fancy equipment but here are a few tips on items you will need.

★ BOWLS ★

These can be of glass, ceramic, or stainless steel, it does not matter which, but what is important if you are using a hand-held electric mixer is that the bowl is tall and deep rather than wide and shallow. Sugar, flour, and especially confectioners' sugar tend to fly out of a shallow bowl.

★ HAND-HELD ELECTRIC MIXER ★

Although not absolutely necessary, a hand-held electric mixer is so handy and quick for creaming butter and sugar and for beating egg whites.

★ MEASURES ★

A set of measuring cups and spoons is vital for measuring quantities down to a fraction of a teaspoon. The amounts given in the recipes are for level cupfuls and spoonfuls unless stated otherwise. A set of scales is also desirable as cookies, like cakes, require accurate measuring of ingredients.

★ COOKIE SHEETS & BROWNIE PANS ★

Cookies can burn easily so it is wise to buy heavy professional quality sheets and pans. Every pan will bake a little differently depending on the weight, thickness, and material it's made from. Lining with parchment paper helps promote even baking as does placing a thin cookie sheet or brownie pan on top of another cookie sheet for extra insulation. Baking sheets should be rimless or with low rims so that it is easy to remove the cookies. Air-cushioned baking sheets bake evenly but they may take a little longer and generally are better when you want to end up with soft chewy cookies rather than crisp ones.

★ TIMER ★

Timing is vital—cookies are easily overcooked if left a few minutes too long, so a timer with a loud ring will keep you alerted.

★ SIFTER ★

A sifter is good to have although not essential. It's often used for sifting confectioners' sugar over the cookies, and if you have a tea strainer that will do the job just as well.

★ PASTRY BRUSH ★

A brush is very handy for brushing away surplus flour, greasing pans, and brushing on egg or glazes. Buy a good quality brush that has firmly fixed bristles.

★ ROLLING PIN ★

Cookie dough is often rolled out to quite a large size so it is preferable to have a rolling pin that is straight and without handles. Other than that choose one that is comfortable for you.

★ CUTTERS ★

Some recipes require cutters. There are many cutters available in myriad shapes and sizes. For best results the cutter should be sharp and have a good clear outline. This generally means that they should be made of metal rather than plastic, but some plastic versions do have a sharp enough edge. To use a cutter, place gently on the dough and then using the palm of your hand press firmly and evenly down on the cutter. Lift the cutter off without twisting it. Some doughs may be slightly sticky or moist so it is a good idea to dip the edge of the cutter in some flour every now and then.

★ KNIVES ★

A large sharp knife is good for cutting cleanly through rolled out or refrigerated dough. Even more useful are a couple of round-bladed spatulas, one large, one small. They are invaluable for spreading and smoothing mixtures, transferring cut out cookies to baking sheets and removing them once cooked. They can also be used for spreading frosting or chocolate onto baked cookies.

★ PARCHMENT PAPER ★

A roll of parchment paper is good to have as it can be used to line baking sheets so cookies don't stick. It's also useful to sandwich soft or sticky dough when rolling out.

★ COOLING RACKS ★

These can be cheap and cheerful, it doesn't really matter. You can even use the grid from the broiler pan, but a cooling rack is necessary if you want crisp cookies as they will go soft if left on the baking sheet.

★ PASTRY BAGS & TIPS ★

Again, these are not essential as only a few recipes in the book require them but if you do a lot of baking they are useful to have. You can buy disposable pastry bags and plastic tips from most specialty kitchen stores.

★ AIRTIGHT STORAGE CONTAINERS ★

Homemade cookies can quickly lose their crispness in humid conditions so a few storage containers are vital.

INGREDIENTS

The finest ingredients make the finest cookies. Don't consider using up your shriveled dried fruit and musty old spices in a batch of cookies. Choose your ingredients carefully and you will have cookies to die for.

BUTTER

Most of the recipes are best made with unsalted butter. Out of all the ingredients (other then chocolate) butter has the most effect on the flavor and texture of cookies so use the best that you can afford. Avoid using tub margarines, butter substitutes, and spreads as these often contain a high percentage of water and will upset the balance of the recipe.

EGGS

Most of the recipes in this book use medium eggs unless stated otherwise. Farm fresh, organic, or free range eggs taste better and give a better result than battery eggs. Always use eggs at room temperature.

FLOUR

Flour does vary so always use a good premium brand and make sure it hasn't been hanging around too long.

These days it is rare to find lumpy flour so sifting isn't always necessary but it does add more air, so making it easier to mix in. Don't sift whole-wheat flour as you will be taking out all the goodness.

BAKING POWDER & BAKING SODA

Some cookie recipes need extra help to rise and so need baking powder or baking soda or sometimes both. Make sure they are fresh as they go stale quite quickly once opened. If you have some that has been hanging around for a while it is best to throw it out and treat yourself to a new pack to avoid disappointing results.

SUGAR

Generally speaking unrefined pure cane sugars have a deeper flavor and are preferable to use but this is not as important as the type of sugar specified in the recipe. The sugar is usually chosen for a particular

reason. For example, superfine sugar has very small crystals which dissolve quickly and easily so it is ideal to use when creaming with fat. You can substitute the sugars in recipes but the results may not be as good.

CHOCOLATE

For the very best flavor always use bittersweet chocolate with at least 70% cocoa solids. Unless stated in the recipe never use chocolate chips to replace chocolate which is to be melted or blended into the batter as they are formulated to keep their shape when cooked and are sweeter and less smooth in texture. Some recipes call for milk or white chocolate so always look for the cooking variety and not confectionery bars.

LEMON & ORANGE ZEST

Always use unwaxed fruit, which has been washed before use.

SPICES & EXTRACTS

All spices should be as fresh as possible. Only buy in small quantities and if they don't smell wonderfully fresh when opened then buy some more. Always use a quality, pure extract, it really makes a difference.

FRUIT & NUTS

Dried fruit should be moist and plump. Fruits such as dates are often better bought whole rather than pre-chopped. Nuts should be as fresh as possible as the oils they contain can turn rancid. Store opened packages in the freezer if you are not going to use them regularly. When chopping or grinding nuts in a food processor always use a perfectly dry bowl and use the pulse button, scraping them down occasionally. Using this method there is no danger of the nuts turning into a paste.

MAKING COOKIES
with kids

Some of the first things young children learn
to cook are little sweets, cakes, and cookies.

when air is beaten into egg whites is science; and decorating with candies and frosting is creative art! So an afternoon spent baking is not frivolous but huge fun and very educational.

Fussy eaters can often be encouraged to be more adventurous if they are allowed to help with cooking. A savory cookie could be made for the child's lunch box—most children love eating the food they have made themselves.

Always allow plenty of time, especially when cooking with very young children, and remember they often lose interest but then come back a few minutes later. It is worth being patient at this stage as a love of cooking and food instilled at a young age is very valuable.

★ REASONS WHY ★

The recipes are simple and don't involve lots of hot pans and sharp knives which are too dangerous for very young children. Not only is baking fun, it can also be a useful lesson in many subjects. Measuring, weighing, and counting cookies is math; washing hands, keeping things clean and tidy is hygiene; seeing what happens

★ SAFETY TIPS ★

Remember a kitchen can sometimes be dangerous for children so there are a few things worth considering.

★ Young children run everywhere so make sure they wear shoes with non-slip soles—trainers are ideal.

★ An apron or even a clean dishtowel will protect their clothes from the food.

★ Make sure they wash their hands and tie back long hair. Keep a clean wet cloth handy for sticky fingers.

★ If they have to stand on a chair or stool to help, make sure it is secure—better if possible to let them mix and stir on a small table suitable to their height.

★ Place a wet cloth under mixing bowls and cutting boards as this will stop them from slipping.

★ Don't leave children alone with knives or electrical equipment.

★ A lot of the cookies in this book can be made much smaller—young children prefer tiny food. Just adjust the cooking time slightly.

★ Small children will find it easier to make drop cookies or those that they can roll into balls. Let older kids be creative with biscuits that are cut out and decorated.

★ The microwave is safer than the stove top for young children to use when doing such things as melting chocolate.

★ Gather all the ingredients together before you start as children are eager to get going but can lose interest if they are waiting around.

★ Encourage a little judicious tasting (avoiding raw egg) to experience new flavors and textures—you don't have to wait until the cookies are cooked. Remember licking out the bowl as a child?

TROUBLESHOOTING

Use these essential questions and answers to dig yourself out of any cookie baking problems you come across.

Q – *The recipe calls for softened butter, what is this?*

A – If you are using an electric mixer the butter should be left at room temperature until it gives slightly when pressed. If you are using a wooden spoon the butter should be the consistency of thick mayonnaise. Butter can be softened in the microwave at 30% power.

Q – *The first tray of cookies I bake are always OK but the cookies on subsequent trays are often deformed.*

A – Always cool cookie sheets before putting on a new batch of raw cookies. Warm sheets will start the dough melting slowly and this will cause the cookies to spread and become deformed.

Q – *I always find it difficult to measure very sticky ingredients such as corn syrup.*

A – To measure corn syrup and molasses accurately open the can or jar and rest the lid on top. Place the can or jar in a bowl and fill with boiling water to half way up the side of the can. Leave for a few minutes and then you will find the syrup is runny and easy to measure accurately.

Q – *I often find my dough to be very sticky and soft, so I add extra flour when rolling out, but then my biscuits turn out tough.*

A – Always refrigerate a dough rather than be tempted to add any extra flour. More flour equals a drier mixture, which will result in a tougher biscuit. Alternatively, roll out the dough between sheets of parchment paper.

Q – *My cookies always seem to bake unevenly.*

A – Always rotate the baking sheets half way through the baking time. If you are baking more than one sheet of cookies at a time then reverse them top to bottom and front to back. Also make sure all the cookies are the same size. If you are unsure of your oven you can fine tune the baking of cookies by test baking 3 or 4 cookies first.

Q – *How can I make sure my drop cookies are all even-sized?*

A – A good trick is to use a small round ice-cream scoop or lightly oiled measuring tablespoon.

Q – *I like to make cookies and usually make the drop variety—occasionally I would like to try other types but I don't have any cookie cutters.*

A – To cut cookie dough rounds without a cutter use a sturdy inverted wine glass. Or form small amounts of the dough into balls and flatten.

Q – *My cookies are often tough and dry, why is this?*

A – There could be a few reasons for this. Make sure your measuring is accurate. Do not over mix the dough once the flour has been added as this will cause the gluten to develop and create a tough cookie. The same applies to kneading and rolling out—keep it to a minimum and do not add extra flour. If the dough is sticky, chill it for a while and roll out between sheets of parchment paper. It could also be that you are leaving the cookies in the oven too long. Even a minute or two extra can make them dry and tough, so remove them just before you think they are done as they will continue to cook for a short time.

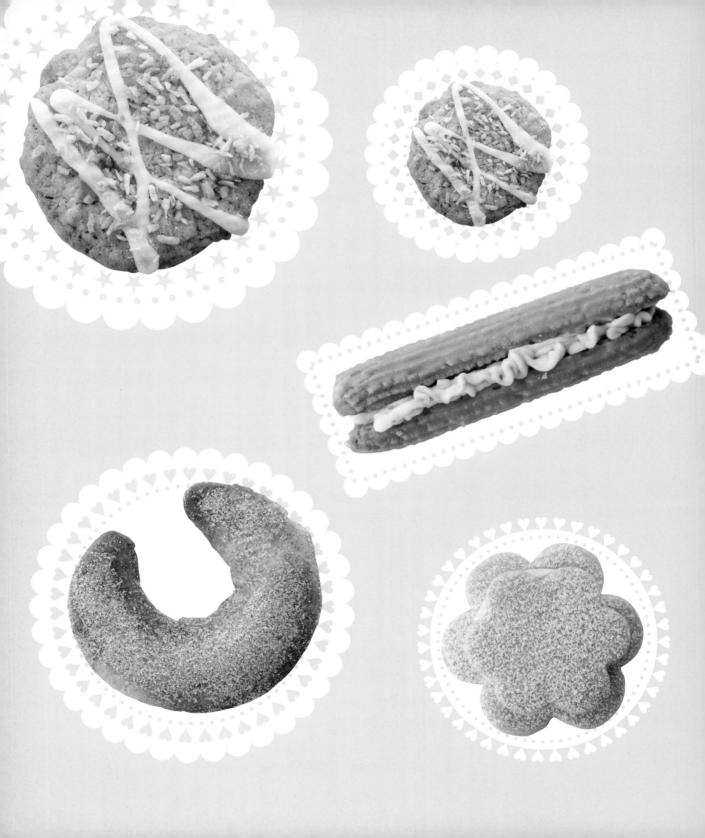

AFTERNOON
TEA

COCONUT
Cookies

Rich cookies, with a strong coconut taste. Decorate them by dipping in chocolate or drizzling a little chocolate over the top.

MAKES: 24
BAKING TIME: 10–12 MINUTES

INGREDIENTS
½ cup/1 stick butter
Generous ¾ cup sugar
¼ cup coconut milk
⅔ cup flaked coconut
Generous 1½ cups all-purpose flour
2 teaspoons baking powder
FROSTING
Scant ¼ cup confectioners' sugar
2 tablespoons coconut milk
Generous ½ cup flaked coconut

1. Preheat the oven to 350°F. Lightly grease two baking sheets.

2. Cream the butter and sugar together until pale and fluffy. Beat in the coconut milk and flaked coconut.

3. Sift the flour and baking powder and work into the coconut mixture. Drop tablespoons of the dough well apart on the baking sheets. Bake until golden, 10–12 minutes. Let cool on the baking sheets for 2–3 minutes, then transfer to a wire rack to cool completely.

4. To make the frosting, sift the confectioners' sugar into a bowl and stir in the coconut milk until smooth. Spread over the cookies, then sprinkle the coconut over the top. Let dry until the frosting sets, 1–2 hours. Store in an airtight container for up to five days.

BANANA & WALNUT Cookies

You could try using other types of nuts, but walnuts work particularly well with the smooth banana taste of these wholesome cookies.

MAKES: **20**
BAKING TIME: **15 MINUTES**

INGREDIENTS
Generous 1½ cups all-purpose flour
1 teaspoon baking powder
½ cup/1 stick butter, cut into cubes
⅞ cup light brown sugar
Scant 1 cup walnuts, coarsely
  chopped
2 small or 1 large banana, peeled
1 egg
¼ cup milk

1. Preheat the oven to 350°F. Lightly grease two baking sheets.

2. Sift the flour and baking powder into a bowl. Add the butter and blend with your fingertips until the mixture resembles fine bread crumbs. Stir in the sugar and walnuts.

3. Mash the banana with a fork and beat in the egg. Stir in the milk. Add to the bowl and mix until well combined.

4. Drop spoonfuls of the dough onto the baking sheets, spacing well apart. Bake until golden, about 15 minutes. Transfer to a wire rack to cool completely. Store in a cool place for up to three days. Suitable for freezing for up to two months.

COOKIE TIP
To make cookie sandwiches, melt some chocolate chips. Using a spatula, spread the chocolate over two cookies and then press them together.

CITRUS CREAM
Clouds

More like little cakes, these cookies would be good for special occasions such as a birthday tea.

MAKES: **18**
BAKING TIME: **5–8 MINUTES**

INGREDIENTS
$^3/_4$ cup/1$^1/_2$ sticks butter
1 teaspoon finely grated lime zest
$^1/_2$ cup confectioners' sugar
2 cups all-purpose flour
$^1/_3$ cup cornstarch
Confectioners' sugar for dusting
FILLING
$^1/_2$ cup/1 stick unsalted butter at
　　room temperature
1 teaspoon vanilla extract
1 teaspoon finely grated orange zest
1 teaspoon finely grated lemon zest
1 cup confectioners' sugar, sifted

1. Beat together the butter, lime zest, and confectioners' sugar until smooth and creamy. Stir in the flour and cornstarch and knead until smooth. Wrap in plastic wrap and chill for 30 minutes until firm.

2. Roll out half the dough between sheets of parchment paper. Using a flower-shaped cutter or a cutter of your choice cut out eighteen 1$^1/_2$-inch shapes.

3. Add any scraps of dough to the remaining pastry and roll out as before and cut out eighteen 2$^1/_2$-inch shapes.

4. Preheat the oven to 350°F. Place the shapes 1 inch apart on baking sheets lined with parchment paper. Bake in the oven for about 5–6 minutes for small shapes and 7–8 for large shapes, until lightly browned. Place on wire racks to cool.

5. Put all the filling ingredients into a bowl and beat together until smooth and creamy.

6. Either pipe or spread the filling on each of the larger cookies. Top each one with a smaller cookie. Dust with confectioners' sugar to serve.

GINGER Crisps

These crisp ginger cookies look very impressive. You will need to work quickly, but once you get the hang of them, they are quite easy to make.

MAKES: **20**
BAKING TIME: **5–6 MINUTES**

INGREDIENTS
¼ cup/½ stick butter
Scant ½ cup all-purpose flour
1½ teaspoons ground ginger
½ teaspoon ground cinnamon
¼ teaspoon ground cloves
½ cup packed brown sugar
2 egg whites

1. Preheat the oven to 375°F. Lightly grease two baking sheets.

2. Melt the butter gently in a pan, then let it cool but not solidify.

3. Sift the flour and spices together, then sift again to ensure that they are well mixed and lightly aerated. Sift the brown sugar to remove any lumps.

4. Beat the egg whites until they stand in soft peaks. Gradually beat in the sugar. Carefully fold in the flour mixture. Drizzle in the butter and fold until just combined.

5. Place 2–3 heaping teaspoons of the dough onto a baking sheet and spread each one to form a 3-inch circle. Bake until just set and beginning to brown around the edges, 5–6 minutes. While one batch of cookies is cooking, spread the next one on the second baking sheet. Oil a rolling pin.

6. When baked, let the cookies stand for a few seconds. Then, working quickly before they set, carefully remove from the baking sheet with a slim spatula and place over the oiled rolling pin; they will cool in a curve. Remove from the rolling pin. Repeat until all the dough is baked. Store in an airtight container for two to three days.

LEMON MACADAMIA NUT Cookies

These cookies have a lovely lemon tang.
They are fabulous served with creamy desserts.

MAKES: 24
BAKING TIME: 10–12 MINUTES

INGREDIENTS

½ cup/1 stick butter, softened
½ cup sugar
2 egg yolks
Grated zest of ½ lemon
¼ cup lemon juice
Generous 1½ cups all-purpose flour
6 tablespoons cornstarch
Scant 1 cup macadamia nuts, lightly
  chopped

1. Preheat the oven to 375°F. Lightly grease two baking sheets.

2. Cream the butter and sugar together until light and fluffy. Beat in the egg yolks, lemon zest, and juice.

3. Sift the flour and cornstarch and beat into the mixture. Add the nuts and stir until well mixed.

4. Drop heaping tablespoons of the dough onto the baking sheets and flatten slightly with the back of a spoon.

5. Bake until golden, 10–12 minutes. Let cool on the baking sheets for a few minutes before transferring to a wire rack to cool completely.

COOKIE TIP

If a recipe calls for both lemon zest and juice, pour the lemon juice over the zest to keep it moist.

MALTED DROP
Cookies

These have a great malty flavor and a chewy texture.
Perfect served with a cup of steaming hot cocoa.

MAKES: 18
BAKING TIME: 10–12 MINUTES

INGREDIENTS
½ cup/1 stick butter, softened
Scant ½ cup sugar
1 egg, lightly beaten
1 teaspoon vanilla extract
5 tablespoons chocolate malt powder
Scant ¾ cup all-purpose flour
½ cup rolled oats

COOKIE TIP
To prevent parchment paper slipping off baking sheets, sprinkle the baking sheet with a few drops of water beforehand.

1. Preheat the oven to 375°F. Line two baking sheets with nonstick parchment paper.

2. Cream the butter and sugar together until light and fluffy. Beat in the egg and vanilla. Sift the chocolate malt powder and flour together and beat into the creamed mixture along with the oats until all the ingredients are well combined.

3. Drop heaping teaspoons of the dough onto the baking sheets, spacing well apart. Bake in the center of the oven until just golden, 10–12 minutes. The lower baking sheet may need slightly longer. Let the cookies cool on the baking sheets for a few minutes, then transfer to a wire rack to cool completely.

SPICY BUTTERMILK
Cookies

The pumpkin pie spice and tangy buttermilk
in these cookies lends a sweet and gentle kick.

MAKES: 20
BAKING TIME: 10–15 MINUTES

INGREDIENTS
6 tablespoons/³/₄ stick butter,
   softened
²/₃ cup sugar
²/₃ cup buttermilk
Generous 1¹/₂ cups all-purpose flour
¹/₂ teaspoon baking soda
2 teaspoons pumpkin pie spice

1. Preheat the oven to 400°F. Lightly grease two baking sheets.

2. Cream the butter and sugar together in a bowl until light and fluffy.
Beat in the buttermilk. Sift the flour, baking soda, and spice together and
beat into the creamed mixture.

3. Drop rounded tablespoons of the dough onto the baking sheets,
spacing well apart as the cookies will almost double in size.

4. Bake until golden, 10–15 minutes. Let cool on the baking sheets for a
few minutes before transferring to a wire rack to cool completely.

COOKIE TIP
*If you prefer not
to use buttermilk,
yogurt is a very good
substitute.*

BASIC SPRITZ
Cookies

Spritz cookies are a firm family favorite and perfect for popping in the mouth at any time. The name derives from the German verb spritzen, meaning "squirt" or to "spray."

MAKES: 24–30
BAKING TIME: 8–10 MINUTES

INGREDIENTS
½ cup/1 stick butter, softened
Scant 1 cup confectioners' sugar
1 egg
½ teaspoon vanilla extract
Generous 1⅔ cups all-purpose flour
Colored sugar crystals for decoration

1. Preheat the oven to 400°F. Lightly grease two baking sheets.

2. Cream the butter and sugar together until light and fluffy. Beat in the egg and vanilla. Fold in the flour.

3. If using a cookie press, chill the dough for about 30 minutes until firm but not hard. Press the cookies onto baking sheets. If you do not have a cookie press you can pipe the cookies, but do not chill the dough first.

4. Decorate with colored sugar crystals and bake until lightly golden, about 8–10 minutes. Let cool on the baking sheets for a few minutes before transferring to a wire rack to cool completely.

COOKIE TIP
Cool cookies on wire racks without touching each other to keep them from sticking together.

CHOCOLATE MINT Creams

A wonderful combination of crisp mint and warm sweet chocolate. If you prefer you could substitute the peppermint extract for orange extract to make Chocolate Orange Creams.

1. Cream the butter and sugar together until light and fluffy. Sift together the flour and cocoa powder and beat in until smooth. Form into a 2-inch thick log and let chill for 1 hour.

2. Preheat the oven to 375°F. Lightly grease two baking sheets. Cut the log into slices ¼ inch thick and arrange well apart on baking sheets. Bake until just firm, about 8 minutes.

3. Let the cookies cool on the baking sheets for a few minutes before transferring to a wire rack to cool completely.

4. To make the filling, place the cream in a mixing bowl and beat in the confectioners' sugar. Add peppermint extract to taste.

5. Sandwich pairs of cookies together with the filling. Store in a cool place for up to three days.

MAKES: 18
BAKING TIME: 8 MINUTES

INGREDIENTS
¾ cup/1½ sticks butter, softened
¼ cup sugar
Scant 1⅓ cups all-purpose flour
2 tablespoons unsweetened cocoa
   powder

FILLING
2 tablespoons milk or light cream
Scant 1 cup confectioners' sugar
½–1 teaspoon peppermint extract

CHOCOLATE & PISTACHIO Fingers

Softer than normal shortbread these cookies
are good served with tea or coffee.

MAKES: 12
BAKING TIME: 15 MINUTES

INGREDIENTS

Scant 1 cup unsalted butter
1/2 cup golden superfine sugar
2 1/4 cups all-purpose flour
1/2 cup unsweetened cocoa powder
1/4 cup shelled pistachio nuts, coarsely
    chopped
Unsweetened cocoa powder for
    dusting

1. Preheat the oven to 350°F. Line a shallow square 7-inch pan with parchment paper.

2. Cream the butter and sugar together until light and fluffy. Sift together the flour and cocoa powder. Add to the butter mixture and work in using your hands until the mixture is smooth. Add the pistachios and knead until soft and pliable.

3. Press the mixture into the pan and smooth the top using the back of a tablespoon. Prick with a fork and mark into bars.

4. Bake in the oven for about 15 minutes. Do not allow to become too brown or the cookies will taste bitter.

5. Allow to cool slightly then cut through the marked sections and remove from the pan. Cool on a wire rack and dust sparingly with cocoa powder.

HONEY & LEMON Cookies

To make these cookies more attractive, you could use star-shaped cutters to give a more sophisticated finish.

MAKES: 16
BAKING TIME: 10–12 MINUTES

INGREDIENTS
Generous 1⅔ cups all-purpose flour
1 teaspoon baking soda
Scant ¼ cup sugar
Grated zest and juice of 1 lemon
½ cup/1 stick butter
5 tablespoons honey

FILLING
4 tablespoons butter, softened
⅔ cup confectioners' sugar
2 tablespoons honey
2 teaspoons lemon juice

1. Sift the flour and baking soda into a bowl. Stir in the sugar and lemon zest. Blend in the butter until the mixture resembles fine bread crumbs.

2. Heat the honey and lemon juice in a small pan until very runny but not too hot. Pour into the flour mixture and mix to form a soft dough. Chill for 30 minutes or until firm enough to handle. Preheat the oven to 375°F. Lightly grease a baking sheet.

3. Roll the dough into small balls and arrange well spaced on the baking sheet. Flatten slightly with a knife. Bake until golden brown, 10–12 minutes.

4. Let cool on the baking sheet for a few minutes before transferring to a wire rack to cool completely.

5. To make the filling, cream the butter and confectioners' sugar together until light and fluffy. Beat in the honey and lemon juice. Sandwich the cookies together in pairs with the filling.

LADY GREY TEA Cookies

The unusual ingredient in these cookies is Lady Grey tea—similar to Earl Grey but with the addition of Seville orange and lemon peel.

MAKES: 18–20
BAKING TIME: 10–15 MINUTES

INGREDIENTS
1/3 cup/2/3 stick unsalted butter, at room temperature
1/4 cup light brown sugar
1 tablespoon Lady Grey tea leaves
1 egg white
1 1/3 cups all-purpose flour

TOPPING
Demerara sugar

1. Preheat the oven to 375°F. Line baking sheets with parchment paper.

2. Put the butter and sugar into a bowl and beat together until creamy. Stir in the tea leaves.

3. Beat in the egg white. Fold in the flour to make a soft but not sticky dough. On a lightly floured surface roll into a cylinder. Flatten slightly to make a cross section that looks like a finger biscuit with rounded ends. Wrap carefully in plastic wrap and chill until firm enough to slice.

4. Cut into thin slices and place on the prepared baking sheets. Sprinkle each biscuit with Demerara sugar. Bake in the oven for 10–15 minutes until lightly browned.

COOKIE TIP
Store delicate cookies between sheets of waxed paper for safe keeping.

NUTTY JELLY
Slices

Sticky and crunchy, these bite-size slices are enjoyable to make and great for teatime snacking.

1. Lightly grease a baking sheet. Cream the butter and sugar together until light and fluffy. Beat in the egg yolk and almond extract. Work in the flour and ground almonds to form a firm dough. Add a little extra flour if the mixture is too soft.

2. Divide the dough in half and roll each into a log about 10 inches long. Place on the prepared sheet.

3. Lightly beat the egg white with a fork and brush over each log. Lightly crush the almonds and press onto the logs. Flatten each log slightly. Use the handle of a wooden spoon to press a channel down the center of each log. Fill the hollows with jelly. Let chill for 30 minutes.

4. Preheat the oven to 350°F.

5. Bake the logs until pale golden brown, 10–12 minutes. Leave on the baking sheet until the jam has set but the dough is still warm. Cut diagonally into slices and transfer to a wire rack to cool completely.

MAKES: **20**
BAKING TIME: **10–12 MINUTES**

INGREDIENTS
$\frac{1}{4}$ cup/$\frac{1}{2}$ stick butter
Scant $\frac{1}{4}$ cup sugar
1 egg, separated
1 teaspoon almond extract
Scant $\frac{2}{3}$ cup all-purpose flour
Scant $\frac{1}{4}$ cup ground almonds
Scant $\frac{1}{4}$ cup sliced almonds
Jelly of your choice

COFFEE & CINNAMON Cookies

The cinnamon flavor and attractive crescent shape of these little cookies makes them perfect for serving at Christmas time.

MAKES: 40
BAKING TIME: 12 MINUTES

INGREDIENTS

1 tablespoon instant coffee granules
1 tablespoon boiling water
1 cup/2 sticks butter
Scant ¾ cup sugar
1 tablespoon Kahlúa or other coffee-
   flavored liqueur
Scant 3 cups all-purpose flour
2 teaspoons ground cinnamon
¼ cup confectioners' sugar

1. Preheat the oven to 350°F. Lightly grease two baking sheets. Dissolve the coffee in 1 tablespoon boiling water.

2. Cream the butter and sugar together until pale and fluffy. Beat in the coffee and liqueur. Sift the flour and 1 teaspoon of the cinnamon together, then beat into the dough.

3. Take small amounts of the dough, each about the size of a walnut, and roll into balls. Shape each ball into a log, then curve it into a crescent. Space well apart on the baking sheets. Bake until golden, about 12 minutes. Let cool on the baking sheets for 2–3 minutes, then transfer to a wire rack to cool completely.

4. Sift the confectioners' sugar and remaining cinnamon together a few times to ensure that the sugar and spice are well mixed. Dust the cookies with the spiced sugar. Store in an airtight container for up to five days.

BUTTERSCOTCH

Fingers

A variation on the Viennese finger these cookies have a delicious butterscotch flavor and a delightful crisp coating.

MAKES: 9
BAKING TIME: 8–10 MINUTES

INGREDIENTS
1 cup/2 sticks unsalted butter
$\frac{1}{2}$ cup dark brown sugar, firmly packed
1 egg white
$1\frac{3}{4}$ cups all-purpose flour
BUTTERSCOTCH CREAM
2 tablespoons butter
1 tablespoon cream
1 cup golden confectioners' sugar, sifted
GLAZE
$\frac{7}{8}$ cup golden confectioners' sugar

1. Preheat the oven to 350°F. Beat the butter and sugar together until light and fluffy. Beat in the egg white. Stir in the flour and mix well.

2. Spoon the mixture into a pastry bag fitted with a $\frac{1}{2}$-inch star tip and pipe eighteen $3\frac{1}{2}$-inch long fingers on lightly greased baking sheets.

3. Bake for about 8–10 minutes or until lightly browned. Cool on a wire rack.

4. To make the glaze, put the confectioners' sugar into a small bowl and add enough water to mix to a pouring consistency. Using a pastry brush, spread the glaze over each biscuit and allow to dry.

5. To make the filling, put the ingredients into a bowl and beat together until smooth. Sandwich the biscuits together with a little of the butterscotch cream.

COOKIE TIP
Make sure you allow the glaze to dry and the filling to set before storing in an airtight container.

ALMOND & VANILLA
FUDGE Crumbles

Crumbly almond cookies with a crunchy topping
have the surprise addition of tiny pieces of fudge.

MAKES: 24
BAKING TIME: 10–12 MINUTES

INGREDIENTS

1½ cups self-rising flour
Pinch of salt
½ cup/1 stick sweet butter
½ cup light brown sugar
1 egg
1 teaspoon almond extract
⅓ cup ground almonds
2 ounces vanilla cream fudge, finely
   diced

TOPPING

2 tablespoons flaked almonds,
   crumbled
2 tablespoons Demerara sugar

1. Sift the flour and salt into a bowl. Blend in the butter. Add all the remaining ingredients (except those for the topping) and mix to a fairly firm dough. Wrap in plastic wrap. Chill for 15 minutes.

2. Preheat the oven to 375°F. Divide the dough into 24 pieces and place, slightly apart on baking sheets lined with parchment paper.

3. To make the topping: mix together the flaked almonds and Demerara sugar and sprinkle a little on top of each cookie, pressing down lightly using the back of a spoon.

4. Bake in the oven for about 10–12 minutes until turning golden at the edges.

5. Remove from the oven and allow to cool for 5 minutes before removing to a wire rack.

GYPSY Creams

A crisp chocolate oat cookie encases a creamy chocolate filling in these hearty, classic, and wholesome sandwich cookies.

MAKES: 10
BAKING TIME: 20 MINUTES

INGREDIENTS

1/4 cup/1/2 stick butter, softened
1/4 cup white vegetable shortening
Scant 1/4 cup sugar
Scant 2/3 cup all-purpose flour
1/2 cup rolled oats
1 tablespoon unsweetened cocoa
   powder

FILLING

1/4 cup/1/2 stick butter, softened
2/3 cup confectioners' sugar
2 tablespoons unsweetened cocoa
   powder

1. Preheat the oven to 350°F. Lightly grease a baking sheet.

2. Cream the butter, shortening, and sugar together until light and fluffy. Beat in the remaining ingredients.

3. Roll the dough into small balls and place on the baking sheet. Flatten with a fork dipped in hot water. Bake until golden, about 20 minutes. Let cool on the baking sheet.

4. To make the filling, cream the butter until fluffy, then gradually beat in the confectioners' sugar and cocoa powder. Sandwich the cookies together in pairs with the filling.

TROPICAL FRUIT
Cookies

Soft cookies packed with tropical fruit
and topped with coconut frosting.

MAKES: 16–18
BAKING TIME: 12 MINUTES

INGREDIENTS
1/2 cup/1 stick butter
1/3 cup superfine sugar
1 egg
1 1/3 cups self-rising flour
1/3 cup ground almonds
9-ounce pack ready-to-eat tropical
   fruit mix, chopped
FROSTING
1 cup confectioners' sugar
2–3 tablespoons coconut cream

1. Preheat the oven to 350°F.
Put the butter and sugar into a bowl
and beat together until creamy.
Beat in the egg.

2. Stir in the flour, ground almonds
and fruit. Place spoonfuls of the
mixture 2 inches apart on a nonstick
baking sheet.

3. Bake in the oven for about 12 minutes or
until lightly browned. Cool on a wire rack.

4. To make the frosting: sift the confectioners' sugar into a bowl. Add the
coconut cream and mix until thick but not too runny. Spoon over the
cookies and leave to set.

COOKIE TIP
*Only store one kind
of cookie in a container.
If you mix crisp and soft
cookies they will all go
soft and end up tasting
the same.*

FRUITY OAT
Bites

These are perfect as a healthy afternoon snack as the dried fruit will give long-lasting energy.

MAKES: 10
BAKING TIME: 20–25 MINUTES

INGREDIENTS
¾ cup/1¼ sticks butter
⅓ cup light brown sugar
⅓ cup honey
6 ounces granola
¼ cup rolled oats
½ cup chopped dried apricots
½ cup chopped dried apple
½ cup chopped dried mango

1. Preheat the oven to 375°F. Lightly grease an 8 x 8-inch square pan and line the bottom with nonstick parchment paper.

2. Melt the butter, sugar, and honey together in a saucepan, stirring until well combined. Remove from the heat and stir in the granola, oats, apricots, apple, and mango.

3. Press the mixture into the prepared cake pan. Bake for 20–25 minutes.

4. Allow to cool for a few minutes in the pan, then cut into bars. Allow to cool completely in the pan before serving. Store in an airtight container for up to two weeks.

LUNCHBOX

CHOC CHIP & MIXED NUT Cookies

A classic recipe for all the family that produces a chewy, melt-in-the-mouth cookie, just like Grandma used to make.

MAKES: 10–12
BAKING TIME: 15–18 MINUTES

INGREDIENTS
1 cup/2 sticks butter, softened
Generous ¾ cup sugar
¾ cup brown sugar, lightly packed
2 eggs
1 teaspoon vanilla extract
Generous 1¾ cups all-purpose flour
1 teaspoon baking soda
1 cup semisweet or milk chocolate chips
Scant ¾ cup mixed nuts (walnuts, pecans, almonds, hazelnuts etc.), chopped

1. Preheat the oven to 325°F. Lightly grease two baking sheets.

2. Cream the butter and sugars together until light and fluffy. Beat in the eggs and vanilla. Sift the flour with the baking soda and beat into the mixture. Add the chocolate chips and nuts and stir until well combined.

3. Drop large rounded tablespoons of the dough onto the baking sheets, five or six per sheet, well spaced as the cookies will spread.

4. Bake until golden, 15–18 minutes. Let cool on the baking sheets for a few minutes before transferring to a wire rack to cool completely.

COOKIE TIP
Only grease the baking sheets when the recipe instructs you to. Otherwise the cookies may spread too much and become flat.

ORANGE & PEANUT BUTTER Cookies

The combination of zesty orange and rich peanut butter in this recipe makes for a fresh yet wholesome, tasty cookie.

MAKES: **24**
BAKING TIME: **18–20 MINUTES**

INGREDIENTS
$\frac{1}{2}$ cup/1 stick butter, softened
Scant $\frac{1}{2}$ cup sugar
1 egg, lightly beaten
$\frac{1}{4}$ cup peanut butter
Grated zest of 1 small orange
$\frac{1}{4}$ cup orange juice
2 cups all-purpose flour
1 teaspoon baking powder

1. Preheat the oven to 350°F. Lightly grease two baking sheets.

2. Cream the butter and sugar together until light and fluffy. Beat in the egg, peanut butter, orange zest, and juice. Sift the flour and baking powder together and beat into the mixture.

3. Drop rounded tablespoons of the dough, spaced well apart onto the baking sheets. Flatten slightly with the back of a spoon.

4. Bake until golden, 18–20 minutes. Let cool on the baking sheets for a few minutes before transferring to a wire rack to cool completely.

COOKIE TIP
For even baking, always bake cookies on the middle rack of your oven.

TRADITIONAL CHOC CHIP Cookies

Enjoy the contrast of white and semisweet chocolate chips in this delicious twist on everyone's favorite cookie.

MAKES: 14
BAKING TIME: 12–15 MINUTES

INGREDIENTS

2 ounces semisweet chocolate chips
2 ounces white chocolate chips
1¼ sticks butter
⅔ cup sugar
1 egg
½ teaspoon vanilla extract
1⅓ cups all-purpose flour
1 teaspoon baking powder

1. Preheat the oven to 350°F. Lightly grease two baking sheets.

2. Cream the butter and sugar together until pale and fluffy. Beat in the egg and the vanilla. Sift the flour and baking powder together and beat into the mixture. Add the chocolate chips and stir until well combined.

3. Drop 5–6 rounded tablespoons of the dough onto each baking sheet, spacing well apart, as the cookies will almost double in size.

4. Bake until golden, 12–15 minutes. Let cool on the baking sheet for 2–3 minutes, then transfer to a wire rack to cool completely. Store in an airtight container for up to five days.

COOKIE TIP
Never drop cookies on to a hot baking sheet. Use two baking sheets if instructed to, or cool the sheet in between batches.

OATMEAL CHOC CHIP Cookies

For an old-fashioned, coarser texture, be sure to use rolled oats. However, if you prefer a smoother cookie, use quick-cooking oats.

MAKES: 10–12
BAKING TIME: 8–10 MINUTES

INGREDIENTS

Generous 1 cup all-purpose flour
1 teaspoon baking powder
¾ cup/1½ sticks unsalted butter, softened
½ cup dark brown sugar, firmly packed
Scant ½ cup sugar
1 large egg, at room temperature
2 teaspoons vanilla extract
2½ cups rolled oats
Scant ½ cup semisweet chocolate chips

1. Preheat the oven to 375°F. Lightly grease two baking sheets.

2. In a large bowl, stir together the flour and baking powder.

3. In a large mixing bowl and using a hand-held electric mixer, cream the butter and sugars together until light and fluffy. Add the egg and beat until combined. Stir in the vanilla. With the mixer on low speed or using a wooden spoon, gradually add the flour mixture until combined. Stir in the oats and the chocolate chips.

4. Drop rounded tablespoonfuls of the dough, well spaced apart onto the baking sheets. Leave space between each one for spreading. Flatten each cookie slightly with the back of the spoon. Bake until golden for 12–15 minutes.

5. Remove the cookies from the baking sheets to a wire rack and let cool.

GINGER & DATE SANDWICH Cookies

Ginger and date makes for a great combination, however, you might like to replace the filling with raisins or even dried apricots instead of dates.

MAKES: 14
BAKING TIME: 12–15 MINUTES

INGREDIENTS
½ cup/1 stick butter
Scant ½ cup sugar
1 tablespoon light corn syrup
Generous 1½ cups all-purpose flour
1 teaspoon ground ginger
½ teaspoon baking powder
FILLING:
Generous ½ cup pitted dates
¼ cup sugar
⅓ cup water

1. Preheat the oven to 375°F. Lightly grease two baking sheets.

2. Place the butter, sugar, and syrup in a pan and heat gently, stirring, until the butter melts. Remove from the heat. Sift the flour, ginger, and baking powder together and stir into the butter mixture to form a dough.

3. Roll the dough into small balls and arrange on the baking sheets. Flatten slightly with a knife. Bake until golden, 12–15 minutes. Let cool on a wire rack.

4. To make the filling, chop the dates. Place in a pan with the sugar and water. Heat gently, stirring, until the sugar dissolves. Bring to a boil, then reduce the heat and cook gently for about 15 minutes until the mixture reduces to a thick, spreadable paste. Remove from the heat and let cool.

5. Use the date mixture to sandwich the ginger cookies together in pairs. Store in an airtight container for up to four days.

CHERRY & CHOCOLATE NUT Slices

Although macadamia nuts taste wonderful alongside the cherries, hazelnuts would work equally well.

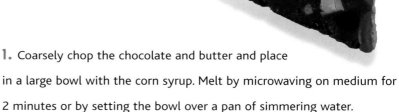

MAKES: 9

INGREDIENTS

7 ounces unsweetened chocolate
½ cup/1 stick butter
½ cup light corn syrup
12 ounces gingersnap cookies
1 cup candied cherries
Generous ¾ cup coarsely chopped, toasted macadamias

1. Coarsely chop the chocolate and butter and place in a large bowl with the corn syrup. Melt by microwaving on medium for 2 minutes or by setting the bowl over a pan of simmering water.

2. Place half the gingersnaps in a food processor and process to fine crumbs. Coarsely chop the remaining cookies and add both to the melted chocolate mixture. Halve the cherries and add with the nuts to the chocolate mixture. Combine thoroughly so that the cookies, cherries, and nuts are coated with chocolate.

3. Line an 8 x 8-inch removable bottomed square cake pan with nonstick parchment paper. Spoon in the chocolate mixture and let set in the refrigerator for 2 hours. Remove from the pan, peel off the paper, and cut into slices.

LEMON Thins

The tangy cream cheese of the filling contrasts beautifully with the zesty lemon of this cookie.

MAKES: 20
BAKING TIME: 8 MINUTES

INGREDIENTS
1¼ cups all-purpose flour
3½ tablespoons cornstarch
½ cup/1 stick butter
Scant ½ cup confectioners' sugar
Grated zest of ½ lemon
1 tablespoon lemon juice
FILLING
Scant ½ cup cream cheese
Scant ½ cup confectioners' sugar
¼ cup lemon curd

1. Preheat the oven to 400°F. Lightly grease two baking sheets. Sift the flour and cornstarch into a mixing bowl. Cut the butter into small pieces and blend into the flour until the mixture resembles fine bread crumbs.

2. Stir in the confectioners' sugar and lemon zest. Add the lemon juice, then bring the mixture together with your hands to form a soft dough. Chill for 20 minutes.

3. On a lightly floured counter, roll out the dough as thin as possible and cut into circles with a 2-inch cookie cutter. Arrange on the baking sheets and bake until crisp and golden, about 8 minutes. Let cool on the baking sheets for 2–3 minutes, then transfer to a wire rack to cool completely.

4. For the filling, beat together the cream cheese, confectioners' sugar, and lemon curd. Sandwich together pairs of cookies with the filling. Store in an airtight container in a cool place for up to three days.

COOKIE TIP
Baked and uncooked shaped cookies can be frozen for up to two months. Thaw baked cookies at room temperature and bake uncooked ones from frozen.

CARAMELITAS

The unbeatable combination of chocolate and caramel makes these bars a firm favorite.

MAKES: **20**
BAKING TIME: **20–25 MINUTES**

INGREDIENTS
2 cups rolled oats
2 cups all-purpose flour
1 teaspoon baking soda
1 ½ cups light brown sugar
½ teaspoon salt
1 cup/2 sticks unsalted butter, melted
10 ounces bittersweet chocolate,
coarsely chopped
1 cup pecans, lightly toasted and
coarsely chopped
1 cup caramel sauce (or Dulce de
Leche)

1. Preheat the oven to 350°F. Base line a 12 x 12-inch shallow baking pan with parchment paper.

2. Put the oats, flour, baking soda, sugar, and salt into a bowl and mix together. Add the butter and mix well. Spread half of the mixture in the base of the prepared pan. Press out evenly using the back of a spoon.

3. Bake in the oven for 10 minutes. Remove and sprinkle the chocolate and nuts evenly over the surface. Drizzle the caramel sauce evenly over the top. Sprinkle the reserved oat mixture on top and press gently with the back of a spoon.

4. Bake in the oven for 20–25 minutes until golden brown.

5. Leave in the pan to cool completely and cut into bars to serve.

COOKIE TIP
*You can always vary nuts
in recipes to suit personal
taste. Pecans could be
substituted with walnuts and
almonds with hazelnuts
for example.*

SNICKERDOODLES

A soft traditional cookie, with a funny name, originating from 19th-century New England.

MAKES: **36**
BAKING TIME: **8–10 MINUTES**

INGREDIENTS
¾ cup/1½ sticks butter, softened
1 cup sugar
1 egg
1 teaspoon vanilla extract
Scant 2 cups all-purpose flour
1 teaspoon cream of tartar
½ teaspoon baking soda

COATING
1 tablespoon sugar
1 teaspoon ground cinnamon

1. Preheat the oven to 400°F. Lightly grease two baking sheets.

2. Cream the butter and the sugar together until light and fluffy. Beat in the egg and vanilla. Sift the flour, cream of tartar, and baking soda together and blend into the butter mixture to form a soft dough.

3. Break off pieces of the dough about the size of a small walnut and roll into balls. Mix the 1 tablespoon sugar and cinnamon together and roll each ball in the cinnamon sugar. Arrange on the baking sheets, allowing room for the cookies to spread.

4. Bake until pale golden, about 8–10 minutes. Transfer to a wire rack to cool.

COOKIE TIP
*You could also try
making whole-wheat
snickerdoodles by substituting
1 cup whole-wheat flour
for 1 cup of the
all-purpose flour.*

SPICED Pretzels

With a lovely spicy flavor and unusual shape, these pretzels are sure to impress guests when offered as a savory snack at a drinks party or impromptu get-together.

1. Preheat the oven to 350°F. Lightly grease two baking sheets.

2. Sift the flour, baking powder, and salt into a mixing bowl and blend in the butter until the mixture resembles fine bread crumbs. Stir the curry paste into ¼ cup boiling water, then add to the flour mixture and mix to form a soft dough.

3. Knead on a lightly floured counter until smooth. Divide into 30 pieces and roll each piece into a strand about 8 inches long. Twist into a pretzel shape by making a circle, then twisting the ends around each other to form a curved letter "B." Press into position to secure and place on the baking sheets.

4. Brush the pretzels with beaten egg. Bake until golden, 18–20 minutes. Carefully transfer to a wire rack to cool.

5. Store in an airtight container for one to two weeks.

MAKES: **30**
BAKING TIME: **18–20 MINUTES**

INGREDIENTS
Scant 1⅓ cups all-purpose flour
½ teaspoon baking powder
Pinch of salt
6 tablespoons/¾ stick butter
1 tablespoon curry paste
¼ cup boiling water
Beaten egg, to glaze

SAVORY
Whirls

You can leave these plain or top with a selection of olives, anchovies, marinated bell peppers, nuts, or sun-dried tomatoes.

MAKES: 15
BAKING TIME: 12–15 MINUTES

INGREDIENTS
½ cup/1 stick butter, softened
1 clove garlic, crushed
2 tablespoons sour cream
Generous 1 cup all-purpose flour
½ teaspoon paprika
Salt and freshly ground black pepper

1. Preheat the oven to 375°F. Lightly grease two baking sheets.

2. Cream the butter until soft, then beat in the garlic, sour cream, flour, paprika, and seasoning. Mix to form a smooth paste.

3. Spoon into a pastry bag fitted with a large star tip and pipe rosettes onto the baking sheets.

4. Bake until golden, 12–15 minutes. Let cool on the baking sheets for a few minutes before transferring to a wire rack to cool completely.

COOKIE TIP
Always measure ingredients accurately. Use glass measuring cups for liquid ingredients as it is more accurate to see the level of liquid.

SAVORY PALMIER
Cookies

These cookies are so versatile—spread them with whatever filling you choose. A little cheese sprinkled over the olives works well.

1. Preheat the oven to 400°F. Roll out the pastry on a lightly floured counter to form a 10 x 12-inch rectangle. Trim the edges with a sharp knife.

2. Spread the pesto in a thin layer all over the pastry, taking care to go right to the edges. Sprinkle with the chopped olives. With the long side facing you, fold about 3 inches of the shorter sides of the pastry so that they reach about half way toward the center. Fold again so that they just meet in the center. Lightly dampen the pastry with a little water and fold again in half down the center.

3. Using a sharp knife, cut the roll into about 20 thin slices and arrange cut-side down, well spaced, on the baking sheets.

4. Bake for 10 minutes, then turn them over and bake until golden and crisp, 5–8 minutes. Transfer to a wire rack to cool.

MAKES: **20**
BAKING TIME: **15–18 MINUTES**

INGREDIENTS

9 ounces ready-made puff pastry, thawed if frozen
2 tablespoons pesto
Generous $\frac{1}{4}$ cup pitted black olives, finely chopped

COOKIE TIP
Palmiers are best served slightly warm, however, if this is not possible, room temperature is fine.

SESAME CHEESE Twists

These classic twists are a favorite at parties and look very professional—however, they are actually unbelievably easy to make!

MAKES: **14**
BAKING TIME: **10–12 MINUTES**

INGREDIENTS
4 ounces cheddar cheese
$\frac{1}{2}$ cup/1 stick butter, softened
Scant 1$\frac{1}{3}$ cups all-purpose flour
Beaten egg, to glaze
2 tablespoons sesame seeds

1. Preheat the oven to 400°F. Lightly grease two baking sheets. Finely grate the cheese, using the fine grater attachment of a food processor.

2. Remove the grating disc and insert the metal mixing blade. Place the butter in the food processor with the cheese and process until pale and creamy. Add the flour and process until the mixture comes together to form a ball of dough.

3. Roll out the dough on a lightly floured counter to about $\frac{1}{8}$ inch thick. Cut into strips about 6 inches long and $\frac{1}{4}$ inch wide. Take two strips at a time and twist together, pinching the ends.

4. Arrange on the baking sheets. Brush with beaten egg and sprinkle with sesame seeds. Bake until pale golden, 10–12 minutes. Let cool for a few minutes on the baking sheets, then transfer to a wire rack to cool completely. Store in an airtight container for up to one week.

CHEESE & TOMATO

Bites

Serve these cheese-filled tomato cookies with pre-dinner drinks. Or why not pack a few into your lunchbox as a savory snack at any time of day?

MAKES: **30**
BAKING TIME: **10–12 MINUTES**

INGREDIENTS
1¼ cups all-purpose flour
½ teaspoon baking powder
6 tablespoons/¾ stick butter
1 teaspoon celery salt (optional)
2 tablespoons ketchup
FILLING
Scant ½ cup cream cheese
1 tablespoon snipped chives
Salt and freshly ground black pepper

1. Preheat the oven to 400°F. Lightly grease two baking sheets.

2. Place the flour and baking powder in a bowl. Blend in the butter until the mixture resembles fine bread crumbs. Stir in the celery salt, then add the ketchup and mix to form a stiff dough.

3. Roll out on a lightly floured counter and cut into 1-inch wafers with a knife or cookie cutter. Arrange on the baking sheets. Bake until golden, 10–12 minutes. Let cool on the baking sheets for a few minutes before transferring to a wire rack to cool completely.

4. Beat together the cream cheese and chives and season to taste. Use to sandwich two wafers together. The wafers will keep unfilled for up to one week in an airtight container; fill just prior to serving.

BLUE CHEESE & POPPYSEED Cookies

Great in a lunchbox these tasty cookies also make delightful cocktail snacks.

MAKES: 25–30
BAKING TIME: 10 MINUTES

INGREDIENTS

1⅓ cups all-purpose flour
Scant ½ cup butter at room temperature
⅓ cup mild full-fat soft blue cheese
2 tablespoons poppyseeds

1. Put the flour, butter, and blue cheese into a bowl and mix well together. Place the mixture on plastic wrap and shape into a cylinder 1½ inches in diameter. Chill until firm.

2. Preheat the oven to 350°F. Unwrap the dough and roll in the poppyseeds. Cut into slices and place 1¼ inches apart on a nonstick baking sheet. Bake for about 10 minutes until lightly browned. Cool on a wire rack.

COOKIE TIP
Always chill cookie dough in the refrigerator when instructed to do so. This will make the dough easier to work with when you are cutting into slices ready to bake.

OAT Cakes

The oaty flavor and texture of these savory treats works very well with cheese and chutney.

MAKES: 12
BAKING TIME: 15–20 MINUTES

INGREDIENTS
1 cup fine oatmeal
Generous ⅓ cup all-purpose flour
1 teaspoon baking soda
1 teaspoon sugar
Pinch of salt
¼ cup/½ stick butter
1–2 tablespoons water

1. Preheat the oven to 350°F. Lightly grease a baking sheet.

2. Put the oatmeal, flour, baking soda, sugar, and salt in a mixing bowl. Place the butter and 1–2 tablespoons water in a small pan and heat until the butter melts. Stir into the oatmeal mixture and combine to form a dough.

3. Turn out onto a lightly floured counter and knead until the dough is no longer sticky, adding a little extra flour if necessary.

4. Roll out the dough until ⅛ inch thick and cut out 3-inch circles with a cookie cutter. Arrange on the baking sheet and bake until golden, 15–20 minutes. Remove to a wire rack to cool. Store in an airtight container for up to two weeks.

CHEWY TRAIL MIX Cookies

Healthy cookies that are truly delicious and will keep you going right till supper

MAKES: 30
BAKING TIME: 20 MINUTES

INGREDIENTS

$^7/_8$ cup butter, softened
1 cup light brown sugar
$^3/_4$ cup granulated sugar
4 tablespoons honey
2 eggs
2 teaspoons vanilla extract
3 cups all-purpose flour
$^1/_2$ teaspoon baking powder
$^1/_2$ teaspoon baking soda
1 teaspoon ground cinnamon
$^1/_4$ teaspoon salt
$^3/_4$ cup unsalted cashew nuts, chopped
$^3/_4$ cup coarsely chopped walnuts
1 cup pumpkin seeds
$^1/_2$ cup sunflower seeds
1$^1/_3$ cups rolled oats
2 cups seedless raisins

1. Preheat the oven to 300°F. Use nonstick baking sheets or line baking sheets with parchment paper.

2. Put the butter, sugars, honey, eggs, and vanilla into a large bowl and beat well together. Sift together the flour, baking powder, baking soda, cinnamon, and salt. Mix into the butter mixture.

3. Stir in the cashews, walnuts, half the pumpkin seeds, sunflower seeds, oats, and raisins. Take pieces of dough about the size of an apricot and roll into balls. Dip one side into the reserved pumpkin seeds, place on the baking sheet and flatten with the palm of your hand.

4. Bake in the oven for 20 minutes. Allow to cool slightly on the baking sheet before removing to a wire rack.

COOKIE TIP
Honey is a great pantry standby and will last with the lid screwed tightly for quite a while. However, if it has crystallized over time, stand the jar in a pan of hot water until it liquifies again.

CHEESY Crumbles

These chewy, cheesy bites are the perfect bite-size snack.

MAKES: **20**
BAKING TIME: **15 MINUTES**

INGREDIENTS
4 ounces Monterey Jack or cheddar
   cheese
4 scallions
¼ cup walnuts
¾ cup all-purpose flour
1 teaspoon wholegrain Dijon mustard
6 tablespoons/¾ stick butter

1. Preheat the oven to 375°F. Grate the cheese coarsely into a bowl. Thinly slice the scallions and finely chop the walnuts and stir into the cheese. Stir in the flour and mustard.

2. Melt the butter and add to the cheese mixture, stirring until well blended. Shape into 1-inch balls and place on lightly greased baking sheets. Flatten slightly with a spatula.

3. Bake for about 15 minutes until golden brown. Leave to cool on the sheets for 2–3 minutes before transferring to a wire rack to cool completely. Best eaten warm or on the day they are made, but they can be stored in an airtight container in a cool place for up to three days.

BUTTER Cookies

Although this recipe for rough puff pastry is ideal for topping savory meat pies, it also makes fabulous cookies.

MAKES: 10-12
BAKING TIME: 8–10 MINUTES

INGREDIENTS
2 cups all-purpose flour
$\frac{1}{2}$ teaspoon salt
1 teaspoon baking powder
Pinch of baking soda
$\frac{3}{4}$ cup/1$\frac{1}{2}$ sticks unsalted butter
6 tablespoons cold buttermilk
1 tablespoon melted butter, for
   brushing

COOKIE TIP
The dough can be made ahead and refrigerated or frozen and then baked fresh to eat with soup, or for breakfast or with roast meat and gravy.

1. Sift the flour, salt, baking powder, and baking soda into a mixing bowl. Cut the butter into dice, add to the flour, and blend together, using your fingertips until the mixture resembles coarse bread crumbs.

2. Stir in half the buttermilk and begin mixing the dough together, adding just enough of the remaining buttermilk to make a soft dough. Turn the dough onto a floured counter and dust with flour. Roll the dough out to 1 inch thick. Lift the dough from the counter and fold it in thirds. Give the dough a quarter turn. Flour the counter and dough again and reroll into a rectangle, of the same thickness. Repeat the folding and turning.

3. Transfer the dough to a baking sheet lined with parchment paper. Cover with plastic wrap and chill, about 20 minutes.

4. Remove from the refrigerator and repeat the rolling and folding twice more. Roll a final time to a $\frac{3}{4}$-inch thick rectangle. Now either cut the dough into triangles or use a cookie cutter to cut the dough into rounds.

5. Put the cut dough about 1 inch apart on the paper-lined baking sheet. Cover with plastic wrap and chill for at least 20 minutes.

6. Preheat the oven to 475°F. Brush the tops of the cookies with melted butter and transfer to the oven. Reduce the temperature to 375°F.

7. Bake until golden all over, 12–15 minutes. Let cool 5 minutes.

PIZZA Chunks

Although the ingredients may seem a little grown-up, these tasty crackers are a firm favorite with children.

MAKES: 24–30
BAKING TIME: 10–15 MINUTES

INGREDIENTS

1½ cups all-purpose flour
⅔ cup butter
¼ cup grated Parmesan cheese
¼ cup grated sharp cheddar cheese
1 tablespoon sun-dried tomato paste
1 ounce sun-dried tomatoes, coarsely
  chopped
1–2 teaspoons Italian dried mixed
  herbs
1 egg yolk
1 tablespoon water

1. Preheat the oven to 350°F. Put all the ingredients into a food processor and process, using the pulse button until the mixture just comes together.

2. Roll out the dough between sheets of parchment paper, to a large rectangle shape.

3. Remove the top piece of parchment paper and lift the dough, using the bottom paper, onto a baking sheet. Leave the bottom paper in place. Using a fork or pastry wheel, mark lightly into squares or bars.

4. Bake in the oven for about 10–15 minutes until lightly browned.

5. Cool on a wire rack on the parchment paper and then break into pieces along the perforations.

COOKIE TIP
Always pay special attention when measuring flour for baking recipes—too much and your cookies will be too hard, and too little and your cookies will be flat.

KIDS'
COOKIES

GIANT M&M

Bites

These fun, giant cookies are perfect for packing in kids' lunchboxes, as a special treat.

MAKES: 12
BAKING TIME: 8–10 MINUTES

INGREDIENTS

½ cup/1 stick butter, softened
⅓ cup sugar
⅜ cup light brown sugar, firmly packed
1 egg
1 teaspoon vanilla extract
Scant 1⅓ cups self-rising flour
1 cup peanut or chocolate M&Ms or candy-coated chocolates

1. Preheat the oven to 375°F. Lightly grease two baking sheets.

2. Cream the butter and sugars together until light and fluffy. Beat in the egg and vanilla. Sift the flour and beat into the mixture. Add the M&Ms and stir until well combined.

3. Drop rounded tablespoons of the dough onto the baking sheets, spacing well apart as the cookies will almost double in size.

4. Bake until golden, 8–10 minutes. Let cool on the baking sheets for a few minutes before transferring to a wire rack to cool completely. These are best eaten the day they are made.

COOKIE TIP
Always stir flour prior to measuring—flour settles as it sits and if you don't stir it you may end up adding too much to your cookies.

PEANUT BUTTER
Cookies

If you prefer a soft, chewy cookie, bake only until the edges have browned slightly.

1. Preheat the oven to 350°F. Lightly grease two baking sheets.

2. Cream the butter and sugar together until pale and fluffy. Add the peanut butter, egg, and corn syrup and beat until well combined.

3. Sift the flour with the baking powder and work into the mixture to form a soft dough. On a lightly floured counter, knead the dough lightly, then shape into a thick log. Cover with plastic wrap and let chill for 30 minutes.

4. Cut the dough into slices ¼ inch thick and space well apart on the baking sheets. Press a crisscross pattern into the dough with the tines of a fork.

5. Bake until golden, 10–12 minutes. Let cool on the baking sheets for 2–3 minutes, then transfer to a wire rack to cool completely. Store in an airtight container for up to five days.

MAKES: **24**
BAKING TIME: **10–12 MINUTES**

INGREDIENTS
6 tablespoons/¾ stick butter
6 tablespoons sugar
½ cup crunchy peanut butter
1 egg
3 tablespoons light corn syrup
1¼ cups all-purpose flour
1 teaspoon baking powder

COOKIE TIP
Use smooth peanut butter if you prefer a creamier texture.

TEDDIES ON a Stick

Younger children will love these cute teddies
and they are great to make for cake sales.

MAKES: 25
BAKING TIME: 8–10 MINUTES

INGREDIENTS

LIGHT DOUGH
1 1/2 cups all-purpose flour
1/2 teaspoon ground cinnamon
1/4 teaspoon baking soda
1/4 cup/1/2 stick butter
1/2 cup light brown sugar
2 tablespoons corn syrup
1 egg, beaten

DARK DOUGH
1 1/2 cups all-purpose flour
1/2 teaspoon ground ginger
1/4 teaspoon baking soda
1/4 cup/1 1/2 stick butter
1/2 cup dark brown sugar
2 tablespoons molasses
1 egg, beaten

TO SERVE
Wooden popsicle sticks
Semisweet and white chocolate chips

1. Preheat the oven to 375°F. Make up the dark and light dough in the same way.

2. Sift the flour, spice, and baking soda into a bowl. Blend in the butter and stir in the sugar. Warm the syrup or molasses in a small pan and add with the beaten egg to the flour mixture. Knead until smooth.

3. Roll out on a lightly floured counter and using a plain round 2 1/2-inch cutter stamp out circles from the light and dark dough. Place on baking sheets lined with parchment paper. Insert a popsicle stick into the base of each circle.

4. Roll out the trimmings from each dough and using a plain round 1-inch cutter stamp out two rounds for each cookie. Use light dough with dark face and vice versa. Place one round on each cookie for the nose. Cut the other in half and place on the face for the ears. Mark the nose with a knife.

5. Bake in the oven for 8–10 minutes. Remove and while still warm position the chocolate chips for eyes.

TUTTI FRUTTI
Cookies

Packed full of fruit, these sweet cookies are adored by young and old alike.

MAKES: 24
BAKING TIME: 10–12 MINUTES

INGREDIENTS

½ cup/1 stick butter, softened
Scant ½ cup sugar
1 egg, lightly beaten
Grated zest and juice of ½ orange
Generous 1½ cups all-purpose flour
Generous ¼ cup candied peel, chopped
Scant ½ cup candied cherries, quartered
¼ cup candied pineapple, chopped

1. Preheat the oven to 375°F. Lightly grease two baking sheets.

2. Cream the butter and sugar together until light and fluffy. Beat in the egg, orange juice, and zest. Add the flour and beat into the mixture. Stir in the fruit.

3. Drop rounded tablespoons of the dough onto the baking sheets, spacing well apart as the cookies will almost double in size.

4. Bake until golden, 10–12 minutes. Let cool on the baking sheets for a few minutes before transferring to a wire rack to cool completely

COOKIE TIP
When making drop cookies, use a spoon from your daily cutlery—not a measuring spoon—to drop them. The deep bowl of a measuring spoon will make the dough harder to remove.

CHOCOLATE & VANILLA whirls

For these cookies, the dough should be quite soft; you may find it easier to handle if you roll it out on nonstick parchment paper. If it is too soft to roll, let chill for 10–15 minutes to firm slightly.

MAKES: **30**
BAKING TIME: **10–12 MINUTES**

INGREDIENTS

¾ cup/1½ sticks butter
¾ cup confectioners' sugar
1 teaspoon vanilla extract
Scant 1½ cups all-purpose flour
2 tablespoons chocolate hazelnut spread, such as Nutella
1 tablespoon unsweetened cocoa powder

1. Preheat the oven to 325°F. Lightly grease two baking sheets.

2. Cream the butter and confectioners' sugar together until pale and fluffy. Beat in the vanilla.

3. Add the flour into the mixture and blend to form a soft dough. Divide the dough in half and work the chocolate hazelnut spread and cocoa powder into one half.

4. Roll each piece of dough on a lightly floured counter to a 6 x 8-inch rectangle. Place one piece of dough on top of the other and press together lightly. Trim the edges and roll up lengthwise like a jelly roll. Cover and chill for 30 minutes.

5. Cut the dough into ¼-inch slices and space well apart on the baking sheets. Bake until golden, 10–12 minutes. Let cool 2–3 minutes on the baking sheets, then transfer to a wire rack to cool completely.

ICE CREAM SANDWICH Cookies

Great to make in the school vacation—either keep the cookies in an airtight container and make fresh sandwiches each time with softened ice cream or make the sandwiches complete with ice cream and freeze.

MAKES: 10
BAKING TIME: 15 MINUTES

INGREDIENTS

½ cup/1 stick unsalted butter at room temperature
½ cup superfine sugar
1 egg, beaten
1¾ cups all-purpose flour
¼ cup unsweetened cocoa powder, sifted
⅔ cup semisweet chocolate chips
Chocolate or vanilla ice cream

1. Preheat the oven to 350°F. Line a baking sheet with parchment paper.

2. Cream the butter and sugar together and beat in the egg. Stir in the flour, cocoa, and chocolate chips to make a firm dough. Roll out on nonstick parchment paper. Cut into 20 rectangles each 3 x 2½ inches.

3. Place on the baking sheet. Bake in the oven for about 15 minutes. Cool.

4. To make the ice cream cookies spread two good spoonfuls of softened ice cream on a cookie and press a second cookie on top. Squeeze so the filling reaches the edges. Eat straightaway or wrap individually in foil and freeze. May be kept up to two weeks in the freezer.

COOKIE TIP
You can use any flavor of ice cream for these sweet treats: choc chip, coconut, raspberry swirl, praline etc.

DOMINO
Cookies

Make chocolate-flavored dominoes by substituting 2 tablespoons unsweetened cocoa powder for the same amount of flour. Pipe dots and lines with white frosting.

MAKES: 14
BAKING TIME: 8–10 MINUTES

INGREDIENTS
6 tablespoons/¾ stick butter, softened
⅓ cup sugar
1 egg
1 teaspoon vanilla extract
Scant 1½ cups all-purpose flour
¼ cup ground rice
1 ounce semisweet chocolate for decoration

1. Cream the butter and sugar together until light and fluffy. Beat in the egg and vanilla. Sift the flour and ground rice together and beat in to form a soft dough. Let chill for 30 minutes.

2. Preheat the oven to 350°F. Lightly grease a baking sheet. Roll out the dough on a lightly floured counter to about ¼ inch thick and cut out rectangles measuring about 2 x 3 inches. Arrange slightly spaced on the baking sheet.

3. Bake until pale golden, 10–12 minutes. Let cool on the baking sheet for a few minutes before transferring to a wire rack to cool completely.

4. To decorate, melt the chocolate in a microwave or in a bowl set over a pan of hot water. Spoon into a pastry bag fitted with a small writing tip. Pipe domino dots and lines onto the cookies and let set.

5. Store in an airtight container for up to one week.

NEAPOLITAN
Cookies

Children love making these simple but fun multicolored cookies.

MAKES: **24**
BAKING TIME: **8–10 MINUTES**

INGREDIENTS
³/₄ cup/1¹/₂ sticks butter, softened
²/₃ cup sugar
1 teaspoon vanilla extract
Generous 1²/₃ cups all-purpose flour
1 tablespoon unsweetened cocoa
   powder
1 teaspoon milk
¹/₂ teaspoon strawberry flavoring
Few drops red food coloring
   (optional)

COOKIE TIP
*If you only have
one baking sheet, make
sure you cool it well
between batches.*

1. Preheat the oven to 375°F. Lightly grease two baking sheets.

2. Cream the butter and sugar together until pale and fluffy. Beat in the vanilla. Add the flour and mix to form a smooth, soft dough. Divide into three equal portions.

3. Beat the cocoa powder and milk into one portion and mix to a smooth dough. Mix the strawberry flavoring and red food coloring, if using, into another portion. Leave the third portion plain.

4. Shape the chocolate-flavored portion into a sausage, then flatten to form a 2 x 10-inch rectangle. Repeat with the plain portion and place on top of the chocolate portion. Finally, repeat with the strawberry portion and stack on top.

5. Cut the bar into about 24 slices and lay flat on the baking sheets, allowing room for the cookies to spread. Bake until just firm, 8–10 minutes. Let cool on the baking sheets for a few minutes before transferring to a wire rack to cool completely.

MERINGUE Critters

Older kids can have fun making these meringue treats while younger ones can help Mum and eat the results!

MAKES: 14–16

BAKING TIME: 45–60 MINUTES

INGREDIENTS

2 egg whites

½ cup superfine sugar

FOR DECORATION

Confectioners' sugar

Licorice

Flaked almonds

Colored sugar sprinkles

Assorted candies for decoration

COOKIE TIP

When making meringue it is easier to separate the eggs when they are cold—but let the whites come to room temperature before using.

1. Put the egg whites in a bowl and beat until they form firm peaks. Gradually beat in the sugar a spoonful at a time. Beat for 15 seconds after each addition. Continue beating until very thick and shiny.

2. Preheat the oven to 300°F. Line a baking sheet with parchment paper.

3. Pipe critters as described below and bake in the oven for 45–60 minutes until dry and crisp.

Mice Spoon meringue into a pastry bag fitted with a 1-inch plain tip. Pipe a blob ½ inch high. Then pipe over this to make a shape like a mouse, taking pressure off the bag at the end to make a pointed nose. Place two silver balls or tiny pieces of candy for the eyes, and a licorice tail.

Hedgehogs Spoon meringue into a pastry bag fitted with a 1-inch fluted star tip and pipe as above. Add on eyes and place flaked almonds in the back for the spines.

Snails Spoon the meringue into a pastry bag fitted with a ½-inch plain tip. Pipe a small blob for the head and then pipe a spiral for the snail shell. Make feelers and eyes from pieces of candy or licorice.

Snakes Fill a pastry bag as for snails and pipe wavy lines about 5 inches long. Bake and allow to cool. When cold, glaze the meringue with a little confectioners' sugar and water and sprinkle with colored sugar sprinkles.

CHOCOLATE
CARAMEL Slices

These delicious marbled slices are perfect for any special occasion.

MAKES: **12**
BAKING TIME: **25 MINUTES**

INGREDIENTS
½ cup butter, softened
¼ cup sugar
1 cup all-purpose flour
3 tablespoons cornstarch

FILLING
6 tablespoons butter
¼ cup packed light brown sugar
1 tablespoon light corn syrup
14oz canned sweetened condensed
  milk

TOPPING
4oz semi-sweet or milk chocolate
1 tablespoon butter
1oz white chocolate

1. Preheat the oven to 350°F. Grease an 8 x 8in square cake pan and line the base with non-stick baking parchment.

2. Cream the butter and sugar together until light and fluffy. Sift together the flour and cornstarch and mix in to form a smooth dough. Press the mixture into the base of the pan. Bake until just golden and firm, about 25 minutes.

3. To make the filling, combine the ingredients in a pan and heat gently, stirring until the sugar dissolves. Bring slowly to a boil and boil the mixture gently for about 5 minutes, stirring constantly with a wooden spoon until thickened. Pour evenly over the cookie base.

4. To make the topping, melt the semi-sweet or milk chocolate in a bowl set over a pan of hot water. Stir in the butter. Spread over the caramel filling. Melt the white chocolate in the same way. Spoon into a pastry bag and pipe squiggles over the darker chocolate. (Alternatively, drizzle the white chocolate from a spoon.) Swirl with a skewer to create a marbled effect and leave to set. Serve cut into squares.

ICEBOX SUGAR
Cookies

The chill-and-bake nature of these cookies means that you can make the dough well ahead of time and bake the cookies as you need them.

1. Cream the butter and sugar together until pale and fluffy. Beat in the egg and vanilla. Add the flour and mix to form a soft dough.

2. Shape into a log about 2 inches thick. Spread the sugar sprinkles on a sheet of nonstick parchment paper and roll the log in the sugar until well coated.

3. Wrap the log in another sheet of parchment paper and chill until firm. At this point the dough can be stored in the refrigerator for up to one week, or placed in a plastic bag and frozen for up to two months.

4. When ready to bake, preheat the oven to 375°F. Lightly grease two baking sheets. Cut the log into slices $1/8$ inch thick and arrange carefully on the baking sheets, leaving enough room for the cookies to spread.

5. Bake until just firm, 8–10 minutes. Let cool on the baking sheets for a few minutes before transferring to a wire rack to cool completely.

MAKES: **45**
BAKING TIME: **8–10 MINUTES**

INGREDIENTS
$1^{1}/_{4}$ cups/$2^{1}/_{2}$ sticks butter, softened
Scant 1 cup sugar
1 egg
1 teaspoon vanilla extract
$2^{1}/_{3}$ cups all-purpose flour
Colored sugar sprinkles for decoration

COOKIE TIP
Preheat the oven for at least 10 minutes prior to baking.

ICED SPRINKLE
Cookies

Fun and colorful, you could also decorate these cookies with melted chocolate instead of the frosting. Use chocolate sprinkles, too.

MAKES: 18–24
BAKING TIME: 8 MINUTES

INGREDIENTS
1/2 cup/1 stick butter, softened
Scant 1/2 cup confectioners' sugar
1 teaspoon vanilla extract
1 1/4 cups all-purpose flour
2 tablespoons ground rice
FROSTING
Scant 1 cup confectioners' sugar
1 tablespoon water or lemon juice
Colored sugar sprinkles

1. Preheat the oven to 400°F.

2. Cream the butter and the confectioners' sugar together until pale and fluffy. Beat in the vanilla. Add the flour and ground rice and mix to form a soft dough.

3. Place the dough between two sheets of plastic wrap and roll out to about 1/8 inch thick. Cut out cookies using a 2–3-inch cookie cutter and carefully transfer to the baking sheets.

4. Bake until crisp and golden, about 8 minutes. Let cool on the baking sheets for a few minutes before transferring to a wire rack to cool completely.

5. Sift the confectioners' sugar into a bowl and add enough water or lemon juice to mix to a smooth frosting. Spread the frosting over the cookies with a metal spatula and decorate with sugar sprinkles. Let frosting set before serving.

COOKIE TIP
Always sift confectioners' sugar prior to use to avoid clumping.

ROCKY ROAD Cookies

Rich cookies, with a strong coconut taste. Decorate them by dipping in chocolate or drizzling a little chocolate over the top.

MAKES: 20
BAKING TIME: 12 MINUTES

INGREDIENTS
Generous 1½ cups all-purpose flour
1 teaspoon baking powder
½ cup/1 stick butter
Scant ½ cup sugar
1 egg
½ teaspoon vanilla extract

TOPPING
1 cup mini-marshmallows
Scant ⅔ cup chopped walnuts
2 ounces semisweet chocolate

1. Preheat the oven to 350°F. Lightly grease two baking sheets.

2. Sift the flour and baking powder together into a mixing bowl. In a separate bowl, cream the butter and sugar together until pale and fluffy. Beat in the egg and vanilla, then work in the flour mixture to form a soft dough.

3. Take small amounts of the dough, each about the size of a walnut, and roll into balls. Space well apart on the baking sheets and flatten slightly. Bake until just golden, about 12 minutes. Reduce the oven temperature to 325°F.

4. To make the topping: mix together the marshmallows and nuts. Melt the chocolate in a bowl set over a pan of gently simmering water, making sure the base of the bowl is not touching the water. Spread a little on top of each cookie and top with the marshmallow and nut mixture.

5. Return the cookies to the oven and bake 1–2 minutes until the marshmallow softens. Let cool on the baking sheets for 2–3 minutes before transferring to a wire rack to cool completely.

6. Drizzle or pipe the remaining chocolate over the cookies.

WHITE CHOCOLATE & CHERRY Cookies

Make up a batch of these scrumptious cookies for when only something sweet will do. Just try not to eat them all at once as they're utterly irresistible!

MAKES: 18
BAKING TIME: 12–15 MINUTES

INGREDIENTS

4 ounces white chocolate
½ cup/1 stick unsalted butter, softened
½ cup superfine sugar
1 egg
1¼ cups rolled oats
1¼ cups all-purpose flour
½ teaspoon baking powder
½ cup dried cherries

1. Preheat the oven to 350°F and grease two baking sheets. Chop the white chocolate into small chunks and set aside. Cream the butter and sugar together in a bowl until pale and fluffy. Beat in the egg, and then add the oats.

2. Sift the flour and baking powder over the mixture, and fold in. Stir in the white chocolate and cherries.

3. Drop dessertspoonfuls of the mixture onto the baking sheets, spacing them well apart. Flatten each one slightly and bake for 12–15 minutes, or until golden. Transfer to a wire rack to cool.

COOKIE TIP
Don't drop cookie dough onto a hot baking sheet as the cookies will spread too much.

CHOCOLATE THUMBPRINT Cookies

Kids love helping to bake these chocolate cookies. Using white chocolate to fill the well in each cookie gives a lovely color contrast. Alternatively, try using peanut butter for a smooth, nutty flavor.

MAKES: 24
BAKING TIME: 10 MINUTES

INGREDIENTS
2 ounces semisweet chocolate
4 tablespoons/$\frac{1}{2}$ stick butter
$\frac{1}{4}$ cup white vegetable shortening
Scant $\frac{1}{4}$ cup sugar
$1\frac{1}{4}$ cups all-purpose flour
FILLING
3 ounces semisweet, milk, or white
   chocolate

1. Melt the chocolate in a microwave or in a bowl set over a pan of hot water. Let cool.

2. Cream the butter, shortening, and sugar together until light and fluffy. Beat in the melted chocolate, then the flour and mix to form a smooth dough. Let chill for 30 minutes.

3. Preheat the oven to 350°F. Lightly grease a baking sheet. Shape the dough into 1-inch balls and arrange well spaced on the baking sheet. Press your thumb into the center of each ball to form a well.

4. Bake for 10 minutes. Let cool for a few minutes on the baking sheet, then transfer to a wire rack to cool completely.

5. For the filling, melt the chocolate in a microwave or in a bowl set over a pan of hot water. Spoon or pipe into the center of the cookies and let set.

SMILIES

Kids will love to make these cookies and they can show off their creative talents by making many different faces.

MAKES: 16
BAKING TIME: 8–10 MINUTES

INGREDIENTS

VANILLA MIX
½ cup/1 stick butter
¼ cup superfine sugar
1¼ cups all-purpose flour

CHOCOLATE MIX
½ cup/1 stick butter
¼ cup superfine sugar
1⅛ cups all-purpose flour
2 tablespoons unsweetened cocoa powder
2 tablespoons drinking chocolate

1. Preheat the oven to 350°F. For each flavor cream together the butter and sugar until light and fluffy. Gradually mix in the remaining ingredients until a soft dough is formed.

2. Roll out the vanilla mixture on a lightly floured board to ¼ inch thick. Using a 3-inch plain cutter stamp out biscuit faces. Place on a nonstick or lightly greased baking sheet. Keep the trimmings.

3. Roll out the chocolate mixture in the same way and cut out mouths, eyes, noses and hair and gently place on the vanilla faces. Curve the mouths up for smiles—maybe one turned down for sad.

4. Then cut out chocolate faces and use vanilla trimmings for the features.

5. Bake in the oven for about 10–12 minutes.

COOKIE TIP
Dip cutters in flour as you go along to keep the dough from sticking to them and tearing the cookies. Reroll as little as possible.

SNOWBALLS

Easy to make and very tasty to eat, these make a great Christmas gift.

MAKES: 12

INGREDIENTS

7 ounces white chocolate
2 tablespoons/¼ stick butter
1 cup sweetened and tenderized
   coconut
3½ ounces leftover sponge cake,
   crumbled
confectioners' sugar

1. Break the chocolate into pieces and place in a bowl with the butter. Put over a pan of gently simmering water.

2. Put ½ cup of the coconut onto a plate. Put the remaining coconut into a bowl with the crumbled cake crumbs. Add the melted chocolate and mix to form a paste.

3. Work quite quickly while the mixture is still warm. Roll the mixture into balls about the size of a walnut and immediately roll in the reserved coconut.

4. Leave to set and then dredge liberally with confectioners' sugar.

COOKIE TIP
Most confectioners' sugar, also known as powdered sugar, is blended with a small amount of cornstarch to prevent major lumping. Even so, it's usually best to sift it prior to use.

HOLIDAY
COOKIES

SWEETHEART
Cookies

These pretty cookies make a delightful gift for a friend or relative. Why not present them in a small basket or giftbox?

MAKES: 8
BAKING TIME: 15–20 MINUTES

INGREDIENTS
1 cup/2 sticks butter
Generous ½ cup confectioners' sugar
1 teaspoon vanilla extract
Scant ¼ cup cornstarch
Generous 1½ cups all-purpose flour
5 ounces semisweet chocolate

1. Preheat the oven to 350°F. Draw four heart shapes on two pieces of nonstick parchment paper. Place ink-side down on two baking sheets.

2. Cream the butter and confectioners' sugar together until pale and fluffy. Beat in the vanilla. Sift together the cornstarch and flour, and beat into the mixture.

3. Place the dough in a large pastry bag fitted with a star tip. Pipe heart shapes onto the parchment paper following the line drawings.

4. Bake until pale gold, 15–20 minutes. Let cool on the baking sheets for 2–3 minutes, then transfer to a wire rack to cool completely.

5. Melt the chocolate in a bowl set over a pan of gently simmering water. Let cool slightly, then dip half of each heart in the chocolate to decorate. Store in an airtight container for up to four days.

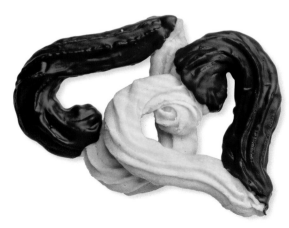

LIPSMACKING KISS Cookies

The perfect Valentine's Day gift for that special someone.

1. Preheat the oven to 400°F. Draw a lip shape onto a piece of card, cut out, and set aside to use as a template.

2. Blend the butter into the flour until the mixture resembles fine bread crumbs. Stir in the sugar, egg, and 1–2 tablespoons cold water to bind the mixture to a soft but not sticky dough. Chill for 20 minutes.

3. Roll out on a lightly floured counter to a ¼-inch thickness. Using the template, cut around it to make 20 kiss cookies. Space well apart on two baking sheets and bake for 7–8 minutes. Allow to cool completely.

4. Roll out the fondant on a surface lightly dusted with confectioners' sugar to a ⅛-inch thickness and cut out 20 kisses using the template.

5. Sift the confectioners' sugar and mix with 2 teaspoons water to a very thick paste. Add a little red food coloring to make a smooth, thick, pink glacé icing. Spoon into a paper pastry bag and snip off the end. Pipe a few dots on each cookie. Lift the fondant kisses and place 1 on top of each cookie. Pipe a fine line of pink icing over each of the fondant kisses to define the outline. Leave to set.

MAKES: 20
BAKING TIME: 7–8 MINUTES

INGREDIENTS
½ cup/1 stick butter, cut into cubes
2 cups all-purpose flour
¾ cup sugar
1 egg, beaten
10 ounces red fondant icing
¾ cup confectioners' sugar
Red food coloring

COOKIE TIP
These cookies could be presented in a pretty giftbox with pretty tissue paper and ribbons.

STAINED GLASS CHRISTMAS Cookies

These cookies are really easy to make and yet look so impressive. They make great gifts for the festive season.

MAKES: **12**
BAKING TIME: **14 MINUTES**

INGREDIENTS

1 ½ cups all-purpose flour
⅓ cup butter
3 tablespoons superfine sugar
1 egg white
2 tablespoons orange juice
8 ounces hard candies in assorted
  colors
Thin ribbon or cord

COOKIE TIP

These cookies look wonderful when hung on the Christmas tree or beside candles, to catch the light.

1. Preheat the oven to 350°F. Line baking sheets with parchment paper.

2. Put the flour into a bowl and blend in the butter. Stir in the sugar, egg white, and enough orange juice to mix to a soft dough. Knead lightly.

3. Roll out the dough on a lightly floured counter and cut into shapes such as stars, hearts, flowers, Christmas trees etc. Cut out the centers of the cookies using a similar shaped cutter or a plain round cutter.

4. Make a hole on the top of the cookie with a skewer. Place on the prepared baking sheet and bake in the oven for 4 minutes. Remove and place a candy in the center of each cookie and return to the oven for an additional 10 minutes or until the cookies are golden brown and the candies have melted and filled the centers of the cookies.

5. Remove from the oven and put a skewer in the holes at the top of each cookies to open them up. Leave the cookies on the baking sheet until cool and set and then peel them off. Thread ribbon or cord through the holes at the top of each cookie.

SNOWFLAKE Cookies

Leave these cookies out for a late-night treat for Santa Claus.

MAKES: 20
BAKING TIME: 6–8 MINUTES

INGREDIENTS
1¼ cups all-purpose flour
½ cup/1 stick butter
1¼ cups confectioners' sugar
½ teaspoon ground cardamom
1 egg yolk
1 tablespoon milk
½ teaspoon vanilla extract
6 ounces white fondant
1 tablespoon sugar
Silver balls for decoration

1. Put the flour, butter, and half the confectioners' sugar into a mixing bowl or food processor and mix until it resembles fine bread crumbs. Add the ground cardamom, egg yolk, milk, and vanilla extract and mix until it forms a soft ball. Chill for 30 minutes.

2. Preheat the oven to 400°F. Roll out the dough on a lightly floured counter to ¼-inch thickness and cut out 20 cookies using a snowflake paper template. Evenly space apart on two baking sheets and bake for 6–8 minutes. Cool on the baking sheets for 10 minutes before transferring to a wire rack to cool completely.

3. Roll out the fondant on a surface lightly dusted with confectioners' sugar to ⅛-inch thickness and cut out 20 snowflakes the same size as the cookies.

4. Mix the remaining confectioners' sugar with 2 teaspoons water to a thick paste, spoon into a paper pastry bag and snip off the tip. Pipe small dots over the cookies and lift the fondant snowflakes on top, pressing down lightly to secure. Push the fondant in all around the shape to leave a small gap between the cookie and the fondant. Use the remaining glacé icing to pipe snowflake lines over the fondant icing. Sprinkle immediately with the sugar and decorate with the silver balls.

GINGERBREAD CHRISTMAS Cookies

To be able to hang the cookies make a hole at the top of each one before baking. Reopen the hole as soon as they come out of the oven.

MAKES: 30–40
BAKING TIME: 10–12 MINUTES

INGREDIENTS

2$\frac{1}{3}$ cups all-purpose flour

1 tablespoon baking powder

2 teaspoons ground ginger

$\frac{1}{2}$ teaspoon ground allspice

$\frac{1}{4}$ cup molasses

$\frac{1}{4}$ cup light corn syrup

6 tablespoons/$\frac{3}{4}$ stick butter

3 tablespoons dark brown sugar, firmly packed

1 egg, beaten

FROSTING

Scant 1$\frac{1}{4}$ cups confectioners' sugar

1 tablespoon lemon juice

1. Lightly grease two baking sheets. Sift the flour, baking powder, and spices together into a bowl.

2. Place the molasses, corn syrup, butter, and brown sugar in a small pan and heat gently, stirring until well combined.

3. Let cool slightly, then beat in the egg. Pour into the dry ingredients and mix to form a firm dough. Let rest for a few minutes, then knead gently until smooth.

4. Preheat the oven to 350°F. On a lightly floured counter roll out the dough to $\frac{1}{4}$ inch thick, and cut out cookies with cookie cutters. Place on the baking sheets and bake until crisp and golden, 10–12 minutes. Let cool on the baking sheets for 2–3 minutes, then transfer to a wire rack to cool completely.

5. To make the frosting, sift the confectioners' sugar into a bowl, add the lemon juice, and mix until smooth. Spread or pipe over the cookies. Let stand until the frosting has set, 1–2 hours. Store in an airtight container for up to two weeks.

SPECULAAS

A traditional Dutch cookie, these are eaten in Holland around the feast of St Nicholas, which is December 6. They are made from a spicy dough wrapped around a soft marzipan filling.

MAKES: 35
BAKING TIME: 35 MINUTES

INGREDIENTS
1½ cups hazelnuts, toasted and
   ground
1 cup ground almonds
¾ cup superfine sugar
1½ cups confectioners' sugar
1 egg, beaten
2–3 teaspoons lemon juice
DOUGH
2¼ cups self-rising flour
1 teaspoon pumpkin pie spice
⅜ cup brown sugar
½ cup unsalted butter
2 eggs
1 tablespoon milk
1 tablespoon superfine sugar
About 35 blanched almond halves

1. Put all the filling ingredients into a bowl and mix to a firm paste. Divide in half and roll each piece to a sausage shape about 10 inches long. Wrap in plastic wrap and chill while making the dough.

2. Sift the flour and spice into a bowl and stir in the sugar. Blend in the butter. Beat one of the eggs and add to the mixture and mix together to form a soft, but firm dough. Knead lightly and chill for 15 minutes.

3. Preheat the oven to 350°F. Line a baking sheet with parchment paper.

4. Roll out the dough to a 12-inch square and cut in half to make two strips. Beat the remaining egg and use to brush all over the pastry strips. Place a roll of filling on each strip and roll up like a sausage roll to completely enclose the filling. Place join side down on the prepared baking sheets.

5. Beat the remains of the egg with the milk and sugar and brush over the rolls. Decorate with halved almonds all along the top. Bake for about 35 minutes until golden brown. Allow to become cold before cutting diagonally into slices.

DEEP FRIED CHRISTMAS Cookies

In Norway these cookies are called reindeer antlers and are made at Christmas, but there are variations all over Europe variously known as "bits and pieces," "rags and tatters" and so on. It is best to make the dough the day before and leave in the refrigerator to firm up.

MAKES: 30

INGREDIENTS
2 egg yolks
¼ cup superfine sugar
4 tablespoons heavy cream
1 tablespoon brandy
1 teaspoon ground cardamom
1 teaspoon finely grated lemon zest
¼ cup/½ stick butter
1¾ cups all-purpose flour
Vegetable oil for deep-frying
Sugar and cinnamon for dusting

1. Put the egg yolks and sugar into a bowl and whisk until thick and pale. Add the cream, brandy, cardamom, and lemon zest. Blend the butter into the flour. Add the egg mixture to the flour and mix to a soft dough. Cover in plastic wrap and leave in the refrigerator overnight.

2. The next day, roll out the dough on a lightly floured counter to ¼-inch thickness. Using a zigzag pastry wheel cut into strips 1½ x 4 inches. Cut a slit 1 inch long lengthwise in the center of each rectangle. Pull one end of the strip through this slit to make a half bow shape.

3. Heat the oil until a cube of bread browns in 1 minute. Deep-fry the cookies a few at a time until golden brown. Remove with a slotted spoon and drain on paper towels. Dust liberally with mixed sugar and cinnamon.

RUSSIAN
Teacakes

These buttery sugar-dusted teacakes are often served at weddings. When made with pecans they are known as Mexican or Portuguese wedding cakes and when made with almonds they are the Greek version known as kourabiedes.

MAKES: 20
BAKING TIME: 15 MINUTES

INGREDIENTS
½ cup/1 stick unsalted butter
2 teaspoons orange flower water
½ cup confectioners' sugar
¾ cup all-purpose flour
1 cup lightly toasted ground walnuts
¼ cup lightly toasted walnut pieces, chopped
Confectioners' sugar for dusting

1. Preheat the oven to 350°F. Line baking sheets with parchment paper. Beat the butter until soft and creamy.

2. Beat in the orange flower water. Add the confectioners' sugar and beat until fluffy. Add the flour, ground and chopped walnuts and mix well using your hand to bring the mixture together. Don't over work the dough. Chill if the mixture is a little soft.

3. Either roll the mixture into balls or shape pieces of dough into sausages about 3 inches long. Curve each one into a crescent shape and place well apart on the prepared baking sheets.

4. Bake in the oven for about 15 minutes or until firm and still pale in color. Cool for about 5 minutes and then dredge liberally with confectioners' sugar.

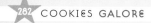

PERSIAN RICE
Cookies

These pretty rose-scented cookies are traditionally offered at special occasions such as weddings.

MAKES: 20
BAKING TIME: 18–20 MINUTES

INGREDIENTS

DOUGH

²/₃ cup confectioners' sugar
1 cup/2 sticks very soft unsalted
   butter
2¹/₂ cups rice flour
²/₃ cup self-rising flour
1 egg yolk
1 tablespoon rose water

TOPPING

²/₃ cup sifted confectioners' sugar
Rose water
Pink food coloring (optional)
Crystallized rose petals for
   decoration

1. Put all the ingredients for the dough into a bowl and mix well together. Wrap in plastic wrap and chill until firm.

2. Preheat the oven to 350°F. Line baking sheets with parchment paper.

3. Shape the mixture into balls the size of large walnuts. Place well apart on the prepared baking sheets and flatten each one slightly.

4. Bake for 18–20 minutes until firm but still pale. Let cool completely on the sheets, as these cookies are extremely crumbly while hot.

5. To make the topping put the confectioners' sugar into a bowl and add just enough rose water to mix to a thick flowing consistency. If desired add a touch of pink coloring to make a very pale shade. Drizzle the icing over the cookies and decorate with crystallized rose petals.

COOKIE TIP
To prevent baking parchment slipping off baking sheets, sprinkle the sheet with a few drops of water beforehand.

EASTER Bonnets

These pretty, colorful cookies make wonderful easter gifts.

1. Cream the butter and sugar together until pale, beat in the egg and stir in the flour, baking powder, vanilla extract, orange zest, and a little of the orange juice to bind to a soft, pliable dough. Chill for 30 minutes.

2. Preheat the oven to 350°F. Roll out on a lightly floured counter to a $\frac{1}{4}$-inch thickness and cut out 18 circles with a $3\frac{1}{4}$-inch round cutter. Space out the circles on two baking sheets and bake for 10–12 minutes. Cool on the baking sheets for 10 minutes before transferring to a wire rack to cool completely.

3. Pinch off small balls of fondant and roll out on a surface dusted with confectioners' sugar to an $\frac{1}{8}$-inch thickness. Cut out tiny flower shapes to decorate the bonnets and push a colored ball into the center of each. Color half the remaining fondant pink and half yellow and roll out to an $\frac{1}{8}$-inch thickness. Cut out nine circles measuring $3\frac{1}{4}$ inches from each.

4. Warm the remaining orange juice and mix 2 tablespoons with the creamed coconut and confectioners' sugar to make a smooth paste. Spoon a teaspoonful of the mixture into the center of each cookie. Cover with the circles of colored fondant and press down lightly to shape the bonnet. Decorate with the ribbon and flowers, securing them with a little confectioners' sugar mixed with water.

MAKES: 18
BAKING TIME: 10–12 MINUTES

INGREDIENTS
$\frac{3}{4}$ cup/$1\frac{1}{2}$ sticks butter
$\frac{3}{4}$ cup sugar
1 large egg, beaten
3 cups all-purpose flour
1 teaspoon. baking powder
1 teaspoon. vanilla extract
Finely grated zest and juice of 1 small orange
$1\frac{1}{4}$ pounds white fondant
Red and yellow food coloring
Colored balls and ribbon for decoration
4 ounces creamed coconut
$\frac{1}{2}$ cup confectioners' sugar

EASTER
Cookies

These currant-filled cookies are traditionally baked for the Christian festival of Easter and in the past they would be eaten after church on Easter morning. They are tied with thin ribbon in bundles of three to represent the Trinity.

MAKES: 18
BAKING TIME: 15–20 MINUTES

INGREDIENTS
1²⁄₃ cups all-purpose flour
¼ cup rice flour
1 teaspoon mixed spice
½ cup/1 stick butter
½ cup superfine sugar
2 egg yolks
⅓ cup currants
1 tablespoon chopped mixed peel
1–2 tablespoons milk
1 egg white, very lightly beaten
Superfine sugar to sprinkle

1. Preheat the oven to 350°F. Use lightly greased or nonstick baking sheets.

2. Mix together the flour, rice flour, and mixed spice. In another bowl cream together the butter and sugar. Beat in the egg yolks and then add the currants and mixed peel. Stir in the flour with enough milk to mix to a fairly stiff dough.

3. Knead lightly and then roll out on a lightly floured counter to ¼ inch thick. Using a 4-inch round fluted cutter cut out cookies and place on the baking sheets.

4. Bake in the oven for 10 minutes then remove from the oven. Brush with the egg white and sprinkle with superfine sugar. Return to the oven for a further 5–10 minutes until lightly browned. Place on a wire rack to cool.

MOTHER'S DAY
Handful Of Love

This is a lovely way to say "thank you" on Mother's Day. Each child can cut out the shape of their hand and decorate with frosting and candies or use purchased frosting in tubes and pipe a message on top.

MAKES: **4–6 HANDS DEPENDING ON SIZE**
BAKING TIME: **10–15 MINUTES**

INGREDIENTS
3 cups self-rising flour
2 teaspoons ground cinnamon
$\frac{1}{4}$ cup honey
1 cup brown sugar
$\frac{1}{4}$ cup/$\frac{1}{2}$ stick butter
1 egg, beaten
Finely grated zest of 1 lemon
1 tablespoon lemon juice

FOR DECORATION
Blanched almonds
Ready made frosting
Candies, silver balls etc.

1. Preheat the oven to 350°F. Line a baking sheet with parchment paper. Put each child's hand on a piece of thin card (cereal boxes are good) and draw around it. Cut out and use as templates.

2. Put the flour and cinnamon into a bowl and mix together.

3. Put the honey, sugar, and butter into a saucepan and heat very gently until melted. Cool slightly. Pour into the flour mixture and add the egg, lemon zest, and juice. Mix to form a soft dough. Knead lightly.

4. Roll out the dough on a lightly floured counter. Using the templates cut out hands from the dough and carefully place on the baking sheet. Reroll the trimmings and using a small heart-shaped cutter, stamp out a heart for each hand. Place a heart between the first finger and thumb of each hand. Press almonds in the fingers to represent fingernails. Bake in the oven for about 10–15 minutes depending on size.

5. When cold decorate as desired.

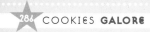

CHOCOLATE PUMPKIN Cookies

For this recipe you need a pumpkin-shaped cookie cutter or draw a pumpkin about 5–6 inches in diameter on some card and use as a stencil.

MAKES: ABOUT 8, DEPENDING
SIZE OF TEMPLATE
BAKING TIME: 8–10 MINUTES

INGREDIENTS
1½ cups all-purpose flour
¾ cup unsweetened cocoa powder
1 teaspoon ground cinnamon
¾ cup/1½ sticks unsalted butter
¾ cup superfine sugar
1 large egg, beaten
10 ounces ready to use fondant,
     colored orange
1–2 tablespoons honey, warmed

1. Sift together the flour, cocoa, and cinnamon. Put the butter and sugar into a bowl and beat until light and fluffy. Beat in the egg. Gradually stir in the flour mixture. Cover in plastic wrap and chill until firm.

2. Preheat the oven to 375°F. Line baking sheets with parchment paper. On a floured counter roll out the dough to ¼ inch thick. Using a cutter or the cardboard stencil and a sharp knife, cut out pumpkin shapes.

3. Carefully place on the baking sheets and bake for 8–10 minutes until crisp but not too browned. Leave to cool on a wire rack.

4. Trim the cardboard templates so they are slightly smaller all round. Roll out the fondant, and using the template, cut out one shape for each cookie.

5. Using the back of a knife mark grooves as on a pumpkin. Using a small pointed knife cut out eyes, nose, and mouth. Brush each cookie with a little warm honey and place a fondant face on each one. Leave to dry.

HALLOWE'EN TOFFEE APPLE Cookies

Great for those Trick or Treat bags at Hallowe'en these cookies are a mixture of chewy oats, soft apple, sweet raisin, and wonderfully crunchy toffee.

MAKES: 18
BAKING TIME: 12–15 MINUTES

INGREDIENTS

²/₃ cup all-purpose flour
¹/₂ teaspoon baking soda
¹/₂ teaspoon ground cinnamon
²/₃ cup unsalted butter
scant 1 cup brown sugar
¹/₂ cup sugar
1 large egg, beaten
2¹/₂ cups rolled oats
Scant ¹/₂ cup raisins
2 ounces ready-to-eat dried apple rings, roughly chopped
2 ounces chewy toffees, roughly cut up

1. Preheat the oven to 350°F. Line baking sheets with parchment paper. Sift together the flour, baking soda, and cinnamon.

2. Put the butter and both sugars into a bowl and beat together until creamy. Add the egg to the butter mixture and beat well. Add the flour mixture and mix thoroughly. Add the oats, raisins, apple, and toffee pieces and stir until just combined.

3. Using a small ice cream scoop or large tablespoon place dollops of mixture well apart onto the baking sheets. Bake in the oven for about 12–15 minutes depending on size, or until lightly set in the center and the edges are just beginning to turn brown,

4. Let cool on the sheets for a few minutes and do not touch as the melted toffee will be extremely hot and will set as the mixture cools down. Using a spatula place the cookies on a cooling rack to cool.

SKELETON Lollipops

These crisp, spiced cookies look very impressive. You will need to cut out a template in the shape of a skull to make these cookies.

1. Cream the butter and sugar together until pale, beat in the egg and stir in the flour, baking powder, and mixed spice. Stir in a little milk if necessary to bind to a soft, pliable dough. Chill for 30 minutes.

2. Preheat the oven to 350°F. Roll out on a floured counter to ¼-inch thickness and cut out 24 circles with a 3¼-inch cutter. Evenly space the circles apart on two baking sheets, slip a wooden popsicle stick 1 inch under each cookie and press down lightly. Bake for 10–12 minutes. Cool on the baking sheets for 10 minutes before transferring to a wire rack to cool completely.

3. Roll out the fondant on a surface lightly dusted with confectioners' sugar to ⅛-inch thickness. Using a skull paper template, cut out 24 skull shapes, rerolling the fondant if necessary.

4. Melt the chocolate in a microwave or a glass bowl set over a pan of simmering water. Spoon into a paper pastry bag and snip off the tip. If necessary, secure the popsicle sticks to the cookies with some of the melted chocolate and allow to set. Pipe small dots over the top half of the cookies and arrange the fondant skulls on top. Pipe the eyes and a nose onto each of the skulls, then paint on the mouth and teeth with the black food coloring.

MAKES: 24
BAKING TIME: 10–12 MINUTES

INGREDIENTS
¾ cup/1½ sticks butter
¾ cup sugar
1 egg, beaten
3 cups all-purpose flour
1 teaspoon baking powder
1 teaspoon mixed spice
Milk
12 ounces white fondant
24 flat wooden popsicle sticks
7 ounces semisweet chocolate
Black food coloring

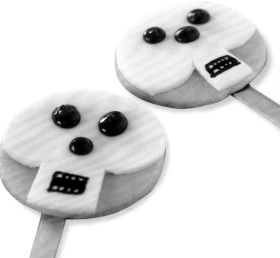

BLUEBERRY SHORTCAKE Cookies

These cookies must be eaten on the day they are made and are especially good warm from the oven. You can substitute with small, halved strawberries or raspberries for a special 4th of July treat.

MAKES: **8**
BAKING TIME: **20 MINUTES**

INGREDIENTS
1¼ cups all-purpose flour
1½ teaspoons baking powder
¼ cup/½ stick unsalted butter
¼ cup granulated sugar
Finely grated zest of 1 lemon
½ cup sour cream
1 cup fresh blueberries
Crushed sugar cubes for sprinkling

1. Preheat the oven to 375°F. Line a baking sheet with parchment paper.

2. Sift the flour and baking powder into a bowl. Blend in the butter until the mixture resembles fine bread crumbs. Stir in the sugar and lemon zest.

3. Stir in the sour cream and blueberries and stir until just combined. Spoon 8 mounds, well apart, on the prepared baking sheet. Sprinkle with the crushed sugar cubes and bake in the oven for about 20 minutes until golden and firm in the center. Serve warm and eat on the day of baking.

COOKIE TIP
Baked and uncooked shaped cookies can be frozen for up to two months. Thaw baked cookies at room temperature and bake uncooked ones from frozen.

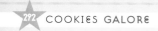

RUGELACH

Little crescents made with a delicious cream cheese dough containing a spicy fruit and nut filling. These cookies are traditionally served during the eight-day Jewish festival of Hanukkah.

MAKES: 24–30
BAKING TIME: 15–20 MINUTES

INGREDIENTS

DOUGH

½ cup/1 stick unsalted butter, chilled
½ cup cream cheese
½ cup sour cream
2¼ cups all-purpose flour

FILLING

¼ cup superfine sugar
2 teaspoons ground cinnamon
4 tablespoons raisins, chopped
4 tablespoons ready-to-eat dried
   apricots, chopped
¾ cup walnuts, finely chopped
Beaten egg for glazing

1. To make the dough put the butter, cream cheese, and sour cream into a food processor and blend until just creamy. Add the flour and blend very briefly, using the pulse button until the mixture just comes together. Remove and wrap in plastic wrap and chill overnight or at least 6 hours.

2. Preheat the oven to 350°F. Line baking sheets with parchment paper. Put the filling ingredients into a bowl and mix together.

3. Divide the dough into four. Take one piece and leave the rest in the refrigerator as it is important to keep the dough as cold as possible as it is very sticky to roll out. Sprinkle a sheet of parchment paper with flour, put the dough in the center and place another sheet of parchment paper on top. Quickly roll out the dough to a circle.

4. Cut into six wedges and sprinkle evenly with a quarter of the filling. Starting at the wide end, roll each triangle up toward the point. Curve each roll into a crescent and place with the pointed side down on the baking sheets. Repeat with the remaining dough.

5. Brush with beaten egg and bake in the oven for about 15–20 minutes or until golden brown. Cool on a wire rack.

CHINESE FORTUNE
Cookies

The messages in these cookies traditionally contain predictions of the future and are popular at the New Year.

MAKES: 35
BAKING TIME: 5 MINUTES

INGREDIENTS

2 egg whites
1/2 cup confectioners' sugar, sifted
1 teaspoon almond extract
2 tablespoons/1/2 stick unsalted butter, melted
1/2 cup all-purpose flour
1/3 cup unsweetened, shredded coconut, lightly toasted
Confectioners' sugar for sprinkling
Tiny strips of paper with good luck and other appropriate messages typed on them

1. Preheat the oven to 375°F. Prepare two or three sheets of parchment paper (they can be used more than once) by cutting them to the size of the baking sheet. Draw two or three circles of about 3 inches diameter on each sheet of paper. Place on the baking sheet.

2. Put the egg whites into a bowl and beat until soft peaks form. Beat in the confectioners' sugar a little at a time. Beat in the almond extract and butter. Stir in the flour and mix until smooth.

3. Place a teaspoonful of mixture in the center of a marked circle and spread out thinly and evenly to fit the circle. Sprinkle with a little coconut. Bake one sheet at a time, in the oven, for about 5 minutes or until very lightly brown on the edges.

4. Remove from the oven and immediately lift the cookies from the sheet and loosely fold in half tucking a message inside. Rest the cookie over the rim of a glass so the cookie bends in the center. Let cool and when firm remove to a cooling rack. Continue to bake and shape the remaining cookies in the same way. Sprinkle very lightly with confectioners' sugar.

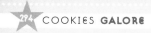

CORN & CRANBERRY Cookies

These little cookies are not overly sweet and have a lovely hint of orange and the delightful addition of cranberry. They make an ideal accompaniment to midmorning or after-dinner coffee.

MAKES: 16
BAKING TIME: 8–10 MINUTES

INGREDIENTS
⅓ cup butter
¾ cup fine cornmeal, plus extra for dusting
1 cup all-purpose flour
¼ cup superfine sugar
1 egg
Finely grated zest of 1 orange
¾ cup dried sweetened cranberries

1. Preheat the oven to 375°F.

2. Put the butter, cornmeal, and flour into a bowl. Blend in the butter. Stir in the sugar.

3. Add the egg, orange zest, and cranberries and mix well together with your hands until the mixture just comes together.

4. Shape into small sticks and roll in cornmeal. Place on nonstick baking sheets and bake in the oven for about 8–10 minutes until just beginning to brown.

COOKIE TIP
Only grease baking sheets when a recipe instructs you to. Otherwise the cookies may spread too much and become flat.

GRANDMA'S
FAVORITES

MAPLE GLAZED
Cookies

These sticky cookies have a soft,
chewy texture that children love.

MAKES: **18**
BAKING TIME: **15 MINUTES**

INGREDIENTS

1 1/4 cups all-purpose flour
1 teaspoon baking powder
1/2 teaspoon baking soda
6 tablespoons/3/4 stick butter, cut into
   cubes
1/3 cup sugar
Scant 1/2 cup pecans, chopped
1 egg, lightly beaten
6 tablespoons maple syrup

1. Preheat the oven to 350°F. Lightly grease two baking sheets.

2. Sift the flour, baking powder, and baking soda into a bowl. Add the butter and blend with your fingertips until the mixture resembles fine bread crumbs. Stir in the sugar and pecans.

3. Add the egg and 4 tablespoons of the maple syrup and mix until well combined.

4. Drop small heaping tablespoonfuls of the dough, slightly spaced apart onto the baking sheets. Bake until golden, about 15 minutes.

5. Brush the cookies with the remaining maple syrup while still hot, then transfer to a wire rack to cool completely.

COOKIE TIP
Always pay special attention when measuring flour for baking recipes—too much and your cookies will be too hard and too little and they will turn out too flat.

SOUR CREAM & RAISIN Cookies

If your raisins are a bit dried out, plump them up by soaking in hot water for about 10 minutes. Rinse with cool water, squeeze dry, and coat lightly in flour from the recipe before adding to the dough.

MAKES: 18
BAKING TIME: 10–12 MINUTES

INGREDIENTS
½ cup/1 stick butter
⅔ cup sugar
6 tablespoons sour cream
1¼ cups all-purpose flour
1 teaspoon baking soda
Scant ½ cup raisins

1. Preheat the oven to 350°F. Lightly grease two baking sheets.

2. Cream the butter and sugar together until pale and fluffy. Beat in the sour cream.

3. Sift the flour and baking soda together, then beat into the mixture. Stir in the raisins.

4. Drop tablespoons of the dough well apart on the baking sheets. Bake until golden, 10–12 minutes. Let cool on the baking sheets for 2–3 minutes, then transfer to a wire rack to cool completely.

COOKIE TIP
Always allow cookies to cool completely before transferring to an airtight storage container.

SPICED MOLASSES Cookies

Rich and spicy, these cookies are delicious served with a cup of coffee.

MAKES: 10–12
BAKING TIME: 12–15 MINUTES

INGREDIENTS
1 1/2 cups sifted all-purpose flour
2 teaspoons baking soda
1/4 teaspoon salt
3/4 teaspoon ground ginger
1 teaspoon ground cinnamon
1/2 teaspoon ground cloves
1 teaspoon pure vanilla extract
1 1/4 cups/2 1/2 sticks butter, softened
1 cup dark brown sugar, firmly packed
1 egg
1/4 cup molasses

1. Preheat the oven to 350°F. Grease two baking sheets.

2. In a large bowl and using an electric mixer, combine the flour, baking soda, salt, ginger, cinnamon, and cloves. Gradually add the vanilla, butter, sugar, egg, and molasses, increasing the speed to medium. Beat for 2 minutes, scraping down the sides of the bowl as necessary.

3. Drop large tablespoonfuls of the dough well apart onto the baking sheets. Bake until the tops are dry, 12–15 minutes. Let cool completely on wire racks.

COOKIE TIP
To prevent molasses from clinging to the side of the measuring cup, lightly grease the cup first or spray it with nonstick cooking spray.

OATMEAL RAISIN

Cookies

These classic American cookies have stood the test of time.
Be sure not to overcook them so that they stay nice and chewy.

MAKES: 10–12
BAKING TIME: 10 MINUTES

INGREDIENTS

Generous 1 cup all-purpose flour
1 1/2 cups rolled oats
1 teaspoon ground ginger
1/2 teaspoon baking powder
1/2 teaspoon baking soda
3/4 cup light brown sugar, lightly
 packed
1/3 cup raisins
1 egg, lightly beaten
1/2 cup vegetable oil
4 tablespoons milk

1. Preheat the oven to 400°F. Lightly grease a baking sheet. Mix together the flour, oats, ginger, baking powder, baking soda, sugar, and raisins in a large bowl.

2. In another bowl, mix together the egg, oil, and milk. Make a well in the center of the dry ingredients and pour in the egg mixture. Mix together well to make a soft dough.

3. Place spoonfuls of the dough well apart onto the baking sheet and flatten slightly with the tines of a fork. Bake until golden, about 10 minutes. Transfer the cookies to a wire rack to cool completely.

APPLE & CRANBERRY
Shortcake

These delicious fruity wedges of shortcake are great served as a dessert accompanied by a spoonful of sour cream.

1. Lightly grease a 9-inch round removable-bottomed pan.

2. To make the filling, peel, core, and slice the apples. Cook gently with 1 tablespoon water for about 5 minutes until the fruit is soft. Stir in the cranberry sauce and allow to cool.

3. Beat the butter and sugar together until light and fluffy. Beat in the egg and vanilla extract. Sift the flour and cornstarch together and beat in to form a soft dough.

4. Divide the dough in half and roll out one piece to fit the base of the prepared pan. Prick all over with a fork. Spread the fruit mixture over the dough, leaving a small border around the edge. Dampen the edges with a little water. Roll out the remaining dough and lightly press over the top. Chill for 30 minutes in the refrigerator or 10 minutes in the freezer.

5. Preheat the oven to 350°F. Bake in the center of the oven for 35–40 minutes until golden. Allow to cool in the pan. When cold, carefully remove from the pan and cut into wedges. Store in a cool place for up to three days.

MAKES: **12**
BAKING TIME: **35–40 MINUTES**

INGREDIENTS
³/₄ cup/1¹/₂ sticks butter, softened
¹/₃ cup sugar
1 egg
1 teaspoon vanilla extract
2 cups self-rising flour
¹/₂ cup cornstarch
FILLING
2 green dessert apples
¹/₃ cup cranberry sauce

BLUEBERRY THUMBPRINT Cookies

The simple, mellow vanilla flavor of these cookies works incredibly well with the tartness of the blueberry jelly. For a really traditional American taste, try filling the thumbprint well with peanut butter and jelly.

MAKES: 36
BAKING TIME: 10 MINUTES

INGREDIENTS
1 cup/2 sticks butter, softened
Scant 1 cup confectioners' sugar
1 teaspoon vanilla extract
Scant 1 cup ground almonds
Scant 1⅓ cups all-purpose flour
Blueberry jelly
Confectioners' sugar for dusting

1. Lightly grease two baking sheets. Cream the butter and sugar together until pale and fluffy, then beat in the vanilla. Blend in the ground almonds and then gradually add the flour, bringing the mixture together with your hands to form a soft dough as you add the last of the flour.

2. Lightly dust your hands with flour and roll the dough into small balls about the size of a walnut. Arrange on the baking sheets and using your thumb, make a deep hole in the center of each cookie. Chill for 30 minutes.

3. Preheat the oven to 350°F. Bake the cookies for 10 minutes, then fill each hole with a little jelly and return to the oven until pale golden, about 5 minutes. Let cool on the baking sheets for a few minutes before transferring to a wire rack to cool completely. Dust with confectioners' sugar to finish.

OATY APPLE
Crunchies

A special favorite with kids and adults, the crunchiness of the oats and moistness of the applesauce gives these cookies great appeal.

MAKES: **18**
BAKING TIME: **10–15 MINUTES**

INGREDIENTS

1¾ cups rolled oats
Generous ⅓ cup all-purpose flour
¾ cup light brown sugar, firmly
   packed
Scant ½ cup chunky applesauce
½ cup corn oil
1 egg

1. Preheat the oven to 350°F. Lightly grease two baking sheets.

2. Place all the ingredients in a large mixing bowl and beat until well combined.

3. Drop rounded tablespoons of the dough onto the baking sheets. Flatten slightly with the back of a spoon.

4. Bake until golden, 10–15 minutes. Let cool on the baking sheets for a few minutes then transfer to a wire rack to cool completely.

COOKIE TIP
If you are cooking with children make sure you clear a large area to work in—a small confined area may cause unnecessary accidents to happen.

MELTING
Moments

These pretty cookies take their name from their fabulous melt-in-the-mouth dough.

MAKES: 20
BAKING TIME: 15–20 MINUTES

INGREDIENTS
¾ cup/1½ sticks butter, softened
Scant ¼ cup sugar
1 egg yolk
1¼ cups all-purpose flour
Grated zest of ½ orange or lemon
1 tablespoon orange or lemon juice
Mixed candied peel for decoration
Confectioners' sugar for dusting

1. Preheat the oven to 375°F. Lightly grease two baking sheets.

2. Cream the butter and sugar together until light and fluffy. Beat in the egg yolk. Work in the flour and orange or lemon zest and juice to form a smooth, thick paste.

3. Spoon the paste into a pastry bag fitted with a large star tip and pipe rosettes measuring about 2 inches across onto the baking sheets. Lightly press some mixed candied peel into each cookie.

4. Bake until pale golden, 15–20 minutes. Let cool on the baking sheets for a few minutes before transferring to a wire rack to cool completely. Dust each cookie with confectioners' sugar.

COOKIE TIP
Only store one kind of cookie in a container. If you mix crisp and soft cookies they will all go soft and end up tasting the same.

STRAWBERRY JELLY Delights

Children will love helping to stamp out the circles and rings in these attractive cookies.

MAKES: 12–16
BAKING TIME: 15 MINUTES

INGREDIENTS
½ cup/1 stick butter, softened
¼ cup sugar
1 egg
½ teaspoon vanilla extract
Scant 1⅓ cups all-purpose flour
6 tablespoons cornstarch
½ teaspoon baking powder
FILLING
Strawberry or raspberry jelly

1. Cream the butter and sugar together until light and fluffy. Beat in the egg and vanilla. Sift the flour, cornstarch, and baking powder together and beat in to form a soft dough.

2. Preheat the oven to 350°F. Lightly grease two baking sheets.

3. Roll out the dough on a lightly floured counter to about ⅛ inch thick and cut into circles using a 2½-inch cookie cutter. Cut a 1-inch circle from the center of half the circles. The trimmings can be rerolled and used to make additional cookies. Make sure you have an equal number of circles and rings. Arrange on the baking sheets.

4. Bake until pale golden, about 15 minutes. Let cool on the baking sheets for a few minutes before transferring to a wire rack to cool completely.

5. When cooled completely, spread the circles with the jelly and place a ring on top, pushing lightly together. Store in an airtight container for up to one week.

SPICY CRANBERRY Cookies

Dried cranberries can be bought sweetened or unsweetened. Sweetened berries resemble red raisins; unsweetened cranberries taste slightly tart.

MAKES: 15
BAKING TIME: 15–18 MINUTES

INGREDIENTS
$\frac{1}{2}$ cup/1 stick butter, softened
Scant $\frac{1}{2}$ cup sugar
1 egg, separated
$\frac{1}{3}$ cup dried cranberries
$1\frac{1}{4}$ cups all-purpose flour
$\frac{1}{2}$ teaspoon pumpkin pie spice
Demerara sugar for sprinkling

1. Preheat the oven to 350°F. Lightly grease two baking sheets. Cream the butter and sugar together until light and fluffy, then beat in the egg yolk. Stir in the cranberries.

2. Sift together the flour and spice. Add to the bowl and mix to form a stiff dough. Roll out the dough on a lightly floured counter to about $\frac{1}{8}$ inch thick and cut into 3-inch circles.

3. Arrange on the baking sheets. Lightly beat the egg white and brush over the surface of each circle. Sprinkle with the Demerara sugar.

4. Bake until golden and brown, 15–18 minutes. Let cool for a few minutes on the baking sheets, then transfer to a wire rack to cool completely. Store in an airtight container for up to one week.

COOKIE TIP
If you have difficulty separating egg yolks from whites, tap the shell sharply and break the egg onto a saucer. Place an eggcup upside down over the yolk and tip the saucer so the white slides into the bowl.

OAT CRUNCH
Cookies

While the cookies are hot, press an indentation into the center of each one with your thumb and fill with a little jelly.

MAKES: **20**
BAKING TIME: **16–18 MINUTES**

INGREDIENTS
Scant 1 cup all-purpose flour
1 teaspoon baking soda
1¾ cups rolled oats
½ cup/1 stick butter
½ cup light brown sugar, firmly
    packed
1 tablespoon light corn syrup
1 tablespoon water

1. Preheat the oven to 350°F. Lightly grease two baking sheets. Sift the flour and baking soda into a mixing bowl. Stir in the oats.

2. Place the butter, sugar, corn syrup, and 1 tablespoon water in a pan and heat gently, stirring until combined. Add to the dry ingredients and stir until well mixed.

3. Take small amounts of the dough, each about the size of a walnut, and roll into balls. Space them well apart on the baking sheets and flatten slightly.

4. Bake until golden, 16–18 minutes. Let cool on the baking sheets for 2–3 minutes, then transfer to a wire rack to cool completely. Store in an airtight container for up to five days.

COOKIE TIP
Cool cookies on wire racks without touching each other to keep them from sticking together.

ALMOND Macaroons

Macaroons are traditionally made on edible rice paper, but if you have trouble finding it, then dust the baking sheets liberally with semolina and flour.

MAKES: **12**
BAKING TIME: **15–20 MINUTES**

INGREDIENTS
$^2/_3$ cup ground almonds
$^3/_4$ cup superfine sugar
2 tablespoons semolina or ground rice
2 egg whites
Few drops of almond extract
$^1/_2$ cup semisweet chocolate chips
Whole blanched almonds for decoration

1. Preheat the oven to 325°F. Line two baking sheets with rice paper.

2. Mix the almonds, sugar, and semolina. In a separate bowl, beat the egg whites until stiff. Add the almond extract.

3. Gradually fold in the sugar and almond mixture until quite stiff.

4. Fold in the chocolate chips. Place tablespoonful of mixture onto the baking sheets, well spaced out. Place an almond on top of each and bake until golden, 15–20 minutes. Cool, then tear the rice paper between each biscuit, or use a wire rack if you're not using paper.

COOKIE TIP
Baked and uncooked shaped cookies can be frozen for up to two months. Thaw baked cookies at room temperature and bake uncooked ones from frozen.

HONEY

Cookies

Orange and walnut flavored cookies dipped in honey for a real old-fashioned taste.

MAKES: 30
BAKING TIME: 15–20 MINUTES

INGREDIENTS

½ cup/1 stick butter
Finely grated zest of 1 orange
⅓ cup superfine sugar
⅓ cup sunflower oil
2 cups all-purpose flour
1 cup self-rising flour
¼ cup finely chopped walnuts
⅔ cup orange juice
1 cup honey
2 tablespoons finely chopped walnuts
　 for sprinkling

1. Preheat the oven to 350°F. Put the butter, orange zest, and sugar into a bowl and beat well together. Gradually beat in the oil until the mixture is light and fluffy.

2. Stir in the flours, nuts, and juice and mix to a soft dough.

3. Using two tablespoons shape the mixture into ovals and place on baking sheets lined with parchment paper. Bake in the oven for 15–20 minutes until lightly browned.

4. Heat the honey in a small saucepan. Making sure the honey is not too hot, dip the warm biscuits in the honey to coat. Place on a wire rack over a tray. Sprinkle with the chopped nuts.

COOKIE TIP
Make sure the honey glaze has set completely before transferring the cookies to a storage container.

DUTCH
Shortcakes

Crisp buttery shortcakes baked in strips and then cut up.

MAKES: 18
BAKING TIME: 15–20 MINUTES

INGREDIENTS
2 tablespoons custard powder (or cornstarch)
1½ cups all-purpose flour
⅔ cup butter
⅓ cup superfine sugar
1 egg yolk

1. Preheat the oven to 350°F. Sift the custard powder and flour together.

2. Cream the butter and sugar together and beat in the egg yolk. Mix in the flour well.

3. Put the mixture into a pastry bag fitted with a large star tip and pipe three flat zigzag lines about 2 x 10 inches on a nonstick baking sheet.

4. Bake in the oven for 15–20 minutes until pale golden brown. While still warm cut each piece into six and cool on a wire rack.

COOKIE TIP
If you are looking out for your health you may be considering replacing the butter with low fat margarine, but be aware that reducing the sugar and fat in the ingredients can make cookies more cake-like.

FIG & DATE Rolls

Short crumbly pastry filled with moist dates and figs. These cookies keep well in an airtight container.

MAKES: 24
BAKING TIME: 20–25 MINUTES

INGREDIENTS

FILLING
1¾ cups dried figs, finely chopped
½ cup stoned dates, finely chopped
½ cup water
Finely grated zest of 1 lemon
½ cup superfine sugar

DOUGH
½ cup/1 stick butter
⅓ cup superfine sugar
1 teaspoon ground cinnamon
1 egg
½ cup ground almonds
2 cups all-purpose flour

1. To make the filling put all the ingredients into a pan and stir over a gentle heat until the sugar is dissolved. Simmer uncovered for about 15 minutes until the mixture is thick and pulpy. Cool.

2. To make the dough beat together the butter, sugar, cinnamon, and egg. Stir in the ground almonds and flour. Knead lightly and divide into four. Wrap each portion in plastic wrap and chill for 30 minutes.

3. Preheat the oven to 350°F. Roll out each portion of dough between sheets of parchment paper to 4 x 8 inches. Spread a quarter of the filling along each rectangle leaving a ½-inch border. Fold the long sides over the filling to meet in the center and press gently together. Tuck the ends under.

4. Place the rolls seam side down, on nonstick baking sheets. Bake for 20–25 minutes until lightly browned. Remove and let cool.

5. When cold cut into slices.

CARDAMOM GINGER Crisps

Ideal for dunking these crisp little fingers have the unusual addition of ground cardamom.

MAKES: 50
BAKING TIME: 10–15 MINUTES

INGREDIENTS
½ cup/1 stick butter
⅔ cup light brown sugar
1 teaspoon ground cardamom
½ teaspoon ground cinnamon
Pinch of ground nutmeg
2 egg yolks
1½ cups all-purpose flour
2 tablespoons candied ginger, finely chopped

1. Put the butter, sugar, spices, and egg yolks into a bowl and beat well together.

2. Stir in the flour and candied ginger. Knead until smooth. Shape into a block about 3 x 11 inches. Wrap in parchment paper and chill until firm.

3. Preheat the oven to 325°F. Cut the dough into ⅛-inch slices and place on baking sheets lined with parchment paper. Bake in the oven for 10–15 minutes until golden. Cool on a wire rack.

COOKIE TIP
Always stir flour prior to measuring. Flour settles as it sits and if you do not stir it you may end up adding too much to your cookies.

APPLE STREUSEL
Bars

These fruity, crunchy bars make a wonderful afternoon snack with a cup of tea.

MAKES: 12–14
BAKING TIME: 45 MINUTES

INGREDIENTS
2 cups self-rising flour
1/4 cup ground almonds
3/4 cup/1 1/2 sticks butter
1/3 cup light brown sugar
2 egg yolks
TOPPING
3 dessert apples
1/2 cup golden raisins (optional)
1 1/2 cups all-purpose flour
1/2 teaspoon ground cloves
3/4 stick butter
1/3 cup brown sugar

1. Preheat the oven to 350°F. Lightly grease an 8 x 11-inch oblong baking pan.

2. Sift the self-rising flour into a mixing bowl and stir in the almonds. Cut the butter into cubes and blend into the mixture until it resembles bread crumbs. Stir in the brown sugar. Add the egg yolks and work the mixture together to form a firm dough. Press out to line the base of the prepared pan. Prick all over and chill while making the topping.

3. To make the topping, peel, core, and roughly chop the apples, then place in a pan with 2 tablespoons water. Cook gently for about 3–4 minutes until tender. Stir in the golden raisins if using.

4. Sift the flour and cloves into another bowl. Blend in the butter until the mixture resembles crumbs. Stir in the brown sugar. Spread the apple mixture over the dough and sprinkle the streusel mixture on top. Bake for about 45 minutes until the topping is golden.

5. Cool in the pan and serve cut into bars or squares. Store in the refrigerator for up to four days.

LAVENDER SCENTED
Shortbread

A popular remedy in traditional medicine, lavender is said to help promote sleep. Try one of these fragrant shortbreads before going to bed and they should really do the trick.

MAKES: 18–20
BAKING TIME: 15–20 MINUTES

INGREDIENTS

1/2 cup superfine sugar
4 dried lavender flowers, natural and unsprayed
1 cup butter
2 cups all-purpose white flour
1 cup ground rice
Pinch of salt
Extra lavender flowers and superfine sugar for decoration

1. Line two baking sheets with waxed paper.

2. Put the sugar and lavender in a food processor and whiz for about 10 seconds.

3. Cream together the butter and sugar until light and fluffy, then stir in the flour, ground rice, and salt until the mixture resembles bread crumbs.

4. Using your hands, gather the dough together and knead until it forms a ball. Roll into a sausage shape and then shape into a long block about 2 inches thick. Wrap in plastic wrap and chill for about 30 minutes, or until firm.

5. Preheat the oven to 375°F. Slice the dough into 1/4-inch squares and place on the baking sheets. Bake for 15–20 minutes, or until pale golden. Sprinkle with sugar and leave on the baking sheets for 10 minutes, then transfer to a wire rack to cool completely.

GOURMET
COOKIES

WHITE CHOCOLATE & NUT Cookies

If you prefer, substitute the macadamias for another variety of nut.

MAKES: 12–15
BAKING TIME: 15–18 MINUTES

INGREDIENTS

Generous 1³/₄ cups all-purpose flour
1 teaspoon baking soda
¼ cup unsweetened cocoa powder
½ teaspoon salt
1 cup/2 sticks unsalted butter, softened
1½ cups light brown sugar, firmly packed
Scant ½ cup sugar
2 large eggs
2 teaspoons vanilla extract
Scant 1¹/₃ cups white chocolate chips
2 cups macadamia nuts, coarsely chopped

1. Preheat the oven to 375°F. Lightly grease two baking sheets.

2. In a medium bowl, sift together the flour, baking soda, cocoa powder, and salt. Set aside.

3. Cream the butter and sugars together until light and fluffy. Beat in the eggs and vanilla. Gently stir in the flour mixture until just combined. Fold in the white chocolate and macadamia nuts.

4. Drop large rounded tablespoons of the dough onto the baking sheets, well spaced apart as the cookies will spread. Bake until firm, 15–18 minutes. Let cool on the baking sheets for a few minutes before transferring to a wire rack to cool completely.

COOKIE TIP
Pack even more of a chocolate punch by adding some semisweet chocolate chips.

ORANGE PECAN Cookies

These cookies will keep in an airtight container—
if you can resist eating them all at once.

MAKES: 24
BAKING TIME: 10–12 MINUTES

INGREDIENTS
6 tablespoons/³/₄ stick butter
6 tablespoons sugar
6 tablespoons light brown sugar,
  firmly packed
1 egg
Grated zest of 1 orange
2 tablespoons orange juice
1¼ cups all-purpose flour
½ teaspoon baking soda
³/₄ cup pecans, coarsely chopped

1. Preheat the oven to 350°F. Lightly grease two baking sheets.

2. Cream the butter and sugars together until pale and fluffy. Beat in the egg, orange zest, and juice.

3. Sift the flour and baking soda together and beat into the mixture. Stir in the nuts.

4. Drop tablespoons of the dough well apart onto the baking sheets. Bake until golden, 10–12 minutes. Let the cookies cool on the baking sheets for 2–3 minutes, then transfer to a wire rack to cool completely. Store in an airtight container for up to five days.

COOKIE TIP
Add a few of the chopped nuts to the top of the cookies before baking to give an extra crunch.

PINEAPPLE
Macaroons

Enjoy these soft, fruity macaroons with midmorning coffee or afternoon tea.

MAKES: 20–24
BAKING TIME: 25–30 MINUTES

INGREDIENTS
14 ounces canned pineapple rings in
  natural juice
10–12 candied cherries
3 egg whites
Scant 1 cup sugar
Generous 2½ cups flaked coconut

COOKIE TIP
*Vary the flavoring in
these chewy cookies or
leave out the pineapple if
you prefer a traditional
macaroon.*

1. Preheat the oven to 325°F. Line two baking sheets with nonstick parchment paper.

2. Drain the pineapple well and chop finely. Place in a strainer and squeeze out as much juice as possible. Halve the cherries.

3. Beat the egg whites to stiff peaks. Gradually beat in the sugar. Fold in the pineapple and coconut until well combined.

4. Drop spoonfuls of the dough onto the lined baking sheets, piling into a pyramid shape. Allow space for the cookies to spread slightly. Top each with half a cherry.

5. Bake until lightly browned and crisp, 25–30 minutes. Let cool on the baking sheets, then carefully remove and store in an airtight container for up to three days. Do not freeze.

SPICED PUMPKIN & PECAN Crisps

These slightly spiced cookies are a great light snack.

MAKES: 24–30
BAKING TIME: 25–30 MINUTES

INGREDIENTS

½ cup/1 stick butter, softened
Scant 1 cup all-purpose flour
¾ cup light brown sugar, lightly
  packed
⅔ cup canned pumpkin or cooked
  and mashed pumpkin
1 egg
2 teaspoons ground cinnamon
½ teaspoon vanilla extract
½ teaspoon baking powder
1 teaspoon baking soda
½ teaspoon ground nutmeg
Scant ½ cup whole-wheat flour
⅔ cup pecans, roughly chopped
1 cup raisins

FROSTING

½ cup/½ stick unsalted butter
1½ cups confectioners' sugar
1½ teaspoons vanilla extract
2 tablespoons milk

1. Preheat the oven to 375°F. Lightly grease two baking sheets.

2. Using an electric beater, beat the butter until fluffy. Add the flour, sugar, pumpkin, egg, cinnamon, vanilla, baking powder, baking soda, and nutmeg. Beat until well combined, scraping down the sides of the bowl. Add the whole-wheat flour, nuts, and raisins and fold in until just combined.

3. Drop the dough in large tablespoonfuls, well spaced apart onto the baking sheets. Bake until golden, 25–30 minutes. Remove from the oven and let cool on a wire rack.

4. To make the frosting, melt the butter over a medium heat in a small pan and continue cooking until light golden brown. Remove from the heat and add the confectioners' sugar, vanilla, and milk. Mix until smooth, adding a little more milk or confectioners' sugar as necessary to make the mixture spreadable. Let cool until thick, then spread generously over the cooled cookies.

DARK CHOCOLATE & PECAN Brownies

Have a batch of these rich, sticky brownies ready for a midnight treat—served with a big scoop of ice cream.

MAKES: 12
BAKING TIME: 20–25 MINUTES

INGREDIENTS
4 ounces bittersweet chocolate
¾ cup/1½ sticks butter
2 cups granulated sugar
3 eggs
1¾ cups all-purpose flour
1½ teaspoons vanilla extract
1 cup pecan nuts

1. Preheat the oven to 350°F. Butter a 13 x 9-inch nonstick baking pan. Break the bittersweet chocolate into pieces and place in a pan with the butter. Melt over a gentle heat, stirring occasionally, and then take the pan off the heat.

2. Add the sugar to the chocolate and stir until dissolved. Beat in the eggs, and then stir in the flour, vanilla extract, and pecan nuts. Pour the mixture into the pan and level the surface.

3. Bake for 20–25 minutes, or until the top of the brownies are shiny and set. Place the pan of brownies on a wire rack to cool, then cut into squares and serve.

COOKIE TIP
If you can keep your hands off them for long enough, these cookies will keep for several days in an airtight container.

WALNUT

Kisses

When grinding walnuts for these cookies, use on and off pulses of the food processor to prevent them from turning to paste.

MAKES: 40
BAKING TIME: 30 MINUTES

INGREDIENTS
Scant ½ cup walnuts
Scant 1 cup confectioners' sugar
2 egg whites

COOKIE TIP
*Almonds
work just as well
as walnuts in this
recipe.*

1. Preheat the oven to 300°F. Line two baking sheets with nonstick parchment paper.

2. Grind the walnuts in a food processor until very finely chopped. Sift the confectioners' sugar into a bowl.

3. Put the egg white in a large, greasefree mixing bowl and beat until frothy. Gradually add the confectioners' sugar and beat until combined.

4. Place the bowl over a pan of gently simmering water and beat until the mixture is very thick and stands in stiff peaks. Remove from the pan and beat until cold.

5. Carefully fold in the ground walnuts until just blended, then spoon into a pastry bag fitted with a large plain or star tip. Pipe small rosettes or balls slightly spaced onto the baking sheets.

6. Bake until the cookies can be easily removed from the paper, about 30 minutes. Let cool and store in an airtight container.

FROSTED COFFEE

Creams

Simple to make with a sophisticated flavor, these frosted cookies are delicious with morning coffee.

MAKES: **20**
BAKING TIME: **15 MINUTES**

INGREDIENTS
½ cup/1 stick butter, softened
Scant ½ cup sugar
¼ cup strong black coffee
Generous 1⅔ cups all-purpose flour
3 tablespoons cornstarch

FILLING
¼ cup/½ stick butter, softened
1⅓ cups confectioners' sugar
2 tablespoons strong black coffee

FROSTING
⅔ cup confectioners' sugar
1–2 teaspoons strong black coffee

1. Preheat the oven to 350°F. Lightly grease two baking sheets.

2. Cream the butter and sugar together until light and fluffy. Beat in the remaining ingredients, bringing the mixture together to form a firm dough.

3. Roll out the dough on a lightly floured counter to about ⅛ inch thick and cut out with cookie cutter shapes of your choice. Arrange on baking sheets.

4. Bake until lightly browned, about 15 minutes. Let cool on the baking sheets for a few minutes before transferring to a wire rack to cool completely.

5. To make the filling, cream the butter until fluffy, then gradually beat in the confectioners' sugar and coffee. Sandwich the cookies together in pairs with the filling.

6. To make the frosting, sift the confectioners' sugar into a bowl and stir in enough coffee to form a smooth frosting. Spread over the tops of the cookies and let set.

LACE
Cookies

You can make these cookies slightly larger than usual as they look lovely piled up and served with ice cream or elegant cream desserts.

MAKES: 12–14
BAKING TIME: 5–7 MINUTES

INGREDIENTS
⅓ cup butter
¾ cup rolled oats
½ cup superfine sugar
1 egg, beaten
2 teaspoons all-purpose flour
1 teaspoon baking soda
½ teaspoon ground cinnamon

1. Preheat the oven to 350°F. Line baking sheets with parchment paper. Melt the butter in a pan and remove from the heat. Stir in all the remaining ingredients.

2. Put 3–4 heaping teaspoonfuls of the mixture onto the prepared baking sheets.

3. Bake in the oven for about 5–7 minutes or until dark golden brown.

4. Leave to cool for a few minutes on the baking sheets and then carefully remove to a wire rack using a large spatula.

COOKIE TIP
Don't be tempted to put more than three or four of these cookies on the baking sheet and make sure they are spaced well apart.

PISTACHIO Biscotti

Decorate these cookies by drizzling a little chocolate over the top.

MAKES: 50
BAKING TIME: 40 MINUTES

INGREDIENTS

Generous 1⅓ cups pistachios
Generous 3 cups all-purpose flour
Generous ⅔ cup coarse cornmeal
2 teaspoons baking powder
½ cup/1 stick butter
Scant ½ cup sugar
3 eggs
1 teaspoon grated lemon zest
1 teaspoon grated orange zest
2 tablespoons orange juice
½ teaspoon almond extract
1 teaspoon fennel seeds, crushed
   (optional)

1. Preheat the oven to 350°F. Lightly grease two baking sheets.

2. Coarsely chop half the pistachios. Sift the flour, cornmeal, and baking powder together.

3. Cream the butter and sugar together until pale and fluffy. Beat in the eggs one at a time. Beat in the lemon and orange zest, juice, almond extract, and fennel seeds. Do not worry if the mixture looks curdled at this stage, as this is normal.

4. Beat in the chopped and whole pistachios. Finally, work in the flour mixture, using your hands to mix it to a soft dough. Divide the dough into four pieces and roll each piece into a log shape about 12 inches long on a lightly floured counter. Place on the baking sheets and flatten slightly.

5. Bake until the logs are risen and golden, about 30 minutes; reverse the baking sheets half way through the baking time. Remove from the oven and let cool slightly.

6. Reduce the oven temperature to 325°F. When the logs are cool enough to handle, cut each one diagonally into ½-inch slices. Arrange cut-side down on the baking sheets and return to the oven until crisp and golden, about 10 minutes. Store in an airtight container for up to two weeks.

LIME BROWN SUGAR Cookies

The lime frosting lends a real tang to these sophisticated cookies.

MAKES: 22
BAKING TIME: 10–12 MINUTES

INGREDIENTS
1/2 cup/1 stick butter
1/2 cup light brown sugar, firmly
   packed
1 egg, beaten
Grated peel of 1 lime
1 tablespoon lime juice
Generous 2 cups all-purpose flour
1 teaspoon baking soda

FROSTING
Generous 1 1/4 cups confectioners'
   sugar
1–2 tablespoons fresh lime juice
Grated zest of 1 lime

1. Preheat the oven to 350°F. Lightly grease two baking sheets. Cream the butter and brown sugar together until fluffy. Beat in the egg, lime zest, and juice.

2. Sift together the flour and baking soda, then beat into the butter mixture. Work together with your hands to form a soft dough.

3. On a lightly floured counter, roll out the dough to 1/4 inch thick and cut out cookies with cookie cutters. Place on the baking sheets and bake until crisp and golden, 10–12 minutes. Let cool on the baking sheets for 2–3 minutes, then transfer to a wire rack to cool completely.

4. To make the frosting, sift the confectioners' sugar into a bowl and mix in the lime juice and zest until smooth. Spread or pipe over the cookies. Let dry for 1–2 hours or until the frosting has set. Store in an airtight container for up to five days.

CHEESECAKE SWIRL Brownies

These are irresistible—a chocolate brownie base topped with brownie mixture and cream cheese. Cut into small squares to serve as they are rather rich but perfectly heavenly and make a great dessert when served with fresh raspberries.

MAKES: 16
BAKING TIME: 30 MINUTES

INGREDIENTS

CHEESECAKE MIX
1 egg
1 cup full-fat cream cheese
¼ cup superfine sugar
1 teaspoon vanilla extract

BROWNIE MIX
4 ounces bittersweet chocolate
½ cup/1 stick unsalted butter
¾ cup light brown sugar
2 eggs, beaten
½ cup all-purpose flour

1. Preheat the oven to 325°F. Grease and base line an 8-inch square shallow cake pan.

2. To make the cheesecake mixture put all the ingredients into a bowl and beat well together.

3. To make the brownie mixture: melt the chocolate and butter together in a bowl in the microwave or over a pan of hot water. When melted, remove from the heat, stir well and stir in the sugar. Add the eggs a little at a time and beat well. Gently fold in the flour.

4. Spread two-thirds of the brownie mixture in the base of the prepared pan. Spread the cheesecake mixture on top. Spoon the remaining brownie mixture on top in heaps. Using a skewer, swirl the mixtures together.

5. Bake in the oven for about 30 minutes or until just set in the center. Leave to cool in the pan and then cut into squares.

FLORENTINES

Sweet and rich these are great with after-dinner coffee and liqueurs.

MAKES: **12**
BAKING TIME: **7–10 MINUTES**

INGREDIENTS

¼ cup/1½ sticks unsalted butter
¼ cup superfine sugar
2 tablespoons heavy cream
2 tablespoons chopped candied angelica
3 tablespoons chopped mixed candied peel
3 tablespoons golden raisins
5 candied cherries, chopped
⅓ cup flaked almonds, lightly crushed
1 tablespoon all-purpose flour
4 ounces bittersweet or white chocolate, chopped

1. Preheat the oven to 350°F. Put the butter and sugar into a small pan and heat gently until dissolved then bring to a boil.

2. Remove from the heat and stir in all the ingredients except the chocolate. Mix well together.

3. Place heaping teaspoonfuls on lightly greased or nonstick baking sheets. Space well apart to allow for spreading. Bake a few at time for about 6–8 minutes until the edges are just beginning to turn brown. Using a large plain metal cookie cutter push the edges of each Florentine in to create a neat round. Bake for 1–2 minutes more until golden brown.

4. Allow to cool on the baking sheet for a few minutes then transfer to a wire rack to harden.

5. Melt the chocolate in a heatproof bowl over a pan of simmering water. Roll the edges of each cookie in the chocolate and place on a sheet of parchment paper until set.

COOKIE TIP
Rolling half the cookies in bittersweet chocolate and the other half in white makes them into a real treat.

BRAZIL NUT
Biscotti

Italians traditionally dunk their biscotti—a cookie native to their country—into espresso or vin santo (sweet wine).

MAKES: **50**
BAKING TIME: **50 MINUTES**

INGREDIENTS

2 eggs
Generous ¾ cup sugar
Grated zest 1 orange
2 tablespoons orange juice
¼ cup light vegetable oil
1⅓ cups Brazil nuts
2⅓ cups all-purpose flour
2 teaspoons baking powder
Scant 1 cup ground rice

1. Preheat the oven to 350°F.

2. Place the eggs and sugar in a large mixing bowl and beat until very pale and thick. Beat in the orange zest, juice, and oil. Stir in the nuts.

3. Sift the flour and baking powder together and add to the bowl with the rice, working the mixture with your hands to form a soft dough. Add a little extra flour if the dough is too sticky. Divide in half and roll each piece to form an 8-inch log.

4. Place the logs on the baking sheets and bake until risen and golden, about 30 minutes. Remove from the oven and let cool slightly. Reduce the oven temperature to 300°F.

5. Using a serrated knife, cut the logs into thin slices and arrange on the baking sheets. Bake the slices, turning once, until crisp and golden on both sides, about 20 minutes. Store in an airtight container for several weeks.

MAPLE SYRUP
Tuiles

These little treats are a great accompaniment to creamy desserts. They do require a little care when cooking. Only cook two or three at a time, as they need to be shaped fairly quickly while still very warm.

MAKES: 20
BAKING TIME: 5–7 MINUTES

INGREDIENTS
¼ cup/½ stick unsalted butter
⅓ cup light brown sugar
1 tablespoon maple syrup
1 tablespoon brandy
⅓ cup all-purpose flour

1. Preheat the oven to 350°F. Put the butter, sugar, and syrup into a pan and heat gently while stirring until the sugar has dissolved. Simmer, uncovered and without stirring, for 2 minutes.

2. Remove from the heat and stir in the brandy and flour. Put 2 or 3 level teaspoonfuls onto lightly greased baking sheets. Bake in the oven for 5–7 minutes until lightly browned.

3. Remove from the oven and cool for just 1 minute and then carefully lift off the baking sheet with a spatula. Drape over a wooden rolling pin or wooden spoon handle and leave to harden. Alternatively, pinch the center together to give a flower shape or drape over upturned eggcups to make little baskets.

COOKIE TIP
These tuiles can soften if left out, so store in an airtight container.

CRACKLE

Cookies

These look stunning and are so easy to make. As a variation try adding some chopped dark candied cherries to the mixture.

MAKES: 24
BAKING TIME: 10 MINUTES

INGREDIENTS
½ cup self-rising flour
¼ cup unsweetened cocoa powder
½ cup superfine sugar
2 tablespoons/¼ stick butter
1 egg, beaten
1 teaspoon cherry brandy
½ cup confectioners' sugar

1. Preheat the oven to 400°F. Sift the flour and cocoa into a bowl and stir in the sugar.

2. Blend in the butter until the mixture resembles fine crumbs. Stir in the egg and cherry brandy and mix well together.

3. Put the confectioners' sugar into a bowl. Shape walnut-sized pieces of dough into balls and drop into the confectioners' sugar. Toss until thickly coated and place on baking sheets lined with parchment paper.

4. Bake for about 10 minutes until just set. Cool on a wire rack.

COOKIE TIP
If you wish you can make the dough ahead of time and keep covered in the refrigerator. Shape and bake the cookies at the last minute and serve warm.

POPPYSEED & HONEY Pinwheels

You can change the nuts and flavorings in these cookies. Try using chopped toasted almonds or macadamias, and for flavor try lemon instead of orange zest or a large pinch of ground cinnamon or ginger.

MAKES: **30**
BAKING TIME: **8–10 MINUTES**

INGREDIENTS
1/2 cup/1 stick butter
1/2 teaspoon vanilla extract
1/2 cup superfine sugar
1 egg
1²/₃ cups all-purpose flour
FILLING
1/3 cup very finely chopped toasted
   hazelnuts
1/2 cup poppyseeds
1/4 cup honey, warmed
1 teaspoon finely grated orange zest

1. Put the butter, vanilla, sugar, and egg into a bowl and beat well together. Stir in the flour and shape into a ball. Wrap in plastic wrap and chill until firm.

2. Put all the filling ingredients into a bowl and mix well together. Cut the dough in half and roll out each portion between sheets of parchment paper, to a rectangle 8 x 10 inches. Spread the filling over the two pieces of dough and roll up from the short side like a jelly roll. Wrap in plastic wrap and chill until firm.

3. Preheat the oven to 375°F. Cut the rolls into 1/8-inch slices and place on nonstick baking sheets. Bake for about 8–10 minutes until lightly browned.

COOKIE TIP
The pastry dough is very soft to handle so make sure it is well chilled before rolling out between sheets of parchment paper.

COOKIES
PLUS

CAPPUCCINO

Bars

The sheer variety of textures in these bars makes for a decadent treat.

MAKES: **12**

INGREDIENTS
⅓ cup golden raisins
½ cup hot strong black coffee
10 ounces graham crackers
½ cup mini-marshmallows
8 ounces semisweet chocolate
¼ cup/½ stick butter

TOPPING
8 ounces white chocolate
¼ cup/½ stick butter
Scant 1 cup confectioners' sugar
Grated semisweet chocolate

1. Lightly grease an 8 x 8-inch square pan and line the bottom with nonstick parchment paper.

2. Soak the raisins in the hot coffee for 5 minutes. Break the graham crackers into small pieces and place in a bowl with the marshmallows. Sprinkle in the coffee and soaked raisins.

3. Melt the chocolate and butter in a microwave or in a bowl set over hot water. Add to the graham cracker mixture and stir until well coated. Press the mixture into the prepared cake pan and let chill until firm.

4. To make the topping, melt the white chocolate in a microwave or in a bowl set over a pan of hot water. Let cool. Cream the butter until soft, gradually beat in the confectioners' sugar. Beat in the melted white chocolate. Spread the mixture over the graham cracker base and let set.

5. Sprinkle with grated chocolate and cut into bars. Store in an airtight container in a cool place for up to four days.

APPLE & RASPBERRY Bars

Apples and raspberries are a wonderfully irresistible combination.

MAKES: 12–14
BAKING TIME: 45 MINUTES

INGREDIENTS

6 tablespoons/$\frac{1}{3}$ cup unsalted butter
$\frac{3}{4}$ cup superfine sugar
3 eggs
1 teaspoon vanilla extract
$1\frac{1}{2}$ cups self-rising flour
4 medium cooking apples (about
   1 pound), grated
6 ounces raspberries

1. Preheat the oven to 375°F. Grease a 15 x 10 x 1-inch baking pan and set aside.

2. In a large mixing bowl beat the butter with the sugar until it resembles fine bread crumbs. Beat in the eggs and vanilla extract until combined.

3. Beat or stir in the flour, and then add the grated apple. Mix thoroughly until well combined.

4. Pour the batter into the prepared baking pan, spreading the mixture evenly. Push the raspberries into the mixture evenly spaced around the tin. Bake for about 25 minutes or until a tester inserted in the center comes out clean.

5. Cool in the pan and serve cut into bars or squares. Store in the refrigerator for up to four days.

CHOCOLATE & MACADAMIA NUT Bars

These bars will set as they cool, but still be wonderfully chewy.

MAKES: 9
BAKING TIME: 30–35 MINUTES

INGREDIENTS
1 cup/2 sticks butter
8 ounces semisweet chocolate, cut up
¾ cup macadamia nuts
1¼ cups light brown sugar
3 eggs
2 cups all-purpose flour
2 teaspoons baking powder
½ teaspoon salt

1. Preheat the oven to 350°F. Melt the butter and chocolate together in a glass bowl over a pan of simmering water until smooth and glossy. Let it cool slightly. Toast the macadamia nuts on a baking sheet in the oven for 5 minutes until just golden, then roughly chop.

2. Beat the sugar and eggs together in a large bowl. Carefully stir in the chocolate mixture. Fold in the flour, baking powder, and salt, then stir in the chopped nuts.

3. Line the bottom of an 8-inch square, nonstick cake pan that is at least 2 inches deep. Pour in the mixture and bake for 30–35 minutes. Allow to cool in the pan.

4. Serve cut into squares with ice cream or cream.

MOCHA MUD Pies

A cookie that's rich and dense in texture like a brownie with a chocolate/coffee flavor has to be divine, and it is. Make sure the mixture is well chilled before baking.

MAKES: **16**
BAKING TIME: **10 MINUTES**

INGREDIENTS

¼ cup all-purpose flour

¼ teaspoon baking soda

7 ounces bittersweet chocolate, coarsely chopped

2 tablespoons/¼ stick unsalted butter

2–3 tablespoons instant coffee granules, according to personal taste

2 large eggs

½ cup superfine sugar

1 teaspoon vanilla extract

2 ounces semisweet chocolate chips

1. Sift together the flour and baking soda. Put the chocolate and the butter into a heatproof bowl over a pan of simmering water or melt in the microwave. When melted remove from the heat and stir in the coffee granules.

2. Put the eggs and sugar into a bowl and beat with an electric beater until pale and very thick. Stir in the chocolate mixture and the vanilla. Add the flour mixture and stir. Mix in the chocolate chips.

3. Cover the bowl and place in the refrigerator for about 1 hour.

4. Preheat the oven to 350°F. Line baking sheets with parchment paper. Place spoonfuls of the mixture well apart on the prepared sheets.

5. Bake for about 10 minutes or until the cookies feel just set when touched lightly with a finger. Cool for a few minutes before transferring to a wire rack.

BLONDIES

These are like brownies but are made with white chocolate and sugar instead of brown—even more irresistible.

MAKES: 18
BAKING TIME: 30–35 MINUTES

INGREDIENTS
1 pound 2 ounces white chocolate
$\frac{1}{3}$ cup butter
3 eggs
$\frac{3}{4}$ cup superfine sugar
1$\frac{1}{2}$ cups self-rising flour
2 cups macadamia nuts, roughly chopped
1 teaspoon vanilla extract

1. Preheat the oven to 375°F. Grease and base line a 10$\frac{1}{2}$ x 7$\frac{1}{2}$-inch baking pan.

2. Roughly chop 12 ounces of the chocolate and put aside.

3. Melt the remaining chocolate and the butter in a bowl over a pan of simmering water. Cool slightly.

4. Beat the eggs and sugar together in a bowl and gradually beat in the melted chocolate. Sift the flour over the mixture and fold in together with the chopped nuts, reserved chocolate, and vanilla extract.

5. Pour into the prepared pan and bake for 30–35 minutes until the center is only just firm to the touch. Cool in the pan. Cut into squares when cold.

COOKIE TIP
Store bar cookies either in tightly covered containers or in the pan in which they were baked. Make sure you cover the pan tightly with aluminum foil.

GRANOLA, HONEY & DATE Health Bars

Although granola is packed full of goodness, it can be very high in calories. Read the labels of packaged granola when buying to make sure that these bars have all the health benefits of granola without the fat!

MAKES: 10
BAKING TIME: 20–25 MINUTES

INGREDIENTS
Scant ¾ cup/1¼ sticks butter
6 tablespoons light brown sugar,
   firmly packed
¼ cup honey
Scant 1¼ cups granola
¾ cup rolled oats
⅔ cup dates, chopped

1. Preheat the oven to 375°F. Grease an 8 x 8-inch square cake pan and line the bottom with nonstick parchment paper.

2. Melt the butter with the sugar and honey in a pan, stirring thoroughly until well combined.

3. Remove from the heat and stir in the granola, oats, and dates. Turn into the cake pan and press down lightly. Bake until firm, 20–25 minutes.

4. Let cool for a few minutes in the pan, then cut into bars and let cool completely. Store in an airtight container for up to two weeks.

COOKIE TIP
*For even cooking
bake the bars on
the middle shelf of
your oven.*

HAZELNUT & CHOCOLATE Bars

Toasting the hazelnuts in this recipe really brings out the nutty flavor.

MAKES: 12
BAKING TIME: 25 MINUTES

INGREDIENTS

3 ounces semisweet chocolate
½ cup/1 stick butter, softened
¼ cup light brown sugar, firmly packed
⅔ cup all-purpose flour
¾ cup rolled oats
12 tablespoons chocolate hazelnut spread, such as Nutella
⅓ cup hazelnuts, chopped and toasted

1. Preheat the oven to 350°F. Lightly grease an 8 x 8-inch square cake pan and line the bottom with nonstick parchment paper.

2. Melt the chocolate in a microwave or in a bowl set over a pan of simmering water. Cream the butter and sugar together until light and fluffy. Beat in the chocolate, then mix in the flour and oats to form a soft dough.

3. Press the mixture into the bottom of the prepared pan and bake until just golden, about 25 minutes.

4. Let cool in the pan. Remove from the pan and spread with chocolate hazelnut spread. Sprinkle with the hazelnuts and press lightly into the spread. Cut into bars. Store in a cool place, in a single layer in an airtight container, for up to one week.

COOKIE TIP
Keep the dough in the freezer for those chocolate cookie urges. Just remember to thaw the dough in the refrigerator for several hours for easier slicing.

NUTTY BUBBLE

Bars

A treat for all those peanut lovers and
a great way to use up leftover cereal.

MAKES: 24

INGREDIENTS
$\frac{1}{2}$ cup/1 stick butter
$\frac{1}{3}$ cup light corn syrup
$\frac{1}{3}$ cup smooth peanut butter
$\frac{1}{2}$ cup superfine sugar
2 cups rice bubble cereal
2 cups coco bubble cereal
2 ounces peanut brittle, chopped
$\frac{1}{2}$ cup chopped toasted hazelnuts
White chocolate, melted, for drizzling

1. Base line a $9\frac{1}{2}$ x 12-inch baking pan with parchment paper.

2. Mix together the butter, corn syrup, peanut butter, and sugar in a medium pan. Heat gently while stirring, until the sugar dissolves. Bring to a boil and simmer very gently, uncovered, without stirring for 5 minutes.

3. Remove from the heat and stir in all the remaining ingredients. Spread into the prepared pan and chill. When set, drizzle over the melted white chocolate and cut into bars.

COOKIE TIP
*To prevent the corn
syrup from clinging to the
side of the measuring cup,
lightly grease the cup first
or spray it with nonstick
cooking spray.*

TANGY CREAM CHEESE Bars

Cream cheese blends best if allowed to soften at room temperature for a good hour before mixing.

MAKES: 18
BAKING TIME: 25–30 MINUTES

INGREDIENTS
¾ cup/1½ sticks butter, softened
4 ounces full-fat cream cheese
¾ cup sugar
1 egg
2 tablespoons orange juice
2 tablespoons lemon juice
Scant ½ cup mixed candied peel
2⅓ cups all-purpose flour
1 teaspoon baking powder

FROSTING
Scant 1 cup confectioners' sugar
1 tablespoon orange or lemon juice

1. Preheat the oven to 375°F. Grease a shallow 9 x 9-inch square pan.

2. Beat the butter and cream cheese together, then add the sugar and continue to beat until pale and fluffy. Beat in the egg. Beat in the fruit juices and stir in the mixed candied peel.

3. Sift the flour and baking powder together and add to the mixture to form a soft dough. Roll out on a lightly floured counter to a square that will fit the bottom of the prepared pan. Place in pan.

4. Bake until golden, 25–30 minutes. Let cool in the pan.

5. Cut into bars. Sift the confectioners' sugar into a small bowl and stir in enough juice to make a smooth frosting. Drizzle the frosting over the bars and let set.

COOKIE TIP
Be sure to store these in the refrigerator as cream cheese is perishable.

GINGER OAT
Squares

A crisp base and a chewy ginger oat topping give these cookies a fabulous contrast of textures.

MAKES: 12
BAKING TIME: 25 MINUTES

INGREDIENTS
1¼ cups all-purpose flour
1 teaspoon ground ginger
½ cup/1 stick butter
¼ cup light brown sugar, firmly
 packed
1–2 tablespoons water

TOPPING
4 pieces preserved ginger in syrup
3 tablespoons preserved ginger syrup
¼ cup/½ stick butter
2 tablespoons light brown sugar,
 firmly packed
1 cup rolled oats

1. Preheat the oven to 375°F. Lightly grease a 9 x 9-inch square pan.

2. Place the flour and ground ginger in a mixing bowl and rub in the butter until the mixture resembles fine bread crumbs. Stir in the sugar. Add enough water to mix to a soft dough. Roll out and use to line the bottom of the pan.

3. To make the topping: chop the ginger. Place in a pan with the syrup, butter, and sugar. Heat gently, stirring until the butter melts and the mixture is well blended.

4. Stir in the oats. Spread the mixture evenly over the dough. Bake until golden brown, about 25 minutes. Let cool in the pan and cut into squares to serve.

APRICOT & ALMOND Slices

For a chewy, nutty flavor that is out of this world, you can't beat these fruit slices.

MAKES: 16
BAKING TIME: 20 MINUTES

INGREDIENTS
2 cups all-purpose flour
3 tablespoons confectioners' sugar
1 teaspoon baking powder
3/4 cup/1 1/2 sticks butter
2 egg yolks

TOPPING
Scant 1/4 cup apricot jelly
2 egg whites
1/2 cup sugar
Scant 1/2 cup ground almonds
Scant 1/2 cup sliced almonds

GLAZE
1/4 cup apricot jelly

1. Preheat the oven to 375°F. Lightly grease a 9 x 9-inch square baking pan.

2. Sift the flour, confectioners' sugar, and baking powder into a mixing bowl. Cut the butter into cubes and blend until the mixture resembles fine bread crumbs. Stir in the egg yolks. Using your fingertips, work the mixture together to form a smooth dough, adding a little cold water if necessary. Roll or press out the dough to fit the bottom of the prepared pan and prick all over with a fork. Bake until just golden, about 10 minutes. Remove from the oven.

3. To make the topping: spread the apricot jelly over the crust. Beat the egg whites until frothy but not stiff. Stir in the sugar and ground almonds. Spread over the jelly and sprinkle the sliced almonds on top. Return to the oven until golden brown, about 20 minutes. Let cool in the pan. Carefully remove the pastry from the pan.

4. To make the glaze: melt the apricot jelly with 1 tablespoon water and brush over the surface to glaze. Cut into triangles to serve.

FIG & CINNAMON
Slices

Delicious on their own these fig slices also make a great dessert served with vanilla ice cream.

MAKES: 24–30
BAKING TIME: 10 MINUTES

INGREDIENTS
$\frac{1}{2}$ cup/1 stick butter
$\frac{1}{4}$ cup light brown sugar
1 teaspoon ground cinnamon
1$\frac{1}{2}$ cups all-purpose flour
2$\frac{1}{2}$ cups dried figs
1 cinnamon stick
$\frac{1}{2}$ cup superfine sugar
Finely grated zest of 1 lemon

1. Preheat the oven to 350°F. Lightly grease and base line a 10$\frac{1}{2}$ x 7-inch baking pan.

2. Beat together the butter, brown sugar, and cinnamon until creamy. Mix in the flour and then press the mixture evenly into the pan pressing down with the back of a spoon or your fingertips. Bake for 15 minutes until golden but not brown.

3. Meanwhile put the figs, cinnamon stick, sugar and 1$\frac{1}{2}$ cups boiling water into a saucepan. Bring to a boil, stirring. Reduce the heat and simmer gently for 15 minutes until the figs have softened and water reduced by about a third.

4. Remove the cinnamon stick. Add the lemon zest. Process the mixture until smooth in a food processor.

5. Spread the fig puree over the cooked base and bake for 10 minutes until set. Cool in the pan. Cut into squares when cold.

COOKIE TIP
Only store one kind of cookie in a container. If you mix crisp and soft cookies they will all go soft and end up tasting the same.

HAZELNUT & CINNAMON Meringues

A soft slightly chewy meringue with a warm spicy flavor.

MAKES: 50
BAKING TIME: 45 MINUTES

INGREDIENTS
3 egg whites
¾ cup superfine sugar
½ cup ground hazelnuts
1 teaspoon ground cinnamon
9 ounces milk chocolate

COOKIE TIP
Alternatively, you can use ground almonds and use bittersweet chocolate instead of milk chocolate.

1. Preheat the oven to 250°F. Line baking sheets with parchment paper.

2. Put the egg whites into a bowl and beat with a hand-held electric beater until the mixture stands in soft peaks. Beat in the sugar a little at a time, beating well between each addition. Fold in the nuts and cinnamon.

3. Put the mixture into a pastry bag fitted with a large plain tip. Pipe in 2-inch rounds on the prepared baking sheets. Flatten the tops with a wetted spatula.

4. Bake in the oven for about 45 minutes until dry to the touch. Turn the oven off leaving the meringues in the oven to dry out.

5. Melt the chocolate in the microwave or in a bowl over a pan of hot water. Either half dip the meringues in the chocolate or just coat the edges. Leave to set on parchment paper.

CITRUS

Squares

These fruity squares pack a real citrus punch to perk up your afternoon.

MAKES: 15
BAKING TIME: 32–40 MINUTES

INGREDIENTS
1$\frac{1}{8}$ cups all-purpose flour
$\frac{1}{3}$ cup confectioners' sugar
Scant $\frac{1}{2}$ cup unsalted butter

TOPPING
2 eggs
$\frac{3}{4}$ cup golden superfine sugar
Finely grated zest of lemon
Finely grated zest of 1 small orange
4 tablespoons lime juice
1 tablespoon all-purpose flour
$\frac{1}{2}$ teaspoon baking soda

1. Preheat the oven to 350°F. Grease and base line a 10$\frac{1}{2}$ x 7$\frac{1}{2}$-inch shallow baking pan.

2. Put the flour, confectioners' sugar, and butter into a food processor. Using the pulse button, process until the mixture comes together to make a firm dough. Press the dough evenly into the prepared pan and bake for 12–15 minutes until golden but not brown.

3. Beat the eggs until frothy. Gradually beat in the sugar and continue until the mixture is thick and foamy. Beat in the lemon and orange zest and lime juice. Beat in the flour and baking soda. Pour over the baked base. Bake for 20–25 minutes until golden brown.

4. Cool in the pan and then cut into squares.

COOKIE TIP
If a recipe calls for both lemon zest and juice, pour the lemon juice over the zest to keep it moist.

NO-BAKE CHOCOLATE FUDGE Bars

The beauty of these bars is their simplicity— and their unadulterated chocolate hit!

MAKES: 12

INGREDIENTS

8 ounces vanilla wafers

$\frac{1}{2}$ cup/1 stick butter

2 tablespoons light corn syrup

2 tablespoons unsweetened cocoa powder

4 ounces milk chocolate, broken into pieces

3 tablespoons confectioners' sugar

2 tablespoons milk

1. Lightly grease an 8 x 8-inch square pan. Place the wafers in a plastic bag and crush to produce fine crumbs with a rolling pin. Alternatively, process the wafers to crumbs in a food processor.

2. Place the butter, corn syrup, and cocoa in a small pan and heat gently until melted and blended, while stirring. Add the crumbs and stir until well combined.

3. Press the mixture into the pan and let chill until firm, at least 1 hour.

4. Melt the chocolate together with the confectioners' sugar and milk in a small bowl over a pan of hot water. Spread over the crumb crust and let set before cutting into bars.

COOKIE TIP

Most confectioners' sugar, also known as powdered sugar, is blended with a small amount of cornstarch to prevent major lumping. Even so, it's usually best to sift it prior to use.

PEPPERMINT CHOC Sticks

These cookies are deceptively easy to make and are absolutely delicious served with coffee at the end of a meal.

MAKES: 12–15

INGREDIENTS

9 ounces bittersweet chocolate
2 ounces clear hard peppermints, crushed
5 ounces Amaretti cookies, crushed

1. Melt the chocolate in a heatproof bowl over a pan of simmering water.

2. Remove from the heat and allow to cool slightly. Stir in the remaining ingredients.

3. Place a 12 x 4-inch sheet of parchment paper on a baking sheet. Spread the mixture evenly over the paper leaving a narrow edge. Let set.

4. When firm use a saw edge knife and carefully cut into thin sticks.

COOKIE TIP
Because this is such an easy recipe to make, it gives you more time to be creative with the shape of the cookie. Instead of sticks the mixture can be spread out and cut into thin squares or disks.

INDEX

RECIPE CREDITS

VALERIE BARRETT
PAGES 200, 208, 211, 214, 216, 218, 230, 238, 241, 244, 250, 254, 258, 267–268, 274, 278–280, 282, 284–286, 288, 290, 292–294, 312, 314–316, 330, 334, 336, 338, 340–341, 347–348, 352, 357–358, 360, 362.

JACQUELINE BELLEFONTAINE
PAGES 198–199, 202–207, 210, 212–213, 217, 222–223, 226– 229, 232–237, 240, 248–249, 252–253, 256–257, 260–262, 264, 266, 272, 277, 298, 300–304, 306–310, 317, 322–325, 328–329, 332–333, 337, 344, 346, 350–351, 354–356, 361.

LORNA BRASH
PAGES 273, 276, 283, 289.

MAGGIE MAYHEW
PAGES 242–243, 311.

GAIL WAGMAN
PAGES 16–18, 20, 22–24, 26–28, 30–32, 34–36, 40, 42–44, 46–48, 50–52, 54–56, 60, 62–64, 66–70, 73–76, 79, 82, 85–88, 90–92, 94, 96–97, 99–102, 104–106, 108–110, 112–114, 118–120, 122–124, 127–128, 130–132, 134–136, 138–140, 142–143, 146, 148–150, 152–154, 156–157, 158–162, 164–166, 168–170, 172–174, 176, 178–180, 183.

JENNY WHITE
PAGES 265, 318, 326.

PHOTOGRAPHY CREDITS

CHRIS ALACK
PAGES 182, 184, 185 BOTTOM, 194 RIGHT, 198, 202, 207, 210, 212–213, 218, 227–228, 233–234, 236–237, 240, 248, 256, 264, 266, 272–273, 276, 283, 289, 300, 303, 307–308, 310, 317, 323, 325, 329, 332–333, 337, 345, 347, 350–351, 355– 356.

MARIE LOUISE AVERY
PAGES 185 TOP, 186–189, 191–192, 194 LEFT, 195, 186–187, 200, 209, 214, 220–221, 225, 230, 239, 241, 244, 246–247, 251, 255, 259, 263, 269, 270–271, 281, 287, 291, 295, 296–297, 299, 305, 313, 319, 320–321, 327, 330, 335, 339, 342–343, 349, 353, 359, 363.

OLIVIER MAYNARD
PAGES 4–8, 10–15, 17, 19, 21–23, 25–26, 29, 31, 33, 35, 37–39, 41–42, 45¬–47, 49, 51, 53, 54, 57–59, 61, 63, 65–67, 69, 71–72, 74–75, 77–78, 80–81, 83,–84, 86, 89, 93, 95–96, 98, 100, 103, 105, 107, 109, 110, 115–117, 119, 121, 123, 125–126, 129, 133–134, 137–138, 141, 143–145, 147, 151–152, 155, 157–158, 163, 167, 171–172, 175, 177–178, 181–182.